The Battle to Control
Broadcast News

The Battle to Control Broadcast News

Who Owns the First Amendment?

Hugh Carter Donahue

The MIT Press
Cambridge, Massachusetts
London, England

Acknowledgments: "The Best Things in Life Are Free," by Lew Brown, Ray Henderson, and B. G. DeSylva, © 1927 Chappell & Company (renewed), all rights reserved, used by permission. "Anything Goes," by Cole Porter, © 1934 Warner Bros. Inc. (renewed), all rights reserved, used by permission. "Ain't Misbehavin'," music by Thomas "Fats" Waller and Harry Brooks, words by Andy Razaf, © 1929 Mills Music, Inc. (renewed), all rights reserved, used by permission of Warner/Chappell Music, Inc. "Are You Lonesome Tonight," words and music by Roy Turk and Lou Handman, © 1926 by Bourne Co. and Cromwell Music, Inc. (renewed), international copyright secured, all rights reserved, used by permission. "Both Sides Now," © 1967, 1974 Siquomb Publishing Corp., used by permission of Warner Bros. Music, all rights reserved. "Mrs. Robinson," © 1968 Paul Simon, used by permission. "New Attitude," words and music by Bunny Hill, Jon Gilutin, and Sharon T. Robinson, © 1984, 1985 by Texascity Music, Inc., Unicity Music, Inc., Brassheart Music, Rockomatic Music, and Robinhill Music, rights administered by Unicity Music, Inc., Los Angeles, Ca., used by permission, all rights reserved. "The People's Key," by Bob Hipkens, © 1976 Flying Fish Records, used by permission.

© 1989 Massachusetts Institute of Technology

This book was set in Bembo by Achorn Graphic Services and was printed and bound by Halliday Lithograph in the United States of America.

Library of Congress Cataloging-in-Publication Data

LIBRARY OF CONGRESS
Library of Congress Cataloging-in-Publication Data

Donahue, Hugh Carter.
  The battle to control broadcast news : who owns the First Amendment? / Hugh Carter Donahue.

     p.   cm.
  Includes index.
  ISBN 0-262-04099-9
  1. Equal time rule (Broadcasting)—United States—History.
  2. Fairness doctrine (Broadcasting)—United States—History.
  I. Title.
KF2812.D66 1988
343.73'09945–dc19
[347.3039945]   88-13279
                                                                CIP

For my brother, John

Contents

Preface

Experience should teach us to be most on guard to protect liberty when the government's purposes are beneficent.

Justice Louis Brandeis

If nothing might be published but what civil authority shall have previously approved, power must always be the standard of truth; if every dreamer of innovations may propagate his projects, there can be no settlement; if every murmurer at government may diffuse discontent, there can be no peace; and if every skeptic in theology may teach his follies, there can be no religion. The remedy against these evils is to punish the authors; for it is yet allowed that every society may yet punish, though not prevent, the publication of opinions, which that society shall think pernicious: but this punishment, though it may crush the author, promotes the book; and it seems not more reasonable to leave the right of printing unrestrained, because writers may be afterwards censured, than it would be to sleep with doors unbolted, because by our laws we can hang a thief.

Samuel Johnson, *Lives of the English Poets,* 1780

In his well-known commentary on Milton's *Areopagitica,* a classic assertion of free speech, Samuel Johnson anticipates many of the issues confronting and defining electronic media in twentieth-century America. Johnson opposes censorship and prior restraint and equivocates on unqualified free speech rights. Even a thinker as orthodox and conservative as Johnson finds it difficult to determine finally the vexed issue of freedom of expression. To be sure, Johnson wrote in an earlier historical period: His was a shrewd Tory pragmatism from Georgian England, as newspapers emerged as a new communications technology, looking back on the Puritan idealism of seventeenth-century England when typeset tracts and pamphlets constituted the latest communications innovation. Even so, Johnson's prudential reservations about free speech are as forceful today, especially among proponents of broadcast content regulation, as they were when he published this commentary.

Justice Brandeis made his observations in a wire tapping case in the 1920s at the height of Prohibition. In an effort to stop illicit importation of Canadian Scotch, police wire-tapped a residence without proper authority. A right of privacy was an essential liberty for Justice Brandeis, so he chided the police for violating an individual's right to privacy in their zeal to enforce "beneficent" prohibition laws.

In twentieth-century America, lawmakers and jurists came to grips with the new mass communications technology of radio and television with beneficently intended rules to ensure equal time and fairness in broadcasting. Neither equal time nor fairness worked. Politicians evaded or manipulated equal time for temporary pragmatic gain. Broadcasters ducked controversial issues for fear of triggering fairness objections, and interest groups of all stripes latched on to fairness to intimidate broadcasters. The public lost more than it gained by having equal time and fairness rules.

In this book I explain the evolution of equal time and fairness in American broadcasting. I present their proponents and detractors. I show that both standards waxed and waned as technology expanded the number of broadcast channels and First Amendment law provided more liberties for speakers. Articulated in earlier times under different conditions, each attempted to enhance average citizens' knowledge of the world they lived in and the issues that affected their lives. In so doing, Congress, the courts, and the Federal Communications Commission put a novel twist on free speech: Because of the scarcity of the spectrum, the rights of the radio listeners and television viewers superseded those of the radio and television speakers to express their views. This assault on broadcasters' First Amendment rights contributed eventually to the erosion of both standards. At the same time, Fairness Doctrine and equal time proponents' deeply held convictions that the airwaves belong to the public animate continuing efforts to sustain a fairness standard. Admittedly, equal time is still on the books. But Congress and the Federal Communications Commission have amended it extensively for the benefit of major party politicians and the public broadcasters. In 1987 the Federal Communications Commission discarded the Fairness Doctrine.

Acknowledgments

My work on this book leaves me indebted to any number of people and organizations. Alan Brinkley and W. Russell Neuman provided superb guidance, directing and perceptively criticizing earlier versions. Edwin Diamond introduced me to broadcast journalism and stimulated my thinking on the implications of this research. Ithiel deSola Pool advised me in the early stages of this study and left a lasting imprint. George Armstrong Kelly gave rich, human intelligence. Milton Cantor, Kevin R. Stoner, Joseph P. McKerns, Linda Lazier-Smith, and Gerald Kosicki commented thoughtfully on several chapters. Stephen B. Oates gave generously of his insights on writing and research methods. Henry Steele Commager gave me a capacious introduction to civil liberties as a student; his continuing encouragement refreshes and stimulates my thinking. Research assistants Deborah Alexander, Eric D. Asel, Lynne Cope, Vincent Garlock, Hamilton Moy, III, and Andrew Plump did yeomen service with library searches. I am especially grateful to Gary Hack of MIT's Department of Urban Studies and Planning and to Walter Bunge, director of Ohio State University's School of Journalism, for their assistance, enabling me to travel to Washington, D.C., for research at the National Archives, Congress, and the Federal Communications Commission. Librarians at the Boston Athenaeum, the Massachusetts Institute of Technology, and Ohio State University were invariably helpful.

I am grateful to Blair Perry, Esq., for his generous counsel, and to John M. Pelkey, Esq., Timothy B. Dyk, Esq., Henry Geller,

Esq., and Lucas A. Powe, Jr., Esq. for their many keen insights and observations.

Several organizations, including the Josephine deKarman Fellowship Trust, the National Association of Broadcasters, the Poynter Fund and the Ohio State University, provided financial support.

My brother, John, and my great aunt, Lottie M. Bourneuf, good friends Sue Barlow, Harvey I. Botman, Christos Coios, John and Priscilla Hicks, Bernard Horn, Frederick E. Hoxie, Phillip and Patricia LaCroix, Juliana Mutti, Sherida Moss, Edward Shoucair, David and Lindsey Toomey, and Martha Trudeau provided constant encouragement and support.

The Battle to Control
Broadcast News

The Emergence of Equal Time

1

Worthwhile things cannot be bought or sold
. . . the stars belong to everyone
They gleam there for you and me
. . . the best things in life are free.

"The Best Things in Life Are Free," music and lyrics by B. G. DeSylva, Lew Brown, and Ray Henderson, 1927

Fiorello LaGuardia stood up. Just 5 feet tall and representing New York's polyglot East Side, Congressman LaGuardia wanted to know that the bill before the House guaranteed free speech over radio. Representative Wallace H. White, architect of the Radio Bill, said it did: "The pending bill gives . . . no power of interfering with freedom of speech in any degree." LaGuardia pressed, "It is the belief of the gentleman and the intent of Congress not to exercise . . . any power whatever in that respect in considering a license or the revocation of a license." Again, White assured him, "No power at all."[1]

In 1926 the United States was struggling to develop a national policy for radio. Radio had come on the national scene with all the energy of the Charleston, the brio of movies, and the popular appeal of automobiles. By 1926 there were over 20 million radios in American homes, up from 50 thousand only 5 years before.[2]

The radio industry needed ground rules to develop radio as a new technology of mass communications. Antiquated federal statutes, dating to 1912, when radio serviced shipping and ship-to-shore communications, inhibited federal regulation. The Clayton and the Sherman antitrust acts prohibited cartelization of the sort that would have enabled radio companies to regulate the airwaves on their own. In December 1926 an Illinois state court ruling, in *Tribune Company v. Oak Leaves Broadcasting Station*, upheld a priority-in-use property right for broadcast licenses, and thus seemed to offer a way out. In a court of equity this common law ruling meant that broadcasters could develop exclusive claims to a radio frequency, based on the length of time they had operated a particular frequency, and could sue for damages other broadcasters who wilfully interferred. By 1927 the law was enacted.[3]

At this early stage America first had to settle systemic issues. Free speech over radio was at the center of competing systemic considerations. Three alternatives emerged: licensing radio frequencies to broadcasters, forming a nationalized system, or providing a common carrier system. A fourth alternative of creating a private market in radio with full free speech rights for broadcasters along the line outlined *Oak Leaves,* was stillborn.

A nationalized radio system, comparable to the British Broadcasting Corporation, appealed to varying interests. Educators and labor activists supported a nationalized system to produce cultural and ideological programming free from the dictates of commercial appeal or censorship by commercial broadcasters. The navy held on to some frequencies from World War I and wanted to extend its control over radio in peacetime. But the navy caught fire from angry Democrats in 1922 after allowing Indiana Republican senator Harry S. New to use a naval radio station in Washington, D.C., to address voters in a hotly contested primary contest. Navy secretary Denby denied charges of favoritism and banned "nonofficial" uses of navy radio to shun further contention.[4] *New Republic* editor Bruce Blevin also called for a nationalized system. These forces never coalesced, and they fought a losing battle against commercial and amateur licensees.[5] Major radio corporations opposed nationalization as well. Many had invested heavily in the new mass communication and resisted efforts to limit radio's commercial possibilities.[6]

In theory, a common carrier system appeared as a system with expansive free speech potential. The common carrier system would have enabled any producer to purchase air time for news, political, public affairs, or entertainment programming. Broadcasters would have had no discretion to accept or reject programming. They would be required to behave much like phone companies, as public utilities.[7] The downside, of course, was that a common carrier system also resembled the American ideal of equal opportunity based on the ability to pay. Offering neither diversity nor excellence, a common carrier system could well have scuttled national radio programming because it short-circuited the economies of networking.

In the odd workings of American politics, opposite ends of the political spectrum backed a common carrier system. Progressives supported it as the system promising the fullest access opportunities for candidates and discussion of public affairs. American Telephone and Telegraph (AT&T), the reformers' nemesis, pressed for a common carrier system until 1926. AT&T had pioneered radio in the United States. It had developed an extensive network of "toll" broadcasting. In the toll system radio programmers and producers paid AT&T a fee or toll for use of the radio waves in much the same way one would pay the telephone company as a common carrier for a long-distance telephone call. But, as radio grew into a medium of mass communication rather than one-to-one communication, radio reaped greater profits by selling time to advertisers to reach potential buyers. AT&T chose not to pursue this market. In 1926 AT&T management decided that the company's future lay in telephones and took AT&T out of broadcasting. AT&T sold its eighteen radio stations to the Radio Corporation of America (RCA) for several million dollars and RCA's promise not to compete in telephones and to use AT&T's wires for interconnecting RCA's radio network.[8]

A licensed system proved more attractive and enduring. Under the Radio Act of 1912, licensing was the existing policy requiring revision for mass communications. Radio manufacturers and nascent amateur and commercial broadcasters backed licensing. An oligopoly, embodied in the Radio Corporation of America, supported licensing and dominated American radio in the 1920s. In 1919 General Electric (GE) formed the Radio Corporation of America with American Telephone and Telegraph, the American Marconi Company, the Federal Telegraph Company, and the United Fruit Company. At that time radio enabled the United States to overtake Great Britain in communications, which remained dominant in the older and slower technology of cable. GE would later claim that it had refused to sell patent rights to the Alexanderson alternator, a device that facilitated transoceanic radio transmissions, to the British-controlled Marconi Company, in deference to Navy Department requests to keep wireless technology in the United States. This claim of patriotism served GE and RCA well, even though the primary corporate motive was to secure licenses to high-powered radio frequencies and to ward off Navy Department proposals to nationalize radio. By 1927, with the navy no longer a player, radio was open for commercial exploitation for mass communications.[9]

Despite America's competitive advantage in radio technology, neither radio manufacturers nor commercial broadcasters could exploit a mass communications market fully without an orderly market. Until then broadcasters' investments would remain a small fraction of their potential value. Of the three systems, licensing promised the best return and most flexibility. Broadcasters, who had already received the coveted privilege to broadcast, embraced licensing on the supposition that they would retain their licenses and gain a competitive advantage over challengers. Licensing also helped broadcasters because it remained unclear whether other state courts would follow the *Oak Leaves* precedent. Other state courts could well have ruled that the length of time that broadcasters operated a frequency and invested in equipment, transmitters, and talent did not provide them exclusive rights to a frequency. General "public interest, convenience, and necessity" obligations eliminated this uncertainty and provided a constitutionally acceptable standard for federal regulation.

Just how a licensed system emerged turned on free speech. Broadcasters pushed for licensing, with the primary goal of ordering the chaotic radio marketplace so that the industry might prosper. Licensing provided them with discretion over politics free of total government control as in a nationalized system and without the burdens of mandated access for the discussion of public affairs as in a common carrier system. Broadcasters would program news, politics, and public affairs in the "public interest" as a quid pro quo for lucrative licenses. However, in striking this deal, broadcasters opened the door for content control because the "public interest" standard provided politicians and future regulators of radio and television a powerful tool with which to control broadcast news and public affairs programming.

Licensing, with an equal time proviso for candidates, emerged in 1927 as the dominant model. This hybrid fell within a political consensus defined by just enough control over speech to prohibit egregious acts of price discrimination and censorship by broadcasters but not so much government control that, it was argued, broadcasters' discretion over programming was violated. Industrial peace was at hand: AT&T and RCA had defined their markets a year earlier. RCA charted its future as a broadcaster; AT&T as a public utility. Both were eager to exploit radio, each accepted equal time as a sensible compromise. A licensed system with equal time also mollified Progressive proponents of a common carrier system.[10]

■ The original federal statute for equal time is:

If any licensee shall permit any person who is a legally qualified candidate for any public office to use a broadcasting station, he shall afford equal opportunities to all other such candidates for that office in the use of such a broadcasting station, and the licensing authority shall make rules and regulations to carry this provision into effect: Provided that such licensee shall have no power of censorship over material broadcast under the provision of this paragraph. No obligation is hereby imposed upon any licensee to allow the use of its station by any such candidate.[11]

Equal time remains in effect to this day with revisions for advertising rates and newsworthy events (chapters 4 and 6).

In 1927 Congress enacted equal time for several reasons. Politicians' ability to mount electoral campaigns over radio, a new mass communications medium, was at stake. Incumbents especially wanted to secure access to broadcasting. Progressive political ideals that an informed electorate reached political decisions by voting on the basis of the fullest information supported arguments that candidates enjoy access to radio during political campaigns. Ideological and sectional politics came into play. Several key Western Congressmen had made their political careers fighting railroad and utility interests and viewed broadcasters suspiciously as the monopolists' latest incarnation. Southern Congressmen protective of the legacy of their region's peculiar institution and anxious about encroaching urbanism, were equally suspicious of Eastern-dominated radio. Perennial Democratic standard-bearer William Jennings Bryan viewed "impartial treatment of candidates" over radio as an effective counterbalance to a Republican press in contested states.[12] All demanded equal time for candidates before a national system of licensing was put in place.

■ Secretary of Commerce Herbert Hoover, architect of American broadcasting regulation, supported licensing, argued for broadcaster discretion within general public interest guidelines, and accepted equal time pragmatically. Although many remember Hoover as a president incapable of coping with the Great Depression, he had a distinguished career as administrator of food relief in Europe following World War I and as a powerful commerce secretary. As commerce secretary, Hoover regulated radio under the 1912 Wireless Act.

Through his power in the Department of Commerce, Hoover attempted to rationalize a rapidly changing, wildly popular, and technologically complex growth industry. He favored a nationally regulated system of commercially financed radio stations and networks along with a portion of radio channels set aside for government and nonprofit uses under control of the secretary of commerce.

Antiquated statutes and the Illinois state court ruling in *Oak Leaves* stood in Hoover's way. The Radio Act of 1912 required the secretary of commerce to grant broadcast licenses to anyone who requested one. But mass communications of the 1920s differed from one-to-one radio communication. In 1923 the courts decided in *Hoover v. Intercity Radio* that the secretary of commerce could only assign frequencies and lacked authority to deny licenses. Then in April 1926, in *United States v. Zenith Radio Corporation,* a federal district court ruled that Hoover was powerless to require a licensee to broadcast at specified times and on designated frequencies. Hoover asked Acting Attorney General Donovan to clarify the secretary of commerce's duties. That July, Donovan agreed with the courts: Hoover was obliged by law to issue licenses on request but was denied authority to assign frequencies. In other words, once someone was granted a license, he was entitled to broadcast on whatever wavelength he wanted whenever he wanted. No matter how bad the interference, the secretary of commerce, as the responsible federal authority, could do nothing.

Following the attorney general's ruling, a period, commonly referred to as the "breakdown of the law," created the urgency for the Radio Act of 1927. During this period radio interference worsened and sales of radio receivers flattened briefly. Here was the opening Hoover needed to expand federal regulatory authority over broadcasting. Few disagreed that interference injured the radio industry and consumers alike. Of course, broadcasters could sue one another under the *Oak Leaves* precedent for deliberate interference. That was an uncertain course, however; it placed radio regulation in state courts and removed it from federal regulatory control. Neither Hoover nor Congress was willing to allow federal licensing authority over broadcasting to slip through their hands, nor were broadcasters willing to play roulette with court decisions.[13]

Hoover began setting the agenda for federal licensing authority by convening four national radio conferences from 1922 to 1925. At these conferences the dynamic, young commerce secretary shaped consensus on policy goals for a system of licensing among amateur and commercial broadcasters and among the competing departments of the federal government and military. Hoover insisted that the secretary of commerce retain authority to issue and revoke licenses. Policy issues turned principally on how to control an advertiser-supported mass medium.

Important for equal time both at these conferences and through lobbying for a revised radio act, Hoover articulated principles of a licensed system. Hoover's themes have become cornerstones of federal policy: public interest, listener sovereignty, spectrum scarcity. At the outset Hoover acknowledged a public interest in radio. At the First National Radio Conference in 1922, he called for regulation so that "there may be no national regret that we have parted with a great national asset into uncontrolled hands."[14] He said that the rights of listeners took priority over those of speakers in articulating a policy of listener sovereignty. "The dominant element in the radio field is, and always will be, the great body of the listening public," he told the Fourth National Radio Conference. Hoover insisted that radio was "too important for service, news, entertainment, education and vital commercial purposes to be drowned in advertising chatter or for commercial purposes that can quite well be served by other means of communication."[15]

Hoover connected the limited number of radio frequencies

with the many consumers of radio programming. He argued that spectrum scarcity (that is, a scarcity of radio frequencies compared with the number of those who wish to broadcast) supported listeners' sovereignty over broadcasters' free expression. "We do not get much freedom of speech if fifty people speak at the same time," Hoover said of the chaotic interference in radio. Jumping quickly to listener sovereignty, he continued, "Nor is there any freedom in a right to come into my sitting room to make a speech whether I like it or not. . . . There are two parties to freedom of the air, and to freedom of speech," Hoover pointed out. "There is the speaker and the listener. Certainly in radio I believe in freedom for the listener. He has much less option upon what he can reject, for the other fellow is occupying his receiving set. The listener's only option is to abandon his right to use his receiver. Freedom cannot mean the license to every person or corporation who wishes to broadcast his name or wares, and thus monopolize the listener's set. No one can raise a cry of deprivation of free speech if he is compelled to prove that there is something more than naked commercial selfishness in his purposes."[16]

Despite the stridency of Hoover's rhetoric on listener sovereignty, in practice Hoover granted more licenses at more powerful frequencies to large commercial broadcasters in preference to smaller educational, religious, or labor broadcasters. In his view commercial broadcasters provided a greater diversity of programming to the public than broadcasters in one special area.

House and Senate Republicans advanced Hoover's principles within a licensed system with broadcaster discretion. "The right of the public to [radio] service," Representative Wallace H. White, Republican floor leader on the Radio Bill, succinctly said, was "superior to the right of any individual to use radio."[17] This position had short-term benefits of providing a rationale for coming to terms with Democrats and Progressives, who were pushing for expansive access for politicians and public affairs. And White's formulation had long-term political and regulatory consequences. It stood the First Amendment on its head by taking free speech from speakers and granting it to listeners in broadcasting. This pragmatic rationale, highly useful in 1927, set in motion more than six decades of law and regulation disputing broadcasters' free speech rights.

Representative White cautioned that "we are here dealing with a new means of communication."[18] White argued that existing regulatory agencies like the Interstate Commerce Commission and the Federal Trade Commission—neither of which had ever indicated any capacity to regulate political speech in broadcasting—could police radio. The Clayton and Sherman antitrust acts protected the public adequately from monopolistic practices in radio, White insisted. "A reasonable doubt [exists] whether we are justified in applying to this industry different and more drastic rules than the other forms of communication are subjected to."[19] He continued, "Laws, narrow, restrictive, destructive to a new industry serve no public good. We should avoid them."[20]

Like White, Representative Arthur M. Free (R-Cal.) warned that burdensome regulation would retard an infant industry: "The question you . . . have got to consider is whether or not you are going to apply special rules to a new and baby industry that you do not apply to any other industry in the United States."[21] The Federal Trade Commission, with its focus on restraint of trade and monopolistic practices, and the Interstate Commerce Commission, with its focus on price fixing, were sufficient federal authority to police monopoly in radio and abuses in political programming by radio broadcasters, Free contended. Only AT&T's 18 out of 536 radio stations licensed to others were cross-licensed according to Republican figures. Two- to three-hundred competing firms manufactured receivers, and over three thousand manufactured radio parts and accessories. These industry dynamics, coupled with the "public interest standards" that suffused the radio bill, were sufficient, Free believed, to ensure the flow of news, political, and public affairs programming to the public.

■ Powerful Senate Progressives Robert LaFollette, Jr. (R/Progressive-Wis.) and Hiram Johnson (R-Cal.) opposed the Hoover plan of imposing nothing more stringent than general public interest obligations on broadcasters. They insisted on common carrier stipulations for candidates' access to the radio airwaves during political campaigns and citizens' access for the discussion of public affairs. They charged that broadcaster censorship and price discrimination limited the diversity of political viewpoints. Each had felt the brunt of broadcaster censorship. Senators Johnson and LaFollette complained that broadcasters in Detroit and Des Moines, respectively, had relegated them to low-power frequencies so that they reached only a fraction of their potential radio audiences. They insisted on a bipartisan commission, not the commanding commerce secretary, to oversee radio and pushed equal time for candidates and public affairs through the Senate Interstate Commerce Committee. The bill also put Secretary of Commerce Hoover on notice of strong support in the Senate for a bipartisan commission as the federal licensing authority.[22]

In the House, Democrats inserted language that radio would be considered as a "common carrier in interstate commerce" for candidates and public affairs. They were at the edge of creating a law that defined politicians' and the public's access rights as prior to the free speech rights of broadcasters. If the bill survived conference, broadcasters would have no choice but to grant equal time to opposing politicians seeking election and to citizens discussing controversial public issues. They also proposed a bipartisan commission of five members, chosen from various sections of the country, to oversee licensing. Such a regulatory body, they claimed, would be more responsive to equal time than the secretary of commerce. Through its bipartisan quality, the commission would also limit the potential for government suppression of freedom of speech, they asserted. Such a commission also put direct control of licenses beyond Hoover's reach for his upcoming presidential bid in 1928. Senator Clarence C. Dill (D-Wash.) remarked, for example, that in placing licensing authority in a bipartisan commission, broadcasters need not be "under the fear which they must necessarily feel, regardless of which party may be in power, when the control is placed in the hands of an administrative branch of the Government."[23]

Fear of media power animated Progressive and Democratic insistence on common carrier provisions for candidates and public affairs within a licensed system. "What greater monopoly," Representative Luther H. Johnson (D-Tex.) asked his House colleagues, "could exist than where a radio company could give the free use of its line to one candidate for office, one contender of some economic theory, and then deny such . . . to those who are on the other side of the question? . . . If the strong arm of the law does not prevent monopoly ownership, and make [price] discrimination by such stations illegal, American thought and American politics will be largely at the mercy of those who operate these stations. For publicity is the most powerful weapon that can be wielded in a republic, and when such a weapon is placed in the hands of one, or a single selfish group is permitted to either tacitly or otherwise acquire ownership and dominate these broadcasting stations throughout the country, then woe be to those who dare to differ with them. It will be impossible to compete with them in reaching the ears of the American people."[24]

Remarking on rapid technological innovations in radio and its diffusion into American society, Johnson continued, "It will only be a few years before broadcasting stations will . . . bring messages to the fireside of nearly every home in America." Broadcasters would use this immense power to shape public opinion: "They can mold and crystallize sentiment as no agency in the past has been able to do." He continued, "The power of the press will not be comparable to that of broadcasting stations when the industry is fully developed."[25]

Johnson advanced equal time for candidates and public affairs. He proposed that "equal facilities and rates, without discrimination, shall be accorded to all political parties and candidates for office, and to both proponents and opponents of all political questions and issues," in essence a common carrier stipulation.[26]

Representative Emanuel Celler (D-N.Y.) supported Johnson by citing price discrimination and censorship. WEAF, AT&T's owned and operated station in New York, charged Celler "$10.00 for every minute [he] desired to use the radio during the last election." Celler said, "I have no knowledge that candidates of the opposing party were asked to pay the same amount for the same use." Representative Ewin Davis (D-Tenn.) complained that broadcasters censored news and politics. He cited congressional testimony by AT&T vice president W. E. Harkness that AT&T routinely rejected applications to use its toll broadcast facilities. Responding directly to LaGuardia's concern about government censorship, Davis told his colleagues, to the applause of the House chamber, "I am even more opposed to private censorship over what American citizens may broadcast to other American citizens. . . . There is nothing in the present bill which even pretends to prevent it or to protect the public against it."[27]

Nor was Progressive and Democratic concern about media

power without foundation. In the protracted fight over radio legislation, dating from 1922, Congress had authorized a Federal Trade Commission (FTC) investigation of monopolistic practices in radio. The FTC study had documented flagrant monopolistic practices. It showed that eight corporations—the Radio Corporation of America, General Electric, American Telephone and Telegraph, Western Electric, Westinghouse, International Radio Telegraph Company, United Fruit Company, and the Wireless Specialty Apparatus Company—had restrained competition and created an oligopoly in the domestic manufacture, purchase, and sale of radio transmitters and receivers as well as in domestic and international radio communication and broadcasting. "There is not any question whatever," Representative Davis said, that "the radio monopoly . . . is one of the most powerful, one of the most effective monopolies in the country . . . a monopoly, the capital stock whose members are quoted on the stock exchanges for $2.5 billion dollars."[28] An infant industry, indeed.

■ Senator Clarence C. Dill (D-Wash.), the heartiest promoter of equal time, introduced the concept as "equal opportunities" for candidates to use radio during election campaigns. "Equal opportunities" quickly transmuted into "equal time." Dill's amendment stipulated equal opportunities for legally qualified candidates. In fact, Dill was so skillful that a journalist would later remark, "He did the one thing that in this day and age gives a man a stranglehold on his job. He became a specialist in a field so new, so complicated, and so interwoven with technicalities of speech and function that there were none to dispute him."[29] So commanding was Dill's technical competence that the senator from Washington became as influential in radio legislation as Commerce Secretary Hoover and Senate giants Hiram Johnson and Robert LaFollette, Jr.

Progressives criticized equal time for political candidates as restrictive, confusing, palliative, narrow, and anemic. Senator Albert B. Cummins of Iowa, a Republican with a career of progressive political reform against the railroad interests, complained that Dill's amendment was confusing. Although radio would not be designated as a common carrier in political programming, Dill's language of equal opportunities would nonetheless require broadcasters to behave as though they were.

Not so, Dill responded: "If a radio station permits one candidate for a public office to address the listener, it must allow all candidates for that public office to do so." This, Dill said, was far different from common carrier stipulations compelling broadcasters to "take anybody who came in order of the person presenting himself and be compelled to broadcast for an hour's time speeches of any kind they wanted to broadcast."[30] Dill's amendment required only that broadcasters provide equal opportunities to all legally qualified candidates if they had granted air time to one candidate. "In other words," Dill told his fellow senators, "a station may refuse to allow any candidate to broadcast; but if it allows one candidate for governor to broadcast, then all the candidates for governor must have an equal right; but it is not required to allow any candidate to broadcast."[31]

Equal time for political candidates was too restrictive, Cummins countered. It allowed broadcasters to regulate political programming. "If we are going to allow [radio] to be used for political purposes at all," Cummins said, "it will become a common carrier as to political service, and . . . Senator [Dill] is simply providing a situation in which broadcasting will be denied to political candidates." Dill parried. He promoted equal time in the spirit of fairness and pragmatism. "I think it would be better to deny [equal time] altogether than to allow the candidate of one party to broadcast and the candidates of the other party not to be able to secure the same right."[32]

Senator Robert B. Howell (R-Neb.), a Progressive advocate of public utility ownership, demanded that broadcasters be required to grant citizens' access for discussion of public issues. Spectrum scarcity vitiated radio industry arguments that broadcasters were like newspapers, he charged. Democracy required a constant flow of news and information to the public, Howell said. He worried about entrusting so important a task to commercial broadcasters. "We are not trying merely to place the privilege of broadcasting within the reach of all so far as cost is concerned," Howell said. "We want to place it within the reach of all for the discussion of public questions when one side or the other is allowed to be presented." He cited the tariff fight. Democrats generally favored free trade and a low tariff, and Republicans defended a protective tariff. Equal time for political candidates was too narrow for full discussion of so vital an issue. "Under this amendment . . . a reduction of the tariff could not be discussed over an eastern radio station. They could prevent it. It might be that in southern sections a discussion of the tariff from the Republican point of view would not be allowed"[33]

Citizens' access for public affairs would doom broadcasting, Dill cautioned. "There is probably no question of any interest whatsoever that could be discussed but that the other side of it could demand time, and thus a radio station would be placed in the position . . . that [it] would have to give all [its] time to that kind of discussion, or no public question could be discussed." He reassured Howell that setting federal policy for public affairs programming and access rights for issue-oriented citizens would be taken up by the Federal Radio Commission once the Radio Act was enacted. Right now, getting the Radio Act on the books was what mattered, and he could not get the bill through Congress with a stipulation that broadcasters be required to act as common carriers for public affairs programming.[34]

Unimpressed, Howell shot back, "Abuses have already become evident. . . . We do not need to wait to find out about these abuses. . . . We ought to meet these abuses now, and not enact a bill which in the future it will be very difficult to change, when these great interests, more and more control the stations of this country; and that, apparently, is the future of broadcasting." Howell continued, "We are discussing a supervehicle of publicity. . . . Unless we now exercise foresight we will wake up some day to find that we have created a Frankenstein monster. . . . The time to check abuses is at the beginning, in the infancy of development of this great vehicle of publicity. . . . Everyday, radio is reaching more and more homes, and there are the great interests, for instance, the General Electric Company, which can thus enter nearly every equipped home in the United States with their radio stations. They have them hooked up so that one station receives what another sends out. Moreover, the General Electric Company and the Radio Corporation of America have been afforded the most powerful stations in the United States. . . . Are we going to allow these great interests to utilize their stations to disseminate the kind of publicity only of which they approve and leave opportunity for the other side of public questions to reach the same audience?"[35]

Howell had offered solutions. He had proposed limiting discussion to one affirmative or negative rejoinder. If a number of people requested time, they could either agree on a representative among themselves or, if no agreement could be reached, they could draw lots. The Senate Interstate Commerce Committee rejected the proposal. The Senate agreed with Dill. Howell had to settle for a clause in Section 18 that "it shall be the duty of the commission to adopt and promulgate rules and regulations" on equal time for candidates.

Senator Howell's rhetoric about Frankenstein is revealing for the anxiety it expresses toward media oligopolists, which, he feared, if uncontrolled, could destroy democratic institutions. The potential dangers of broadcaster manipulation of public opinion assaulted the Progressives' identification of good government with an informed electorate capable of making independent political decisions after digesting news and public affairs, hence Howell's insistence along with that of Senators Hiram Johnson and Robert LaFollette, Jr., that radio broadcasters be designated as common carriers in radio news, political, and public affairs programming.

This Progressive position differed appreciably from Commerce Secretary Hoover's. The difference turns on common carrier stipulations within a licensed system or broadcaster discretion in a system of licensing. Howell, Johnson, and LaFollette supported common carrier stipulations as a means of sustaining an informed electorate. Hoover, by contrast, advocated broadcaster discretion. In his view broadcaster abuses could best be curbed after a broadcaster had violated the "public interest" in the quality of his radio service or in the partiality of his news and political programming.

Dill emerged triumphant in Senate debate. Dill's amendment emerged as Section 18 of the Radio Act of 1927, which became Section 315 of the Communication Act of 1934, cornerstones of mass communications law in the United States. Equal time extended to candidates but not public affairs. Politicians could command equal time only if broadcasters had granted or sold air time to legally qualified candidates for the same office. Rather than deal with the statute's ambiguities, Congress empowered a bipartisan commission, the Federal Radio Commission (FRC), to make rules and regulations implementing the compromise rule.

By distinguishing broadcaster regulation from broadcaster discrimination, Dill succeeded in creating a law that provided broadcasters some discretion in political programming and ensured candidates' access. Such a course seemed wholly reasonable. Broadcasters entered the radio industry voluntarily. Listeners paid nothing for radio service beyond the cost of receivers. The radio marketplace encouraged broadcasters to provide equal time to build their own reputations among listeners. With such incentives and constraints, common carrier stipulations were gratuitous. "It seemed unwise," Dill said, "to put the broadcaster under the hampering control of being a common carrier and compelled to accept anything and everything that was offered to him as long as the price was paid."[36]

■ As president, Hoover vetoed a law to extend equal time to public affairs and stymied provisions for procedural changes and greater administrative authority for the FRC. The broadened legislation included equal time for people to speak for and against candidates, referenda, and public issues.[37]

The Federal Radio Commission realized Hoover's architectural scheme. Commercial broadcasters won more licenses at stronger frequencies than educational, labor, and religious organizations. First, the FRC redesigned licensing. Louis G. Caldwell, the FRC's first general counsel, proposed a license reallocation plan in 1928, designating forty "clear channels" with as much power as 50,000 watts, cutting back the number of existing frequencies, and effectively ending previous time sharing among some licensees. Many of the forty channels went to broadcasters affiliated with the National Broadcasting Company (NBC), the Columbia Broadcasting System (CBS), or commercial broadcasters. Educational, labor, and religious broadcasters competed for space on fifty additional channels that reached local and regional audiences. Second, the FRC articulated Hoover's policy of listener sovereignty, based on spectrum scarcity, as federal regulation. In *Great Lakes Broadcasting Company,* a regulatory ruling, the FRC stated that it would favor broadcasters serving "the entire listening public" with "well rounded" programming, which listeners, responding in a marketplace, could and would determine. Because of spectrum scarcity, broadcasters would be expected, the FRC noted, to cooperate with educational, religious, social, and labor groups so that the public would receive a diversity of information. "There is not room in the broadcast band for every school of thought, religious, political, social, and economic, each to have its separate broadcasting station, its mouthpiece in the ether."[38]

Educators split into a group that pushed for cooperation and a group that demanded frequencies for educational programming. The latter group demanded a clear national channel under government control, modeled after the BBC, that, they claimed, would provide public affairs programming and a quality alternative to the commercial networks. Commercial broadcasters censored controversial public affairs, they asserted; such "private" censorship in mass communications jeopardized democracy. In 1931 and 1932 they pushed unsuccessfully for 15% of the radio spectrum. In another setback the FRC reported that cooperation was the ideal way to reach mass audiences and that broadcasters depended on advertising to operate.[39]

■ At this early stage of broadcast regulation, politicians tended their own garden. Congress imposed licensing and enacted equal time for legally qualified candidates during electoral campaigns. Congress empowered a bipartisan commission, the Federal Radio Commission and its successor the Federal Communications Commission, with considerable discretion to regulate a system of commercial licensees.[40] The FRC and FCC relied on this enabling legislation to cow commercial broadcasters by granting and revoking licenses. Consequently commercial licensees promised greater compliance with politicians and regulators than religious, educational, or labor broadcasters with partisan agendas, operating either on nationalized or common carrier systems. Equal time was icing for the licensing cake. In the eyes of a subsequent observer, equal time was the "most human" and "amusingly specific" section of the Radio Act "bespeaking delightfully the solidarity of the political fraternity."[41]

Equal time, coupled with "public interest" obligations, proved to be the functional compromise between broadcasters, politicians, and regulators that enabled commercial broadcasters to dominate American radio. Western Progressives and Southern Democrats had won their point to the extent that equal time imposed common-carrier-like obligations on broadcasters for legally qualified political candidates. At the same time, Hoover, with his vision of a national system of licensees regulated "in the public interest," also emerged as a partial victor. Radio took the commercial direction, providing mass entertainment which Hoover, and later the Federal Radio Commission and Federal Communications Commission, supported with licensing policies that favored larger commercial broadcasters.

Listener sovereignty and spectrum scarcity were twin pillars supporting the regulatory scaffolding. Congress enacted law making listeners, rather than speakers, sovereigns of broadcasting due to spectrum scarcity. To be sure, Congress created the scarcity by empowering the FRC to control allocation and assignment of radio frequencies. Policymakers dismissed broadcasters' free speech rights. Both the Progressives' position for common carrier stipulations and Hoover's in favor of broadcaster discretion in a commercially based system of licensees abrogated the free speech rights of radio broadcasters. Hoover's position on listener sovereignty is coincidental with Supreme Court decisions on "clear and present danger" in political speech. Both in Hoover's criterion and Court rulings the First Amendment rights of speakers may be justifiably abridged to achieve the public interest.

In agreeing to meet "public interest" obligations and equal time, broadcasters retained limited discretion in political programming. As Senator Dill put it, "a station [could] regulate, but it [could not] discriminate."[42] To be sure, it might be a negative power to deny access to all candidates. But it might be sound business sense to allow access to any number of politicians to indicate evenhandedness on public affairs to listeners. In either case, by accepting the quid-pro-quo of serving vague "public interest" obligations and providing candidates' access, broadcasters freed themselves to exploit radio's commercial potential and shackled themselves to FRC and FCC regulation.

This regulatory architecture promised confusion.[43] Equal time ensured broadcaster discretion and provided common-carrier-like guarantees for political candidates. The FRC was to be empowered to cope with difficult interpretative tasks that balanced these contradictory requirements. Equal time partisans would champion differing interpretations of congressional intent to manipulate commission decisions, and the commission behaved similarly for its own institutional purposes. Although precise in its provisions, the very name "equal time" suggested common carrier obligations exceeding broadcasters' responsibilities as licensees.

FDR, Equal Time,
and Public Affairs

2

Times have changed. . .
The world has gone mad today,
And goods bad today
And blacks white today
And days night today
When most guys today
That women prize today
Are silly gigolos
. . . Anything goes.
Cole Porter, "Anything Goes"

In his first inaugural address, Franklin Delano Roosevelt claimed extraordinary powers to combat the Great Depression. "In the event the national emergency is still critical," Roosevelt said, "I shall not evade the clear course of my duty."[1] With these words, Roosevelt sent a collective shiver through the spine of the nation's broadcasters. FDR might visit their worst fears of nationalization on them. Using the fullest powers of the presidency, Roosevelt could take their licenses to marshal broadcasting as a public utility in the national recovery.

How much was current exigency and how much the long reach of navy plans to nationalize radio, RCA officials, as owners of NBC, may well have wondered. As Wilson's assistant secretary of navy, Roosevelt had participated in discussions in 1919 between the navy and General Electric when GE was setting up RCA. Roosevelt gave tentative approval to GE's cross-licensing and patent-sharing plan to establish RCA that April. The following month, Navy Secretary Josephus Daniels, just returned from Europe with President Wilson, overruled Roosevelt and called for a nationalized radio system controlled by the navy.[2] As president of a country suffering economic paralysis, FDR might well reach back to Daniels's nationalization plan.

Cooperation emerged even more strongly as industry policy. William S. Paley, the young, dynamic president of the Columbia Broadcasting System, wired President Roosevelt with his willingness to lend CBS support in coping with the emergency.[3] "President Roosevelt if he chose to do so might have commandeered the radio for the government as though the nation were at war," observed the radio trade journal *Broadcasting,* "but the immediate cooperation extended by radio obviated any suggestion that such a need would arise."[4]

FDR manipulated broadcasters against proponents of nationalization within his administration, including Secretary of Interior Harold Ickes, Secretary of Labor Frances Perkins, and Secretary of Agriculture Henry Wallace, to get the maximum radio coverage for his New Deal programs. With the help of White House insiders Louis Howe, Marvin McIntyre, and press secretary Stephen Early, FDR muscled commercial broadcasters and broadcast networks to provide national coverage of his fireside chats by forcing the radio networks to interconnect his broadcasts with all their affiliates. That way FDR reached a national audience, something neither Father Coughlin nor Huey Long could do with their popular broadcasts. The president also outdistanced himself from other political foes. For example, in the court-packing fight in 1937, FDR and the attorney general both commanded a national audience, whereas FDR's opponents proved unable to reach the entire nation.[5]

President Roosevelt used the Federal Communications Commission as a tool to keep broadcasters jittery and compliant. He appointed Herbert L. Petty, former director of radio publicity for the Democratic National Committee, as executive secretary of the FRC in 1933. That July, the FRC, responding to a suggestion from the president's secretary Louis Howe, requested that licensees submit copies of public affairs speeches. The commission renewed licenses for six-month periods during part of the 1930s. The FCC dropped a proposal obligating broadcasters to provide specified amounts of educational programming in 1934 after NBC showed that it had aired 871 administration broadcasts, amounting to 250 hours for no fee as "educational programming." In 1936 the White House helped Massachusetts Democrat James Michael Curley and the Chicago Federation of Labor to win more powerful frequencies for friendly broadcasters. In the late 1930s the FCC began to investigate broadcast monopoly, specifically exploring NBC's dominant red and blue networks and CBS's emergence as a strong number two. Under activist chairman James Lawrence Fly, the Commission investigated newspaper ownership of radio licenses. In October 1941 Fly notified Roosevelt that neither isolationist nor interventionist foreign policy received an upper hand on network public affairs programs, a clear indication that the FCC was monitoring networks and that broadcasters accommodated a significant interest group.[6] Nor did Roosevelt want to tackle broadcasters frontally. By the 1930s broadcasters marshaled an effective lobby in Washington, and President Roosevelt enjoyed ready compliance through FCC monitoring and licensing authority.[7]

Nationalization did not repay Congress. Broadcast industry policy of cooperation succeeded in creating a system in which major party politicians reached the public. Although FDR's opponents uniformly failed to wrest broadcast time that reached national audiences, they succeeded in winning a great deal of time for political addresses carried regionally or locally. The radio networks, or "chains" as they were called in the thirties, willingly granted time in order to sustain impartiality and avoid threats to their licenses. As radio prospered, entertainment celebrities such as Jack Benny, Fred Allen, and Fibber McGee and Molly and respected news commentators such as H. V. Kaltenborn, John MacVane, and Elmer Davis, all commanded national audiences. No congressman or senator chose to assault such popularity. Congress was also reluctant to tackle compensation for broadcast studios and transmitters if radio was to be nationalized, and hugely popular broadcasters had to be bought out.[8]

Fireside chats, another tool in the president's arsenal, enabled Roosevelt to speak directly to the public without triggering equal time. During his presidency, Roosevelt delivered approximately thirty fireside chats. Six, from March 1933 to September 1934, covered bank closings and economic recovery. Ten, from 1941 to 1943,

(top) President Calvin Coolidge with Secretary of Commerce Herbert Hoover addressing participants of a national radio conference at the White House, October 1924. Courtesy of the Library of Congress.

(bottom) Secretary of Commerce Herbert Hoover, architect of American radio and television regulation. Courtesy of Herbert Hoover Presidential Library.

(top) Senator Clarence C. Dill, architect of equal time, in the late 1920s. Courtesy of UPI/Bettmann Newsphotos.

(bottom) Senator Hiram Johnson (R/Prog.–Calif.), an advocate of common carrier rules for public affairs for radio. Courtesy of the United States Senate.

(top left) Senator Robert LaFollette, Jr. (R/Prog.-Wis.), an advocate of common carrier rules for public affairs for radio. Courtesy of the United States Senate.

(top right) Fiorello H. LaGuardia. As a congressman, LaGuardia warned of censorship of radio through licensing. Courtesy of LaGuardia Archives, Fiorello H. LaGuardia Community College.

(bottom left) Senator Wallace H. White (R-Me.), a Republican leader on communications regulation from the 1920s to the 1940s. Courtesy of the United States Senate.

(bottom right) Congressman Luther A. Johnson (D-Texas), an advocate of common carrier rules for public affairs for radio. Courtesy of the Library of Congress.

Senator Robert B. Howell (R/Prog.-Neb.) had his automobile equipped with a radio transmitter for his 1928 reelection bid. Advance men went from town to town circulating handbills informing radio owners of the times of Howell's broadcasts. Howell advocated common carrier rules for public affairs for radio. Courtesy of UPI/Bettmann Newsphotos.

William S. Paley, president of CBS, making the contact that opened the world's then-largest hookup of radio stations. Courtesy of UPI/Bettmann Newsphotos.

President Franklin Delano Roosevelt gets a helping hand from Massachusetts governor James Michael Curley during a radio address from Boston. As president, Roosevelt made numerous regional and local broadcasts during his extensive travels throughout the country. Courtesy of the Mayor's Office of Public Service, Boston.

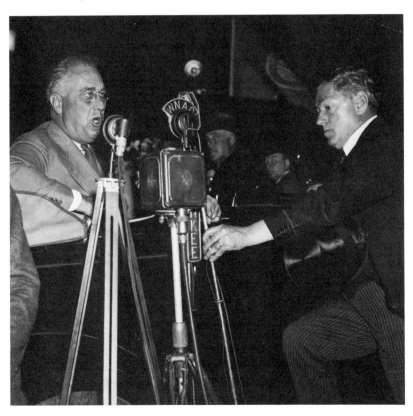

explained US policy toward the Allies and the Axis, US entry into World War II, domestic policy, the coal crisis, and a report on the Cairo conference. Only one, "On Conserving Soil, Water and Life," in September 1936 took place when FDR was a candidate for reelection. When Los Angeles stations KFI and KECA refused to carry the chat unless the Democratic National Committee paid for the air time under equal time, Federal Communications commissioner George Henry Payne blasted the licensee as a "censor."[9] In 1938 the FCC issued rules and regulations on Section 315 of the Communications Act that sustained congressional language that candidates enjoyed equal time, but the discussion of public affairs did not invoke the law, thus freeing Roosevelt from national responses to his fireside chats.

Roosevelt carefully orchestrated regional and local broadcasts so as not to overuse the popular fireside format. In October 1934 White House advisers cautioned FDR that his extensive use of radio was diluting his impact. Roosevelt delivered only two chats in 1935 and 1936. He increased regional and local broadcasts during his many travels about the country. White House press secretary Stephen Early routinely notified broadcasters of the president's itinerary, regional times, the length of any remarks, and whether the president wanted local, regional, or national hookups.[10]

Broadcasters tended their reputations unfailingly to assure popular esteem and defuse possible nationalization demands. NBC broadcast only live entertainment, and required any entertainer performing after 6 pm to wear evening clothes and black tie. As a rule, NBC, CBS, and Mutual refused advertising for "beer, wine, liquor, deodorants, depilatories, undertakers, cemeteries or any financial schemes."[11]

Congressional progressives—New York Democrat Robert Wagner and Henry D. Hatfield (R-W.V.)—failed to extend equal time to public affairs. The Wagner-Hatfield amendments to the Communications Act of 1934 mirrored those of Southern Democrats and Western progressives in the 1920s. They called for "equal opportunities" for access for issue-oriented citizens to discuss candidates, election issues, and referendum questions.

The Wagner-Hatfield amendments designated one-quarter of the radio channels for nonprofits, a position Senators Dill and White (formerly Representative White) and the radio industry attacked.

Dill and White argued that broadcasters with specific interests would discriminate against those who did not share their points of view. They cautioned against government discrimination in assigning licenses to some educational, religious, labor, and cooperative organizations but not to others. They predicted that programming costs for full-time radio stations would force the nonprofits to become like commercial broadcasters. Commercial broadcasters devoted significant programming to religious and educational programming.[12] In short, Dill and White said that the commercially dominant model of licensees produced a greater quantity of balanced programming for general public service as well as news, political, and public affairs programming.

The radio industry cited cooperation to defend broadcasters' discretion. "Almost every one recognizes that, despite minor defects, the Radio Act of 1927, and the court decisions under it, have established a solid, workable and sound basis for government regulation of radio," an industry spokesman told a Senate hearing. "The National Association of Broadcasters," commented another, "fully agrees that the facilities of broadcasting should be made available in the fullest possible measure, as it maintains they are now, and either free of all charge or at the lowest possible cost, in the service of education, religion, or other activities for human betterment, but it insists that these facilities should be those of stations serving the public as a whole." Educators failed to mobilize behind the legislation.[13]

Wagner and Hatfield relented. In the end, Section 315 of the Communication Act of 1934 on equal time was identical with Section 18 of the Radio Act of 1927. The statutory language covered political candidates, not public affairs. They settled on a compromise on nonprofits, which called on the FCC to deliver a study on reserving a fixed percentage of the spectrum for nonprofits by February 1, 1935.[14] The FCC report, to no one's surprise, reaffirmed FRC policy that commercial stations served the public interest more effectively than nonprofits. Commercial broadcasters convinced the commission that they devoted approximately 15% of broadcast time to nonprofit and educational programming. Because of such cooperation, spectrum limits, questions about public demand, and the difficulties nonprofits would experience running nonprofit stations without becoming commercial broadcasters themselves, the commission decided that the wiser course lay in the existing co-operative arrangement. "It would appear that the interests of the non-profit organizations may be better served by the use of existing facilities, thus giving them access to costly and efficient equipment and to established audiences, than by the establishment of new stations for their peculiar needs."[15]

During the second world war President Roosevelt kept his distance from journalists. When meeting with British Prime Minister Churchill to draft the Atlantic Charter, FDR excluded American reporters. At the Casablanca conference in January 1943 President Roosevelt arrived in North Africa buffeted by criticism from radio commentators and newspaper columnists, many of whom supported his liberal policies, for failing to unite rival factions of the French resistance under Generals de Gaulle and Giraud. FDR distrusted de Gaulle as a right wing egotist, and wanted to leave open the issue of France's future government until after the war. But FDR needed the appearance of unity between the rival French leaders to mollify public opinion. After protracted negotiations, de Gaulle agreed to a photo with Giraud, with Roosevelt and Churchill looking on. Reporters were allowed in for the ceremonial photo and a final day FDR-Churchill press conference.[16]

The armed services refused to cooperate with the Office of War Information. Established in June 1942, six months after the war began, to centralize often chaotic reports, the Office of War Information ran aground of parochial army and navy interests, which continued releasing information as each service wished. Respected broadcaster Elmer Davis, whom Roosevelt appointed to run OWI, failed to rein in the services. The army went so far as to state that as creators of wartime news it deserved unique consideration "in the way [news] [was] reported and edited."[17]

By the end of the war the dominant system of commercial broadcasters flourished. Industry policy of cooperation succeeded in fending off the appeals of nationalization advocates during the Great Depression. Cooperation provided the FCC with a rationale for supporting commercial broadcasters and for extending its own authority. In the 1940s FCC policing powers over content would come back to haunt broadcasters, but it served them well in the 1930s by deflecting proposals for nationalization.

Franklin Delano Roosevelt mastered broadcast regulation by sidestepping equal time. As the only national leader capable of reaching a national audience, FDR enjoyed unparalleled range. FDR displayed a cunning grasp of communications law. With the exception of one fireside chat, Roosevelt delivered these seemingly intimate broadcast talks when he was not a candidate, so his opponents could not demand equal time. This worked well for broadcasters. They accommodated Roosevelt's opponents with regional and local responses and mollified his foes by passing the blame for incomplete network carriage on to unwilling affiliates. The system was open but selectively closed.

Industry cooperation, FDR's mastery of the radio, and failed efforts to legislate public affairs responsibilities in the Communications Act set the stage for the Fairness Doctrine, which came in the 1940s. By the late 1930s, the FCC's network inquiry and its investigation of newspaper ownership of radio stations were well underway. Although the investigation proved fruitless, the Court ruled the network inquiry inevitable. Indeed, FCC and Justice Department worries that oligopoly limited public affairs drove both investigations.

The Articulation of Fairness

3

I don't stay out late, don't care to go,
I'm home about eight, just me and my radio,
Ain't misbehavin', I'm savin' my love for you.
"Ain't Misbehavin'," 1941 pop hit. Music by Thomas "Fats" Waller and Harry Brooks. Words by Andy Razaf. 1929.

The Fairness Doctrine (1949) imposed two obligations on broadcasters: It required broadcasters to provide controversial news and public affairs, and it required broadcasters to provide reasonable opportunities for the presentation of contrasting viewpoints. This second obligation imposed contingent access obligations on broadcasters to provide reply time to issue-oriented citizens and organizations whenever broadcasters covered a controversial issue or editorialized on public issues. Thus broadcasters could trigger Fairness Doctrine compliants without editorializing. Spectrum scarcity was the doctrine's technological rationale. Because more people wished to broadcast than available frequencies could accommodate, broadcasters' "public trustee" obligations required explicit regulatory clarification, the FCC reasoned. The commission required neither of the Fairness Doctrine's obligations before 1949. Until then broadcasters had to satisfy only general "public interest" standards of the Communications Act.

■ The Fairness Doctrine had its beginnings in a noisy fight between Boston politicians and Boston radio commentator Leland Bickford, who blasted politicians relentlessly, sometimes unfairly and, at least once, foolishly over the Yankee Network's WAAB. On April 29,

1937, Bickford pressured Massachusetts governor Charles F. Hurley to veto legislation outlawing advertisements for painless oral surgery. The Massachusetts legislature had just passed a bill regulating dental practices. Hurley later told FCC hearing examiners that Bickford had visited him at the State House to complain that the new law would cost WAAB some of its advertising revenues. Hurley quoted Bickford's threats, "I have a powerful political factor in my radio station, and if you disregard my wishes . . . you will have to take the consequences." Hurley responded, "If that's the way you feel about it, I'm signing this bill right now," and kicked the cheeky broadcaster out of his office.[1]

Two years later, when the Yankee Network, licensee of WAAB, came before the Federal Communications Commission for license renewal, Boston's political elite turned out to castigate Bickford. WAAB also broadcast Father Charles E. Coughlin's partisan and, toward the end of Coughlin's career, anti-Semitic addresses. Hurley, by then a former governor, blamed Bickford's editorials for scuttling his 1938 reelection bid. Former Boston mayor Frederick W. Mansfield complained that WAAB unfairly denied reply time to a Bickford broadside in which the commentator had accused the outgoing mayor of padding the city payroll and making last-minute personnel transfers and promotions to embarrass incoming mayor Maurice Tobin. That hardy perennial of Boston politics, James Michael Curley, sent his campaign manager Francis B. Masterson, who testified that Curley found Bickford's editorials "violently slanderous and vituperous."[2]

Another applicant, Mayflower Broadcasting Company, had come to the fore. Mayflower petitioned the FCC for the Yankee Network's license. Yankee Network management had violated the public interest by peppering WAAB's news with Bickford's strident editorials, Mayflower charged. The FCC had a duty, according to Mayflower backers, to revoke WAAB's license. If the FCC failed to do so, the Yankee Network could use the scarce resource of its radio frequency to express the Yankee Network management's private views. Anxious to keep its lucrative license, Yankee Network management became contrite. The Yankee Network testified that management had stopped editorializing in mid-1938, and its attorney promised FCC hearing officers that the Yankee Network management would never again allow WAAB commentators to make editorial statements on its behalf.[3]

The Federal Communications Commission ruled in its *Mayflower* decision in 1941 that the Yankee Network could keep its license so long as Yankee Network management did not broadcast editorials on public issues and political candidates over WAAB. By accepting a license, the FCC ruled, broadcasters "assumed the obligation of presenting all sides of important public issues, fairly, objectively and without bias." By broadcasting opinionated editorials on public officials without providing reply time, the Yankee Network had neither fully nor objectively informed the public and hence was derelict as a public trustee. "Freedom of speech on the radio must be broad enough to provide full and equal opportunity for the presentation to the public of all sides of public issues," the FCC ruled. "Radio can serve as an instrument of democracy only when devoted to the communication of information and the exchange of ideas fairly and objectively presented."[4]

The FCC relied on spectrum scarcity as the technological basis for its *Mayflower* decision. Because of "the limitations in frequencies inherent in the nature of radio, the public interest can never be served by a dedication of any broadcast facility to support of [broadcasters'] own partisan ends. . . . The public interest—not the private—is paramount. . . . A truly free radio cannot be used to advocate the causes of the licensee," the FCC wrote. "It cannot be used to support the candidacies of his friends. It cannot be devoted to support the principles [the broadcaster] happens to regard most favorably. In brief, the broadcaster cannot be an advocate."[5]

Spectrum scarcity was hardly novel. In its *Mayflower* decision the FCC reiterated policy and court precedents that a scarcity of channels placed the flow of information to the public above the free speech rights of broadcasters. The Federal Radio Commission had stated such a policy as early as 1929 and as recently as its 1940 annual report; the FCC noted, "Stations are required to furnish well-rounded rather than one-sided discussions of public questions."[6]

In its reach, however, the *Mayflower* decision was quite novel. The FCC forbade licensee editorials entirely. The FCC went beyond its customary practice of policing public affairs programming at license renewals and of reviewing any abuses on a case-by-case basis after they had occurred. It placed a prophylactic ban on broadcasters' views. In so doing, the FCC exceeded statutory provisions in the Radio and Communications acts, neither of which specified public affairs programming or mentioned broadcaster editorials.

Its grasp was wholly formal. The FCC barred broadcast licensees from editorializing, but it did not forbid commentators like Bickford from editorializing on public issues. The *Mayflower* decision applied to commentators only if they spoke for licensees. Commentators continued to remark on the news, public affairs, and politicians as individuals, not as licensees' advocates. In striking this balance, the FCC sought to limit licensees' power while not violating the free speech rights of commentators, even those as foolish as the then-silenced Bickford.[7]

■ In June 1941 William S. Paley, president of CBS, complained that the FCC was terrorizing broadcasters. "In every other field of American industry," Paley told a congressional committee, "before one can be . . . stigmatized and punished as a monopolist, he must be made the subject of a judicial proceeding either by indictment or complaint. Here, the Commission . . . has chosen to act as complaining witness, prosecutor, judge, jury, and hangman, and we find ourselves . . . stigmatized as a monopolist and the most important practices of our business sweepingly abolished by administrative fiat. . . . We [broadcasters] are at a loss as to how to operate a network successfully under the new rules, either from our own selfish, economic point of view or from the standpoint of the public interest and good programming."[8]

An FCC report on chain broadcasting and new rules on network programming struck at the heart of broadcasting revenues. The FCC sought to break up NBC's red and blue networks and to end exclusive programming contracts between networks and affiliates. In so doing, the FCC jeopardized the ability of networks, specifically NBC and CBS, to sell national advertising. Although NBC proved the ultimate target of the report and a subsequent suit, FCC figures showed that NBC's dominant red and its smaller blue channel together with CBS blanketed 86% of evening radio. After factoring in the third-ranked Mutual Broadcasting System, FCC figures showed that the three networks saturated national evening programming, with 97% of the offerings. Once again, nationalization lurked as a possibility.[9]

To meet so grave a challenge to network operations, Paley offered four striking proposals: (1) license the networks, (2) enact a fairness law for public affairs, (3) redefine FCC discretionary authority, and (4) remove common carrier oversight from a restructured commission. Each served a purpose. Licensing networks would remove some of the sting of FCC accusations that networks were interlopers. Enacting a fairness law for public affairs strove to mollify isolationists, including Senator Burton K. Wheeler, chairman of the Senate commerce committee charged with overseeing broadcast regulation. Wheeler claimed that too many radio commentators were interventionists. Paley also intended the fairness proposal to assuage FDR's foes, who resented the president's ability to propagandize his programs with national coverage through fireside chats without triggering equal time. Restructuring of the FCC aimed to redefine the commission so that an activist chairman like Fly would no longer be able to claim discretionary authority beyond the commission's congressionally delegated powers.[10]

Public affairs dominated the fight. The FCC's *Report on Chain Broadcasting* and its 1941 exclusivity rules aimed to boost public affairs by individual broadcasters by breaking network dominance. Again Paley presented the broadcasters' argument. "The real heart of the charge of domination is the implication that the networks either can or do somehow manipulate public opinion to serve their own ends or the ends of favored persons or causes," Paley testified. "Long before the FCC looked at the issue [favoritism]," he continued, broadcasters "dealt with it voluntarily at great cost. . . . Except for declaring that all political candidates must be treated alike, the radio law itself is silent on this whole phase of broadcasting. . . . We recognized our ethics had to differ from those of press and other media of mass communication because of the physical limitations that Nature had put on broadcasting facilities. Thereupon Columbia publicly proclaimed that it would be forever noneditorial and free from bias and would never seek to promote its own views or those of others on controversial public questions."[11]

Paley's adroit strategy advanced broadcaster control while maintaining the appearance of a common carrier medium. Paley deftly increased broadcasting's influence by accommodating significant interest groups such as isolationists with impartial news and balanced commentary and educators and religious organizations through cooperation. CBS adhered to its policy of "having no editorial views of its own and not seeking to maintain or advance the views of others." "An excellent example of how fair and comprehensive broadcasting can be," Paley told Congress the summer before US entry into the war, "was furnished [in 1939] . . . when there were speeches from London, from Paris, and from Canada, but none from Germany which were made available for broadcasting. We succeeded in obtaining the text of various Hitler proclamations and statements and presented his side perhaps as well as if he had spoken."[12]

Prominent commentator William L. Shirer has complained that CBS's policy left Americans ignorant of Hitler's grave dangers. Shirer has asserted that broadcasters feared that controversial programming would scare away advertisers. The lengths to which Paley went to appease isolationists indicates that CBS attached equal seriousness to regulation. Had CBS editorialized for the allies before Pearl Harbor, it would have faced the immediate wrath from congressional isolationists. And CBS featured commentators like Shirer, who warned of the Nazi peril.[13]

Shortly thereafter, Paley retracted his proposal for a fairness law. A fairness law would vitiate its purpose, he warned. "For a year now we have struggled for a tenable suggestion as to how to write such a law and to create machinery to administer it without utterly destroying the freedom of radio broadcasting. I am simply afraid it cannot be done. I believe whoever has this power and however it is sought to be exercised, the only result can be to throttle free speech in the very commendable effort to make it free."[14] Spectrum scarcity was no grounds for a fairness law, he said. More than 900 radio broadcasters could program their own news and public affairs in 1941, if they chose. He credited listeners with adequate intelligence to choose other broadcasters if they disliked one's editorials. He cautioned against mathematical measurements of fairness. The better course lay in broadcasters' control and discretion, he said. Nothing came of Paley's four proposals.

■ In 1942 Henry Luce sat down to lunch with Robert Hutchins. The influential *Time* publisher wanted to discuss journalism's role in America with the energetic and thoughtful president of the University of Chicago. Luce told Hutchins that he was worried about further government regulation unless media corporations put their houses in order. Justice Department cases against NBC and the Associated Press for monopolistic practices were wending through the courts. With the war on, America would emerge as an international leader. For the country to function, media organizations had to inform Americans of a vastly more complicated world. Some sort of study was needed, one by the best people, Luce told Hutchins, to guide the press with its new responsibilities. Hutchins agreed. Any number of thoughtful people shared their concerns, he acknowledged, people like Harold Laswell, Arthur M. Schlesinger, Archibald MacLeish, Reinhold Niebuhr, Canada's John Grierson, and France's Jacques Maritian. Yes, he would assemble such a commission to look into things.

Five years later, the Hutchins commission offered its recommendations. The commission recommended that radio and films enjoy First Amendment freedoms comparable to print. It promoted new technologies as ways to increase media competition. It called for sparing use of antitrust law to break up monopolies and, in communities with natural media monopolies, for some mechanism for public access. It recommended more professionalism and mutual criticism. The Hutchins commission singled out broadcasting for its dependency on advertising and chided broadcast executives to exert more control for public affairs and quality programming. It recommended that an independent group assess press performance annually.[15]

Years later, at his Center for Democratic Institutions, Hutchins reprimanded broadcasters for failing to provide Americans with public affairs and high-quality entertainment. Television did nothing more than bring Coney Island into the American living room, the learned man complained.

■ At the Supreme Court in 1943, Justice Felix Frankfurter welcomed NBC's suit against the United States, a suit testing FCC authority to force the radio network to break up its red and blue channels. In *National Broadcasting Company v. United States,* Frankfurter affirmed FCC authority in expansive language. Congress had established the FCC to effect maximum efficiency of the radio spectrum through licensing. Accordingly the FCC was applying its licensing authority over NBC as "a proper exercise of its power over commerce."

Justice Frankfurter rejected NBC arguments that breaking up its dominant channels constituted a violation of its First Amendment freedoms and exceeded the FCC's statutory authority. As radio's "unique characteristic," spectrum scarcity legitimated application of the FCC's public interest standard, Frankfurter ruled.[16]

Justice Frank Murphy was not as sure. He questioned whether breaking up NBC would produce more public affairs and better entertainment. He doubted that Congress intended the FCC to exercise so much power. He acknowledged radio's pervasiveness and persuasiveness. And he worried that Frankfurter's affirmation of FCC powers could lead to censorship. "Events in Europe show that radio may readily be a weapon of authority and misrepresentation, instead of entertainment and enlightenment," Murphy observed. "It may even be an instrument of oppression. In pointing out these possibilities I do not mean to intimate in the slightest that they are imminent or probable in this country, but they do suggest that the construction of the instant statute [the Communications Act] should be approached with more than ordinary restraint and caution, to avoid an interpretation that is not clearly justified by the conditions that brought about its enactment, or that would give the Commission greater powers than the Congress intended to confer."[17]

In 1945, in *Associated Press v. United States,* the Supreme Court ruled that the Associated Press was engaging in monopolistic practices by offering its wire service to selected newspapers and denying it to their competitors. In the suit the Court combined antitrust law with the First Amendment to place the rights of the public to receive information above those of the press. "Surely a command that the government itself not impede the free flow of ideas does not afford non-governmental combinations a refuge if they impose restraints upon that constitutionally guaranteed freedom. Freedom to publish means freedom for all and not for some. Freedom to publish is guaranteed by the Constitution but freedom to combine to keep others from publishing is not."[18] The Court's standard of freedom of expression was virtually identical with the arguments, dating back to the national radio conferences and congressional debates in 1926 about freedom of speech over radio, in favor of listener sovereignty because of the technological constraints of a scarce radio spectrum. Only now the Court applied those standards to a wire service.

Both decisions, *NBC* and *AP,* became twin towers supporting expansion of FCC authority to public affairs programming.[19] The *NBC* case buttressed FCC licensing authority; the *AP* case provided further precedent for the FCC to police content on grounds of limiting private censorship.

The following year, 1946, the FCC flexed its public affairs muscle. In a book of standards that became known as the blue book,[20] the FCC deplored the preponderance of radio soap operas over news, public affairs, and classical music. It documented that network affiliates routinely rejected network-produced public affairs (sustaining) shows for music and light entertainment. Broadcasters' dependencies on advertising and the advertisers' insistence that radio offend no segment of any potential market combined to limit radio to banality and trivia, the FCC observed. In three rulings the FCC made public affairs programming a license requirement.[21]

■ In 1947 a petition from Cornell University radio station, WHCU, requesting the right to editorialize, provided the FCC with an opportunity to reconsider its *Mayflower* decision and to articulate a fairness policy.[22] At hearings the following year, issues moved from congressional concerns about patent monopoly and price discrimination, which dominated the Radio Act debate in the 1920s, to content regulation in broadcasters' news and public affairs. Spectrum scarcity, although less pressing than in 1926, played the critical technological role extending FCC authority to editorial content. Twelve hundred radio stations broadcast after World War II, up from about six hundred at the time of WAAB's editorials in 1937 and FCC fact finding for its *Report on Chain Broadcasting.*

The players changed. Regulators, broadcast executives, trade unionists, religious groups, academic experts, and, above all, attorneys emerged as key players. Former judge Justin Miller, representing the National Association of Broadcasters (NAB), former FCC chairman James Lawrence Fly, speaking for the American Civil Liberties Union, and Louis G. Caldwell, counsel for the Federal Radio Commission in the early days of broadcasting and Mutual Broadcasting's attorney at the Supreme Court in its successful collaboration with the FCC to break up NBC, shined as policy experts.

NAB director Justin Miller argued that broadcasters should enjoy the same First Amendment freedoms as print and that the

FCC had no authority to oblige broadcasters to carry news or editorials or to provide reply time. "It is entirely consistent with the concept of the First Amendment . . . that . . . the station operator may maintain his own editorial policy and expression, exclusively; that, as the Supreme Court has indicated . . . his editorials may be silly, grotesque and amateurish; perhaps his partisanship and bias may most effectively balance similar inadequate editorialization by other station operators or newspapers in his community. That is of the essence of freedom of speech and press, and it is thus that truth proves itself in the marketplace of ideas. Any other procedure means government interference, which violates the First Amendment."[23]

Broadcasters controlled public affairs and editorials with no reply time requirement, Miller insisted. "Whether he broadcasts formal programs, which he calls editorials, is a matter for him to decide, in his own judgment. Whether he does or not, he exercises editorial control, editorial selection and choice every hour of the day. It would be impossible for him to exercise the discretion vested in him by law, without using the methods of editorial control . . . [that are] consistent with, and appropriate to, the provisions of the First Amendment."

The FCC was overreaching by extending the public interest standard to broadcast editorials, Miller insisted. "It is absurd to say each outlet . . . must, as a condition of being allowed to speak, undertake to speak for everyone. The First Amendment recognizes the right of the individual listener or reader to make his own balance . . . or to make no balance at all, as he chooses." The FCC was powerless to lawfully challenge any licensee, Miller argued, until a broadcaster had been convicted of creating a clear and present danger through his public affairs programming and editorials. "In granting a license," Miller told the FCC, "you have no power to say anything about freedom of speech, one way or the other. All you are supposed to do is to grant a license so that a man can operate on a frequency, just as you would grant a license to sail a boat on a river." Miller blasted the FCC for intolerance and charged it with fashioning its fairness policy to control broadcasters. Only in small communities where one corporation controlled all media outlets could Congress legislate specific remedies for monopolistic practices, Miller asserted.[24]

James Lawrence Fly, ACLU attorney at the hearings and FCC chairman at the time of the *Mayflower* decision, countered that the FCC had full authority to require controversial news and public affairs and reply time to broadcaster editorials. NAB director Miller stood on "pathetic ground," amounting to little more than broadcaster censorship, Fly charged. Broadcasters enjoyed enormous institutional advantages in getting messages to the public; full editorial privileges would give them too much influence, Fly cautioned. "To permit a broadcaster to harangue the public with his own pet projects, candidacies and philosophy and exclude opposing views," Fly warned the FCC, "is to . . . endow the licensee with . . . a private property right . . . and would strike at the very roots of the First Amendment." To mute Miller's assault on an obligation to balance every issue, he pointed out that the commission historically supported "the right of citizens to hear diverging points of view" as part of the public interest standard. Broadcasters enjoyed no more right to editorialize than anyone else, Fly insisted. He recommended that the FCC enable them to do so as individuals, not as corporations.[25]

Louis G. Caldwell, former general counsel for the Federal Radio Commission, urged the FCC to lift the *Mayflower* decision on First Amendment and administrative grounds. As FRC general counsel, he testified that he had written "fair play" rulings for and against license renewals on substantially similar evidence. He warned that the FCC would be placing a prior restraint on freedom of expression by stipulating reply time, of the sort the commission later adopted in the Fairness Doctrine, as a condition for granting editorial privileges. Such a policy, Caldwell advised, would create impossible administrative problems by placing the FCC in the untenable position of policing content through a fairness standard. Miller and Fly agreed.[26]

Broadcasters divided on editorial privileges. One group, headed by CBS president Frank Stanton, championed unrestricted editorial rights, held out long-standing industry policy of cooperation, and argued that the FCC should concern itself exclusively with technical issues. Radio was "only half free," claimed Stanton, until broadcasters could editorialize. CBS's fairness policy in its news programming would not change with the right to editorialize, Stanton assured the FCC, nor would CBS alter its policy of providing free use of its facilities for controversial spokesmen. He merely resisted any FCC requirement to do so. It would be "constitutionally unsound," Stanton warned presciently. ABC president Woods maintained that broadcasters should be free to reject reply time to editorials if other media in their communities presented those views. "Radio . . . is only one of many effective means . . . for the expression of ideas."[27]

Others were willing to accept an FCC requirement to provide reply time to editorials. Nathan Straus, licensee of WMCA radio, supported editorial rights so long as stations programmed editorials for no more than fifteen minutes each day, labeled editorials as such at the beginning and end, granted rebuttal time, and read letters from the public following editorials. All licensees, save those stations controlled by absentee owners, should enjoy editorial rights, Straus testified. Morris Novick of WNYC favored editorial rights so long as the FCC required broadcasters to seek out people critical of editorials and provide them with reply time. Gordon P. Brown, licensee and general manager of WSAY in Rochester, urged abolition of the *Mayflower* decision for individual licensees but told the FCC that the editorial ban should still apply to networks.[28]

Farm and labor groups, heirs to Progressive and Democratic concerns about media monopoly, cautioned the FCC about granting broadcasters too much liberty. Joseph A. Breine, president of the Communications Workers, cited the influential Hutchins commission to argue that broadcasters' dependency on advertising revenues prevented "fair and reasonable" editorial policies. Eric Barnouw, president of the Radio Writers Guild, feared that independent editorial voices would be unable to assert themselves in huge entertainment corporations. The CIO's Henry C. Fleisher complained that "radio treated controversy as a form of leprosy, at best to be avoided, at worst to be handled under carefully prescribed conditions." Broadcasters "place[d] controversy in carefully sterilized cells," he said, so that "as few listeners as possible may be 'contaminated' by the expression of ideas."[29]

In the absence of the *Mayflower* decision, Charles Siepmann, *Blue Book* author and Columbia professor, worried that broadcasters would further stifle liberal commentators. CBS commentator William L. Shirer had lost his sponsor and had resigned from

CBS a year earlier, following his critical commentaries opposing the Truman Doctrine. "Know-how, institutional prestige, production skills, [and] command of people with public reputations" all gave broadcasters great advantages in shaping public opinion. To allow broadcasters to control public affairs programming, Siepmann advised the FCC, would grant them too much influence. "*Mayflower* should stand, broadcasters should content themselves with profits, and in the public interest forego the pleasure of the power conferred by editorial license," the wry Englishman testified.[30]

Reply time to broadcaster editorials coupled with an obligation to present news and public affairs emerged as the middle ground. This is the root meaning of "fairness." To the FCC "fairness" meant freedom of expression through broadcast editorials combined with a twofold duty to present controversial public issues in news programming and to provide access for a variety of views on controversial public issues.[31] The Fairness Doctrine was born.

In the Fairness Doctrine the FCC increased its control by changing the rules on broadcast news and public affairs. The FCC attached an affirmative obligation to seek out and present controversial public affairs programming as a license requirement. It replaced an a posteriori standard of public affairs programming with an a priori condition for maintaining a license. The FCC went beyond congressional definitions of broadcaster discretion "in the public interest" in 1926 and again in 1934. Broadcasters won those fights to classify themselves as licensees and not as common carriers precisely so they could decide what issues to cover and what news to present within the "public interest" standard. Long after Senator Howell had fruitlessly recommended a law requiring broadcasters to present "public questions" to radio listeners, there now stood a regulatory rule requiring broadcasters to behave as Howell had lectured an unwilling Congress twenty years earlier.

The FCC argued that spectrum scarcity was the sole reason why broadcasters enjoyed any control for radio news, public affairs, and political programming. Congress enacted a policy of licensing, which granted discretion to broadcasters, to provide broadcasters with legal protection to refuse requests for access to the scarce medium, the FCC wrote.

The FCC said it would implement the Fairness Doctrine in terms of overall news and public affairs programming, not on a case-by-case basis. Implementation turned on "the reasonableness of [a] station's actions" not "any absolute standards of fairness." What mattered, the FCC wrote in reference to hypothetical legislation, was whether "the licensee had permitted only advocates of the bill's enactment to utilize its facilities to the exclusion of its opponents. . . . No independent appraisal of the bill's merits by the Commission would be required to reach a determination that the licensee had misconstrued its duties and obligations . . . to serve the public interest." On content, however, the FCC drew the line at "stack[ing] the cards" in favor of one view. The FCC acknowledged no formula for measuring fairness or stacking. It noted that broadcasters should rely on their "good judgment," and that as a rule, good judgment would foster programming on all shades of opinion. In the end the FCC said that decisions on licenses could turn on the reasonableness of broadcasters' actions to achieve the practice of providing access to "responsible" individuals and organizations to address controversial public issues. It held up reasonableness as a "flexible standard" well within Anglo-American law. If broadcasters thought that the FCC enforced standards of fairness in an arbitrary or capricious manner, they could use "procedural safeguards" under the Communications Act and the Administrative Procedures Act and in the end resort to the courts.

The FCC rejected the broadcasters' arguments that reply time obligations were a prior restraint. In language comparable to the *Associated Press* decision, the FCC rebutted Justin Miller, Frank Stanton, and others: "The freedom of speech protected against government abridgement by the First Amendment does not extend any privilege to government licensees or means of public communications to exclude the expression of opinions and ideas with which they are in disagreement. We believe, on the contrary, that a requirement that broadcast licensees utilize their franchises in a manner in which the listening public may be assured of hearing varying opinions on the paramount issues facing the American people is within both the spirit and letter of the First Amendment."[32]

FCC extension of editorial rights to broadcasters was notably limp. The FCC ruled that "within reasonable limits" broadcaster editorials were "not contrary to the public interest." The commission noted that it was "not persuaded" that broadcasters' editorials "may not be actually helpful" in promoting informed public opinion. Nowhere in the Fairness Doctrine did the FCC renounce the *Mayflower* decision.

The Fairness Doctrine suffered deficiencies of form. The FCC announced its fairness rule as a regulatory memorandum, subject to agency revision. This gave the Fairness Doctrine a hazy status. Subsequently fairness proponents and opponents cited the doctrine's status as a regulatory memorandum to expand or diminish FCC authority, depending on their partisan interest.

In a blistering concurrence, Commissioner Robert F. Jones excoriated fellow commissioners for poor thinking and procedure and warned of implementation problems. He criticized the Fairness Doctrine for vagueness by conflating news, commentary, and editorialization. "Neither the general policy created nor the qualifications on the right to editorialize are made clear in terms free from ambiguity," Jones blasted. "Background, policy, example, qualification are commingled." He criticized reply time as an ambiguous and unenforceable prior restraint. It was one matter to enforce a specific decision after the fact of an abuse and another to hold up a standard of fairness that would be difficult to apply to daily news operations, he warned. He warned of FCC censorship by imposing its standards of "reasonableness" as a litmus test of broadcasters' freedom of expression. The FCC failed to follow correct administrative procedures by issuing the Fairness Doctrine as a regulatory memorandum, Jones charged. He chastised fellow commissioners for temerity by failing to repudiate the *Mayflower* decision as a previous censorial error. And he voted for fairness as an improvement over *Mayflower*'s prophylactic ban.

Nor was articulation of "fairness" as a doctrine firmly supported. Commissioner E. M. Webster voted for the Fairness Doctrine despite qualms that it left a "licensee in a quandary and a state of confusion." Commissioner Frieda Hennock cast the sole dissent: The doctrine would prove to be unenforceable, she cautioned. Two others, including Chairman Coy, were out of the country at the time and did not participate.[33]

■ Broadcasters responded cautiously. After pushing for abolition of the *Mayflower* decision, broadcasters now wondered if a fairness rule might become some sort of Frankenstein turning against them. *Broadcasting* worried that the doctrine's fairness requirement would foster conformity in public affairs programming by inhibiting broadcasters from taking partisan stands on controversial issues.[34]

■ Evidence suggests that the Fairness Doctrine reflected the cold war. The commission issued the Fairness Doctrine in 1949, four years after the Allies had defeated the Axis, within three years of Winston Churchill's warning of an iron curtain descending across Europe and George Kennan's long telegram on the Soviet threat, and just short of two years after the Truman Doctrine. A totalitarian Soviet foe threatened the United States. Freedom of expression was a major component of American internationalism. A democratic polity included "freedom of speech and religion" among other liberties, whereas a totalitarian system, in President Truman's words, "relie[d] on . . . a controlled press and radio" and other means of suppression to deny human rights.[35] As the Hutchins commission showed, classic democratic theory of an informed electorate reaching political decisions emerged even more strongly as the consensus in the late 1940s. In 1943, midpoint in the war, Judge Learned Hand, in his district court ruling in the *Associated Press* case, reaffirmed this democratic faith that "right conclusions are more likely to be gathered out of a multitude of tongues, than any authoritative selection. To many this is, and always will be folly, but we have staked upon it our all."[36]

Momentum ran toward content regulation for avowedly beneficent purposes of promoting democracy. In the dominant democratic ideology, broadcasters, while flashy capitalists, were not so far removed from totalitarians. The FCC viewed broadcasters as an undemocratic elite enjoying monopolistic privileges and inordinate influence and pushing for total control of the airwaves. In the *Mayflower* hearings, for example, James Lawrence Fly warned that NAB director Justin Miller "turn[ed] the right of exclusion over to the licensee. . . . With a thousand tongues free to criticize the government, democracy is secure," Fly advised the commission.[37]

By embracing content regulation, the FCC moved government involvement from the boardroom into the newsroom. To some extent, this course was as normal as it seems frightening. Twenty-two years earlier, grappling with radio as a new technology, Congress concerned itself with structural regulation to cope with oligopolistic practices in patents, transmitters, and receiving sets, cross-licensing arrangements, RCA's exclusive traffic arrangements with foreign governments and nations, and price discrimination against political candidates. Congress left questions of content regulation to the commission. The FCC deferred to FDR during the New Deal. The FCC participated in the dominant ideology of the cold war so fully that it imposed a prior restraint on broadcasters through the Fairness Doctrine, putting the FCC squarely in the newsroom.

First Amendment law supported FCC articulation of fairness. *NBC v. US* sanctioned FCC licensing authority, and *AP v. US* buttressed FCC thinking of broadcasters as monopolists. Beyond those cases indictments were issued in 1948 for *Dennis v. US,* ultimately decided in 1951, which revived arguments dating from the 1920s that speakers' rights may be justifiably abridged to protect the state. Broadcasters' free speech rights claimed no special exemption.[38]

The movement toward content regulation coincided with a movement away from nationalization. By 1949 few called for nationalization and instead promoted balance within news programs of commercial licensees. Gone was the New Deal faction promoting nationalization; gone, too, was any hint of nationalization from the FCC's 1941 proposed rules. Instead the FCC emerged as guardian of the constellation of public affairs concerns that had comprised the animating vision of both nationalization and common carrier models. James Lawrence Fly, ever mindful of FCC authority and anxious about commercial broadcasters, asked, "who knows, so far as CBS is concerned, what the future management will be and what its full policy will be, indeed who the future owners will be?" In the absence of such certainty and the probability that without regulation future owners could well exclude the public interest, the FCC moved toward content regulation. In issuing the Fairness Doctrine, the FCC went no further than what a majority of broadcasters evidently supported, according to a *Broadcasting* poll.

The FCC entered a legal and regulatory swamp by rejecting advice that a fairness policy would prove impossible to enforce despite warnings from partisans as antagonistic as James Lawrence Fly, Justin Miller, Frank Stanton, and Charles Siepmann. The Fairness Doctrine's spectrum scarcity rationale led to a unit of measurement that eventually eroded the doctrine's foundation. The individual broadcasters became the unit of measurement for fairness in public affairs because the FCC premised scarcity on the scarcity of frequencies compared to the number of individuals who wished to broadcast. As the number of media outlets expanded and provided many methods for listeners to receive information, this spectrum scarcity rationale wore thin.

The fairness battle shows that regulatory in-fighters won more clout, broadcasters won and lost some discretion, and the public would have to wait and see if the Fairness Doctrine would produce public affairs programming. Although politicians would remain dominant, following the Fairness Doctrine regulators, legal experts, partisans of any number of issues, and broadcasters exerted more influence on regulatory policy. Broadcasters won half a victory in the Fairness Doctrine because the FCC removed the *Mayflower* decision's prophylactic ban on editorials and acknowledged broadcasters' discretion, if not full control, concerning rights of reply. Things did not change much for the public. As vast entertainment corporations, broadcasters were first of all entertainment programmers. Public awareness of the Fairness Doctrine and its impact on news and public affairs awaited concrete tests.

The public interest and the image of Frankenstein are two themes running through fairness. "Public interest" suffuses the Radio and Communications acts. It figured importantly in Justice Frankfurter's Supreme Court imprimatur in *NBC v. US* for FCC licensing authority. In 1949 the FCC relied on "public interest" to impose a fairness doctrine on news and public affairs.

Frankenstein suggests a fabricated creature beyond control. Progressives employed the image of Frankenstein to argue that broadcasting would become an uncontrollable capitalist monster unless Congress classified it as a common carrier or, failing that, imposed stringent access obligations. Politicians such as LaGuardia, Dill, and White feared the Frankenstein of uncontrollable government censorship. They were reluctant to vest the Federal Radio Commission and the FCC with too much authority over news and public affairs for fear of violating broadcasters' free speech rights. Broadcasters feared that, in lobbying to lift the *Mayflower* decision, they had created a Frankenstein in the Fairness Doctrine. All interest groups shared two concerns, control and fear.

■ By 1959 television replaced radio as the dominant mass communications system in the United States. Equal time regulated political programming over television and inhibited television from its fullest uses. If equal time stayed in place, would television fail to serve the public interest? If Congress changed equal time, would television become a monster in American politics, setting public opinion and determining election results? If Congress changed equal time, would the major parties become uncontrollable monsters in American political life? Or would they merely become boring as the public digested television news and public affairs as light entertainment? And with boredom, would television produce opportunities for novel candidates and parties, capable of meeting the public's insatiable appetite for novelty, melodrama, and scandal? "No one," P. T. Barnum, that genius of popular psychology, once remarked. "ever went broke by underestimating the taste of the American public." Or with reduced regulatory controls and more independence, would television news subject candidates to unprecedented scrutiny and provide voters with information, unalloyed by party operatives, that voters might vote on issues as well as a candidate? "I am waiting for a rebirth of wonder," beat poet Lawrence Ferlinghetti wrote in 1955, one year following Joe McCarthy's censure in the Senate and five years before John F. Kennedy's election. "I am waiting for a new symbolic western frontier."[39] Ferlinghetti would not have to wait long. It was on American television in 1960.

Lar Daly, Codification Confusion, and the Kennedy-Nixon Debates

4

Are you lonesome tonight?
Do you miss me tonight?
Are you sorry we drifted apart?
. . . Is your heart filled with pain?
Shall I come back again?
Tell me dear, are you lonesome tonight?
"Are You Lonesome Tonight?" Elvis Presley, 1960 pop hit

Snow hit Mayor Daley's face. Together with city officials and International Harvester executives, Chicago mayor Richard Daley braved a snowstorm to welcome Argentine president Frondizi at Chicago's Midway Airport in February 1959. Crews from Chicago television stations filmed the event for evening newscasts. The story was brief: a few handshakes, President and Mrs. Frondizi waved; in the stormy weather Mayor Daley had enough time to say only, "How do you do?" Dignitaries entered limousines, which lumbered through the Windy City's snow-clogged streets carrying their passengers to the Drake Hotel.[1]

Lar "America First" Daly, a perennial candidate for many political offices and an opponent of Mayor Richard Daley in Chicago's upcoming Democratic primary, did not like what he saw on television that night. Lar Daly felt that Chicago television treated him poorly. Chicago broadcasters reported Mayor Daley performing official duties while denying candidate Lar Daly equal time. None had broadcast news stories on Lar Daly's unprecedented filing in both the Democratic and Republican mayoralty primaries, but they had broadcast stories of Mayor Daley filing his petitions for the Democratic primary and former Congressman Timothy P. Sheehan filing his for the Republican.

Lar Daly requested equal time from several Chicago broadcasters. He was a candidate, too, he said. Admittedly he had none of Mayor Daley's organizational strength. Some might dismiss him as a crackpot, he acknowledged. But he was a mayoral candidate nonetheless, deserving equal time. Congress had intended it so by enacting equal time, Lar Daly insisted. It was the law. WBBM and WNBQ refused Daly. He petitioned the Federal Communications Commission to require both stations to devote as much time to him as they had to Mayor Daley and former Congressman Sheehan in their newscasts.[2]

The FCC ordered WBBM and WNBQ to provide Lar Daly with roughly ten minutes each of air time. A candidate's appearance in a newscast was a political "use" of television, the FCC ruled, triggering equal time. "Unequivocal" language in Section 315, commission discretion for rule making for political uses of broadcasting, *AP v. US,* which supports maximum flow of news and information to the public—all support this expansive ruling, the FCC maintained. However, television's persuasive powers mattered more. "While not always indispensable to political success . . . television may enjoy a unique superiority in selling a candidate to the public in that it may create an impression of immediacy and intimate presence, it shows a candidate in action, and it affords a potential for reaching large audiences." By withholding news coverage, broadcast journalists put a candidate at a disadvantage because of television's "ability to reach widespread audiences and to create an illusion of intimate presence by placing the candidate, as it were, in the home of the viewer."[3]

The FCC decision came as a surprise. A majority of commissioners wanted Congress to grapple with candidates' "uses" and voted deliberately in Lar Daly's favor. Two years earlier the FCC had ruled that broadcasters controlled news content. So long as a candidate did not initiate coverage, news fell under broadcaster control or discretion. In October 1958 the FCC restated its position exempting newscasts covering candidates performing ceremonial duties from equal time. It would review broadcast news reports on candidates on a case-by-case basis, the FCC said, but precedent and practice had excluded newscasts from equal time.[4]

FCC chairman John C. Doerfer opposed so literal an application of equal time. His fellow commissioners were subordinating the public's right to receive information to an idealized standard, Doerfer charged. The FCC was taking a giant step backward and imposing common carrier requirements on broadcasters, a course Congress had rejected historically. "A broadcaster should be given some discretion other than a Hobson's choice. This is either a plethora of political programming ad nauseam or a complete blackout," Doerfer argued.[5]

WBBM refused, and CBS asked the FCC to review its Lar Daly decision affecting its owned and operated Chicago station. There was not enough time in newscasts to accommodate all candidates, CBS protested. The FCC was creating "unequal opportunities," CBS complained, by requiring equal time in newscasts irrespective of a candidate's seriousness. Broadcast news reports fell properly within broadcasters' control and discretion, not politicians'. The FCC's decision would cause a blackout of television news coverage of the 1960 Republican and Democratic national conventions and presidential election, network news executives warned, besides making it impossible for broadcasters to cover incumbent politicians performing official duties. RCA chairman Sarnoff cautioned politicians to take comfort in journalists' discretion lest the public tire of repetitive political programming should television news be required to provide time for every legally qualified candidate.[6]

The FCC's ruling drew intense criticism. President Eisenhower called it ridiculous. Joining their television confreres, the national press decried the decision for violating the First Amendment. Senator Dill came out of retirement to say that Congress never intended equal time to cover broadcast news, only uses initiated by candidates.[7]

To major party politicians Senator Hubert Humphrey's plight with the Lar Daly ruling proved that the FCC had overstepped. In July 1959, less than a week after fellow Minnesotans Senator Eugene McCarthy and Governor Orville Freemen had announced Senator Hubert Humphrey's candidacy for the Democratic presidential nomination, CBS, on its counsel's advice, withdrew an invitation for Humphrey to appear on "Face the Nation." Evidently CBS feared an equal time demand from Lar Daly, who was running for president after his unsuccessful bid for mayor of Chicago earlier in the year, and from Henry Krajewski, a Secaucus, New Jersey, tavern keeper who had announced his candidacy on the Poor Man's Party ticket. "This decision," said CBS news vice president Sig Mickelson, "is impelled [because] we would be required . . . to devote 'Face the Nation' to insignificant or obscure or now unknown aspirants for the Democratic presidential nomination . . . destroy[ing] 'Face the Nation' as an important information program." Lar Daly also sought time in network newscasts equal to that devoted to Vice President Nixon and Soviet prime minister Nikita Khrushchev's kitchen debate. CBS rejected the request, saying the peripatetic Daly failed to demonstrate that he was a legally qualified Republican presidential candidate.[8]

Congressmen quickly filed a raft of bills to amend Section 315 lest the FCC *Lar Daly* rule exclude broadcasters from reporting their activities. The Senate held hearings on four different bills three days after the FCC refused to reconsider its initial ruling. "We are practically in the twilight of this session. . . . If we do not do something . . . about [the *Lar Daly*] situation, we shall have a very chaotic situation come next election," Senator Spessard L. Holland (D-Fla.) warned. A House subcommittee considered eight bills to modify the FCC's decision two weeks later. CBS supported one giving most control to broadcasters. NBC and ABC said their news divisions could function with a law reversing *Lar Daly*. The Radio and Television News Directors Association advocated abolition of equal time. According to the American Civil Liberties Union, newscasts, documentaries with incidental attention to candidates, and commentaries should be excluded from equal time, but debates and panel discussions should not. The Democratic and Republican parties differed in how far to go in amending equal time. As the poorer majority party, Democrats favored more equal time restrictions; as the wealthier minority party, Republicans wanted fewer. Among minority parties, Norman Thomas recommended that broadcasters be legally required to provide time for discussion of election issues five to six weeks before elections. The Socialist Labor Party backed the FCC. Speaking for New York's Liberal Party, Senator Kenneth Keating urged that debates and panel discussions remain under equal time. Lar Daly urged retention of the rule bearing his name on the grounds that broadcaster control of newscasts constituted a "subjective determination" of news, placing tyrannical power with broadcast journalists.[9]

■ The Justice Department and the Federal Communications Commission warned Congress not to lift broadcasters' Fairness Doctrine obligations to carry controversial news and public affairs in their haste to modify equal time. "Care should be taken lest [the agency's] present requirements for fair treatment for public issues be weakened," the Justice Department advised. Under the public interest standard, "the Commission requires a licensee to be fair in the presentation of opposing views on controversial public issues."[10] Neither recommended incorporating the Fairness Doctrine into a new equal time law.

Senator William Proxmire (D-Wis.) pushed for more regulatory control over public affairs in news content. He sought to make the Fairness Doctrine part of the equal time law. In floor debate he tried to modify the Senate bill by adding that it is "the basic intent of Congress [that] . . . all sides of public controversies shall be given as equal an opportunity to be heard as is practically possible" in broadcast newscasts, interviews, documentaries, and on-the-spot news coverage. Later, the language was changed in floor debate from "as equal an opportunity" to "as fair an opportunity" and adopted as the Senate bill. The House bill addressed candidates' uses of broadcasting, not public affairs. It exempted broadcast news, interviews, documentaries with incidental attention to candidates, and on-the-spot news coverage of events from equal time.[11]

Senate and House conferees agreed with the Justice Department and the FCC that new equal time exemptions for candidates should not disturb the FCC's Fairness Doctrine for public affairs. Senator Proxmire's amendment went too far, many believed. It was not "the basic intent of Congress" to take away broadcasters' control over the content of public affairs newscasts, interviews, documentaries, and on-the-spot news coverage. Senator John O. Pastore (D-R.I.), chairman of the Senate committee regulating broadcasting, said the public interest standard made Proxmire's amendment unnecessary. The conference committee accepted the House bill. Heeding the Justice Department and the FCC's advice, the conference committee modified Senator Proxmire's amendment with

Justice Felix Frankfurter wrote the NBC v. US decision. Courtesy of the Supreme Court Historical Society.

FCC commissioner Frieda P. Hennock cautioned that the Fairness Doctrine would prove unenforceable. Courtesy of Broadcasting Magazine.

(left) FCC commissioner Robert F. Jones worried that the Fairness Doctrine muddied distinctions between news, editorialization, and commentary. Courtesy of Broadcasting Magazine.

(right) Justin Miller, director of the National Association of Broadcasters. Courtesy of Broadcasting Magazine.

James Lawrence Fly, activist chairman of the Federal Communications Commission for President Roosevelt. Courtesy of Broadcasting Magazine.

CBS president Frank Stanton at the time of the FCC *Mayflower* hearings in the late 1940s. Courtesy of CBS Television Network.

(top) Presidential candidate John F. Kennedy looks out from the backseat of a car during a two-day campaign swing through Indiana as perennial candidate Lar "America First" Daly (partially obscured) protests for equal time, February 1960. Courtesy of UPI/Bettmann Newsphotos.

(bottom) Adlai Stevenson, an advocate of televised candidate debates, 1960. Courtesy of Broadcasting Magazine.

(left) Senator John O. Pastore (D-R.I.), chairman of the Senate commerce committee charged with overseeing broadcast regulation and Democratic leader on communications regulation at the time of the *Lar Daly* amendments to equal time, 1959. Courtesy of the United States Senate.

(right) Senator Hugh Scott (R-Pa), a Republican leader on communications regulation at the time of the *Lar Daly* amendments to equal time, 1959. Courtesy of the United States Senate.

John Fitzgerald Kennedy and Richard M. Nixon at the first of four televised debates, WBBM, Chicago, 1960. Courtesy of WBBM-TV, CBS Television, Chicago.

the proviso that new equal time exemptions did not "reliev[e] broadcasters [from] operat[ing] in the public interest and . . . afford[ing] reasonable opportunity for the discussion of conflicting views on issues of public importance." This language retained FCC authority to enforce the Fairness Doctrine as a regulatory rule, restated a standard of fairness while not codifying the Fairness Doctrine as law, and got major party candidates and broadcasters off the hook with *Lar Daly*.[12]

Within three months of the FCC's Lar Daly order on candidate uses of broadcasting, Congress authorized the first major change in equal time in fifty years. Congress exempted "bona fide" news events, interviews, documentaries in which a candidate's appearance is incidental to the story, and on-the-spot coverage of news events from equal time. Congress accepted a proviso, or savings clause, stating that the FCC's fairness rule for public affairs still applied to broadcast newscasts, interviews, documentaries, and on-the-spot news. Congress defined "bona fide" as either regularly scheduled or special newscasts that broadcasters initiated. Under the 1959 amendments, either a politician's "use" by purchasing air time promoting his candidacy or a broadcaster's "use" by granting or selling air time for expressly political programming favoring one candidate still triggered equal time. In changing the rules, major party politicians ensured broadcast news coverage and paved the way for "media events" staged to gain broadcast news coverage.[13]

■ In 1960, however, broadcast candidates' debates still fell under equal time. Congress had not exempted debates along with newscasts, interviews, documentaries with incidental attention to candidates, and on-the-spot news coverage from the inhibiting rule. President Eisenhower was completing his second term, so no incumbent was running for president and hence unlikely to participate in televised debates lest he give a lesser known opponent undue exposure. Reeling from quiz show scandals two years before, broadcasters pushed for televised candidate debates between Democratic and Republican nominees in an effort to repair their tattered image. In April NBC offered eight hours of an expanded version of "Meet the Press" to prospective Democratic and Republican candidates. CBS and ABC followed with similar offers. CBS president Stanton mollified South Carolina's Strom Thurmond, 1948 Dixiecrat presidential candidate, saying that substantial third-party candidates would receive equitable if not equal time in addition to routine news coverage.[14]

Inadequate, rebutted Adlai Stevenson to NBC's proposal. Journalists would control the issues to be discussed. Candidate debates were preferable. Congress should impel broadcasters to provide Democratic and Republican presidential nominees with an hour of prime time to debate once a week for eight weeks preceding the election. Donating time in the public interest "would hardly be so expensive as to be beyond [broadcasters'] endurance." According to the Hamlet-like candidate, his proposal would reduce the influence of campaign contributions and enable voters to "make a direct comparison" of candidates.[15]

Republican leaders viewed Stevenson's proposal for televised candidate debates warily. With more money to spend, they worried that televised debates might give the Democrats free publicity and stuck by the 1959 equal time exemptions for newscasts, interviews, documentaries with incidental attention to candidates, and on-the-spot news. Former New York governor Thomas Dewey labeled Stevenson's proposal "expropriatory." Former president Hoover complained that it violated Republicans' First Amendment rights as a minority party.[16]

In July all three networks offered time for debates to Nixon and Kennedy following their presidential nominations. Kennedy accepted immediately; Nixon did so through spokesman Herbert Klein within a day. In August Congress suspended equal time for the 1960 presidential election, paving the way for broadcasters to invite the 1960 Democratic and Republican presidential candidates to debate without minority party candidates. After election day equal time would go back on the books. President Eisenhower signed the joint resolution two days later. In this moment of congressional reprieve, Kennedy and Nixon squared off. The first of four televised candidate debates took place on September 26, 1960, at CBS's WBBM.

Senator John F. Kennedy looked great. Tanned and just back from Cape Cod after a campaign swing through Florida, Kennedy stepped on stage of Chicago's WBBM-TV for the first nationally broadcast presidential debate with Vice President Richard M. Nixon. The vice president looked pallid. When stepping out of his car to enter the television studio, Nixon hit his knee, causing his face to contort with pain. Earlier in the day, Nixon had addressed an unenthusiastic audience at a United Brotherhood of Carpenters and Joiners convention. He had kept his own counsel on this first ever television debate between presidential candidates, accepting a phone call from running mate Henry Cabot Lodge in which patrician Lodge reportedly urged Nixon to erase his "assassin image." Nixon consulted his television advisers during the car ride to the studio.

Senator Kennedy had the first say. Kennedy told the television audience that America could do better. "I'm not satisfied when the United States had last year the lowest rate of economic growth of any major industrialized society. . . . I'm not satisfied when the Soviet Union is turning out twice as many scientists and engineers as we are . . . when many of our teachers are inadequately paid . . . when I see men like Jimmy Hoffa . . . still free. . . . If a Negro baby is born . . . , he has about one-half as much chance to get through high school as a white baby. He has one-third as much chance to get through college [and] . . . four times as much chance that he'll be out of work in his life as the white baby." Kennedy tied the idea of a bustling America of racial equality to effective national government, saying that an active, effective federal government was America's and the world's best guarantee of freedom. He quoted Roosevelt's 1933 inaugural speech, saying that an earlier generation had a rendezvous with destiny. "Our generation has the same rendezvous. It's time America started moving again."[17]

Vice President Nixon told the audience of some 80 million that he and the Massachusetts senator agreed on goals but differed on means. Americans prospered under Eisenhower. Their wages had gone up five times as much with Ike than with Truman but goods cost them five times more under Truman than Eisenhower, he said. "Now, that's not standing still." Blasting Kennedy's proposals as Truman "retreads," Nixon complained that they would stifle "creative energies" and drew a look of perplexity on Kennedy's face. Racial equality and medical care for the aged were important, he acknowledged. "Senator Kennedy feels as deeply about these problems as I do, but our disagreement is not about the goals for America but only about the means to reach those goals."[18]

The four debates accelerated a trend toward Kennedy. Kennedy's crowds had been growing in numbers and enthusiasm a week before; they grew phenomenally and frantically afterward. Ten Democratic governors from the South, at best indifferent and at worst hostile, wired their congratulations from a regional conference. Later, Kennedy credited television debates for energizing his campaign and recommended discarding equal time restrictions on candidate debates. Nixon qualified their importance.[19]

■ By placing the decision to cover minor party politicians with broadcasters, major party politicians won greater news coverage for themselves without repeated occurrences of heavy-handedness. Broadcasters came away from this fight with renewed statutory recognition of their discretion and control in determining how they covered politics. In terms of mutual self-interest, the dynamic worked well: Votes indicated newsworthiness, newsworthiness legitimated coverage. Politicians, at least from the major parties, reached voters through television newscasts. Although captured in entertainment corporations, broadcast news commanded attention for its mass reach. The public did not fare badly. The 1959 equal time exemptions increased the flow of news about candidates. Until the exemptions broadcasters were reluctant to cover candidates for fear that fringe or splinter candidates would demand news time. Minor party candidates retained equal time privileges in cases of candidates' advertisements and broadcaster favoritism. If minor party candidates met a threshold of newsworthiness, broadcasters reported their activities, as would be borne out with candidates as different as John Anderson and Lester Maddox, Eldridge Cleaver and George Wallace.

In terms of technology, spectrum scarcity remained so firmly ensconced as the technological rationale for regulation that individual broadcasters rather than media outlets in a community remained the unit of measurement for policing equal time.

As for fairness, congressional haste amending equal time produced vague statutory language, suggesting that Congress had codified the Fairness Doctrine. In accepting the fairness proviso, Congress did no more than preserve the FCC's fairness rule for public affairs from the equal time exemptions affecting candidates. However, because the proviso referred to broadcast opportunities for discussion of conflicting views on issues of public importance, many argued subsequently that Congress made the Fairness Doctrine a law in the 1959 equal time amendments. This ambiguity grew into a controversy, setting the stage for fairness fights in the 1980s.

Televised candidate debates increased a trend toward plebiscitary politics, beginning with Eisenhower. Kennedy emerged from this first television debate as something of a movie star. Beyond the enthusiastic crowds following his first debate with Nixon, Kennedy's example showed that speaking directly to voters in an adversarial situation with opponents guaranteed public attention. Television performance joined organizational might as a crucial variable and altered the chemistry of electing an American president. Candidate debates enabled voters to evaluate candidates. As Theodore White observed, "Let the voters decide, by instinct and emotion, which pattern of behavior under stress they preferred in their leader."[20] In 1964, 1968, and 1972, Lyndon Johnson and Richard Nixon refused to debate their opponents on television, believing they had more to lose than gain by doing so.[21] Following Watergate, the public demanded scrutiny of presidential candidates, and in 1976 televised debates emerged as a feature of presidential politics.

The 1960 televised candidate debates also continued the stubborn resistance in broadcasting to realizing the First Amendment by providing information to the public or by providing an electronic forum to all who wished to speak. In waiving equal time for candidate debates, Congress limited the First Amendment rights of such minor party candidates as Lar Daly of the Tax Cut Party, Orval E. Faubus of the National States Rights Party, Whitney Harp Slocomb of the Greenback Party, and William Lloyd Smith of the American Beat Consensus to debate with Kennedy and Nixon either together or separately. However, it is equally clear that the waiver enabled more Americans to learn about candidates Kennedy and Nixon. The brevity of the waiver suggests that politicians were so anxious about the power of television to shape electoral outcomes that they granted minimal discretion to broadcasters for candidate debates.

The Cresting Tide
of the Fairness Doctrine

I've looked at love
from both sides now
from up and down
and give and take
and win and lose,
and still somehow
it's love's illusion I recall,
I really don't know what
love's about at all.

"Both Sides Now," Joni Mitchell, 1967

The 1960s witnessed a remarkable extension of the Fairness Doctrine to advertisements (see chapter 8), appearances of candidates' spokesmen, and finally, as law of the land in a 1969 Supreme Court ruling (*Red Lion Broadcasting v. FCC*), upholding the doctrine's constitutionality.

Distinguished reporter and commentator Edward R. Murrow fired a first salvo from within broadcasting for public affairs programming. In an address to the Radio and Television News Directors Association in 1958, Murrow insisted on public affairs programming as an essential ingredient in broadcasting. He spoke as an intelligent, influential insider, going public after stormy bouts with CBS management over public affairs. Murrow alluded to broadcaster shyness about editorializing but did not advocate increased government scrutiny. Quite the contrary, Murrow viewed equal time as a governmental intrusion (see chapter 7). Nonetheless, the tone of Murrow's remarks, coming as quiz show scandals beset broadcasting and as broadcasters prepared to beef up news and public affairs lest Congress or the FCC intercede, bolstered FCC expansion of the Fairness Doctrine three years later in the Kennedy administration.

Complaining that broadcasting was an "incompatible" mix of show business, advertising, and journalism, Murrow criticized broadcast management for timorousness in acquiescing to the government, particularly a "fiat" from Secretary of State Dulles banning American journalists from Communist China. He complained that corporate interest routinely dominated the public interest, remarking critically about CBS's and NBC's delayed broadcasts of an address by President Eisenhower on "the probability of war between this nation and the Soviet Union and Communist China" in order to avoid disrupting entertainment programming. He stated flatly that many broadcasters had "welshed on [their] promises" to televise news and public affairs programming because of greed.

Murrow believed fervently that broadcast journalism could and should inform the public about serious issues. The United States was "wealthy, fat, comfortable and complacent. We have currently a built-in allergy to unpleasant or disturbing information," Murrow warned. "Our mass media reflect this. But unless we get off our fat surpluses and recognize that television in the main is being used to distract, delude, amuse and insulate us, then television and those who finance it, those who look at it and those who work in it, may see a totally different picture too late."[1]

Murrow proposed that advertisers devote a share of their advertising money to public affairs and that the networks absorb the production costs. By doing so, Murrow asserted, both advertisers and broadcasters would come out ahead in terms of the "corporate image" so important to them. He offered a solution within the existing framework that did not threaten the profitability of broadcasters, advertisers, or producers and was far less invasive than a congressional or FCC mandate. Eventually broadcasters produced more news and public affairs, but only after scandals had rocked their industry.

■ In the early 1960s the FCC pushed broadcasters to provide more news and public affairs through a number of policy statements. To many people stiff regulation seemed necessary. Late in the Eisenhower administration, two FCC commissioners, including the chairman, were forced to resign because of improper dealings with broadcasters. In 1960 the nation elected a vigorous, optimistic president, who espoused the positive role of government in directing the nation's future.

In 1960, the last year of the Eisenhower administration, the FCC issued a policy statement calling for more public affairs. In part, the FCC sought to repair its damaged reputation as a regulatory agency captured by the industry it was charged to regulate. The FCC specified a number of formats, including editorials, public affairs, educational, political, and news programs, that, it said, served the public interest. The statement also designated "service to minority groups" as a public interest responsibility.[2]

In 1961, the first year of the Kennedy administration, FCC chairman Newton Minow's "Vast Wasteland" address to the National Association of Broadcasters had a more dramatic impact. Minow spoke for the New Frontier. He told broadcasters to "help prepare a generation for great decisions . . . , [to] help a great nation fulfill its future." He urged broadcasters "to put the people's airwaves to the service of the people and the cause of freedom."[3] He warned broadcasters that news, public affairs, and local programming were critical to successful license renewals. In 1964 the FCC published the *Fairness Primer*. The *Primer* compiled a number of "typical" fairness cases and provided broadcasters with information on FCC decision making on fairness complaints.

FCC activism during the Kennedy administration had at least two sources. President Kennedy asked James Landis, a key New Deal supporter and protégé of Supreme Court Justice Felix Frankfurter, his advice on regulatory agencies. In a well-publicized report Landis recommended that the president reinvigorate regulatory agencies, such as the FCC, following the lassitude of the Eisenhower years. For the FCC this meant expanding its Fairness Doctrine responsibilities to include policing the "traffic," as Frankfurter had written in *NBC v. US* in the early 1940s. Second, right wing fundamentalists attacked the president virulently with anti-Catholic editorials and assailed New Frontier initiatives, for example, the Nuclear Nonproliferation Treaty. These attacks led to the Fairness Doctrine's Cullman corollary (see chapter 8), FCC prosecution of Red Lion Broadcasting in the Johnson administration, and ultimately Supreme Court approval of the Fairness Doctrine by the decade's end.[4]

■ The FCC expanded the Fairness Doctrine through administrative actions much in the spirit of the Fairness Doctrine's authors, who intended subsequent FCCs to modify it as public interest required. In 1963, in its letter to the Honorable Oren Harris, the FCC changed fourteen years of Fairness Doctrine administration by announcing that it would review fairness complaints on specific issues on a case-by-case basis and would not withhold decisions until license renewals. This policy was fairer to broadcaster and public alike, the FCC said. Broadcasters could seek legal relief in the courts if they wanted to contest specific fairness decisions, and it lessened broadcasters' risk of losing their licenses. The public benefited by timely disposition of fairness cases, rather than waiting until license renewal, when a controversial issue may have waned in public importance, the FCC wrote.[5]

Substantive problems beset the FCC. Because of the new case-by-case review, the FCC found itself involved directly in the content of controversial news programming. Although the FCC had written Congressman Harris that case-by-case review would require the FCC to deal only with the reasonableness of a broadcaster's efforts to ensure a balance of conflicting views, in practice its new fairness policy created myriad bureaucratic problems. The FCC had to determine what constituted a reasonable balance of conflicting views on individual topics. To do that, the FCC had to document time allotted to controversial issues and analyze the balance of conflicting views within those presentations. It had to weigh a complainant's direct access to a relatively small audience of issue-oriented viewers through a public affairs program against access to a significantly larger audience that an "unbalanced" program might reach during prime time broadcast.

Case-by-case review did not work so well for organizations and citizens with fairness complaints. In making the rule, the FCC required complainants to document a broadcaster's unfairness, but it did not require broadcasters to release information. Individuals or groups with fairness complaints had to go through time-consuming documentation to allege a broadcaster's unfairness. Despite these procedural problems, the FCC received more fairness complaints.[6]

The FCC expanded the Fairness Doctrine to broadcast uses of

candidates' spokesmen in the *Zapple* decision in 1970. Nicholas Zapple, chief counsel to a Senate commerce subcommittee, had asked for equal time for spokesmen for candidates. Zapple wanted broadcasters to provide equal time for one candidate's spokesmen if they had provided time for another's. Because equal time applied solely to candidates during political campaigns, Zapple asked the FCC to rule that the Fairness Doctrine ensured a candidate's spokesmen equal time. The FCC ruled that broadcasters must sell time to one candidate's spokesmen if they had sold it to another's. Unlike the Cullman corollary, which dealt with ballot issues (see chapter 8), the *Zapple* decision ruled out any requirement to provide free time to a candidate's spokesman. "Any such requirement would be an unwarranted and inappropriate intrusion of the Fairness Doctrine into the area of political campaign financing," the FCC reasoned. In the Cullman corollary, by contrast, the FCC thought that the public's right to hear information on ballot issues overrode potential abuses of the corollary by partisans.[7]

■ Three court decisions—one enabling citizen participation in license renewals, another stripping the license of a right wing broadcaster, and a third upholding the constitutionality of the Fairness Doctrine—crested a Fairness Doctrine wave by 1971.

In the *United Church of Christ* case (1966), the United States Court of Appeals in Washington, D.C., upheld the right of citizens to participate in the FCC's licensing, opening the door for greater public participation in licensing renewals. The United Church of Christ contended that WLBT in Jackson, Mississippi, was broadcasting racist news and public affairs programming and that the FCC had acted irresponsibly in renewing WLBT's license. The FCC had granted a provisional license renewal to WLBT on the condition that WLBT management change its ways. Specifically the FCC required WLBT to "comply strictly with the . . . Fairness Doctrine, . . . to observe strictly its representations to the Commission in this [fairness] area, . . . [to] have discussions with community leaders, including those active in the civil rights movement . . . as to whether its programming is fully meeting the needs and interests of its area, [and to] cease discriminatory programming patterns."[8]

The court of appeals instructed the FCC to consider new applicants for WLBT's frequency. The decision showed that the Fairness Doctrine supplemented other legal remedies, such as libel, slander, or defamation, as an effective tool to challenge broadcasters. It put broadcasters on notice in no uncertain terms that their licenses could be challenged not only by other broadcasters competing for the same license but also by groups of entrepreneurs and public interest proponents.[9]

In *Red Lion* (1969) the Supreme Court upheld the FCC's personal attack rule and decided that the Fairness Doctrine did not unconstitutionally abridge broadcasters' free speech rights.

The personal attack rule requires broadcasters to provide reply time to persons or groups whose honesty, integrity, or character is attacked in editorials on controversial public issues. The FCC requires broadcasters to notify the person or group of the editorial within a week, provide a transcript, and offer a "reasonable opportunity" for response over the broadcaster's station. The personal attack rule includes political editorials dealing with a broadcaster's editorial endorsement of or opposition to political candidates. In such cases the rule requires broadcasters to notify all legally qualified candidates of their editorial opinion, provide each with a tape or transcript, and offer each "a reasonable opportunity" to respond over the broadcaster's station. It specifically exempts commentaries that were within newscasts, but it does apply to editorials a broadcaster might make on his own following a newscast.

The Court held that the public's free speech rights to receive information supersedes the free speech rights of broadcasters. Hence the personal attack rule did not violate broadcasters' First Amendment rights. Writing for a unanimous court, Justice Byron White ruled that "it is the right of the public to receive suitable access to social, political, aesthetic, moral and other ideas, which is crucial here." Like Frankfurter in the *NBC* case, White wrote, "There is nothing in the First Amendment which prevents the government from requiring a licensee to share his frequency with others and to conduct himself as a proxy or fiduciary with obligations to present those views and voices which are representative of his community and which would otherwise by necessity, be barred from the airwaves." And, like the *AP* ruling, White saw "no sanctuary in the First Amendment for unlimited private censorship operating in a medium not open to all." The Court dismissed broadcasters' arguments that the rule chilled their free speech rights as "at best speculative."[10]

The Court based its ruling on spectrum scarcity by denying the broadcasters' argument that the number of broadcast outlets in a community is a more useful measure of editorial diversity, and relieved individual broadcasters of their responsibilities to provide "a reasonable opportunity" for response. In the Court's opinion broadcasters held licenses to scarce airwaves as public trustees and, as such, were obligated to provide reply time for expressing controversial editorial views. In other words, each broadcast licensee was the unit of measurement: "The First Amendment confers no right on licensees to prevent others from broadcasting on 'their' frequencies and no right to an unconditional monopoly of a scarce resource which the government has denied others the right to use." Accordingly, the Court ruled that broadcasters must follow the FCC's personal attack rules and notify an individual that he has been the subject of a personal attack and offer him reply time. However, the Court noted it would reconsider the constitutionality of the Fairness Doctrine when technology provided more spectrum.[11]

The Court expanded FCC authority. Justice White found broad authority for the FCC to make rules, such as the personal attack rule. Justice White noted that the FCC had promulgated the personal attack rule in 1967; it fell, therefore, within the FCC's congressionally delegated authority to make rules. This distinction was critical because the FCC's own rule-making capacities and the scope of FCC authority were being tested. History and law favored the FCC, Justice White wrote. In the *Great Lakes* case of 1929, the Federal Radio Commission ruled that "the public interest requires ample play for the free and fair competition of opposing views, and the commission believes that the principle applies . . . to all discussions of issues of importance to the public." In the 1930s, Justice White noted, the FCC had denied license renewals or refused construction permits for broadcasters who wanted to broadcast special interest programming because of regulatory insistence that broadcasters carry programming for a diversity of people.[12]

The Court equivocated on the hard question of whether Congress codified the Fairness Doctrine in the 1959 equal time amendments. Justice White noted that Senator Proxmire's original amendment imposed statutory fairness obligations on broadcasters but that a conference committee altered the amendment to "the present merely approving language." He described the Fairness

Doctrine and the personal attack rule as "complementary" to statutorily imposed equal time responsibilities. But Justice White also wrote that the "amendment vindicated the FCC's general view that the Fairness Doctrine inhered in the public interest standard. Thirty years of consistent administrative construction left undisturbed by Congress until 1959, when that construction was expressly accepted, reinforce the natural conclusion that the public interest language of the Act authorized the Commission to require licensees to use their stations for discussion of public issues, and that the FCC is free to implement this requirement by reasonable rules and regulations."[13]

In *Brandywine Main Line Radio* (1971), the FCC issued its only license denial in connection with a fairness violation. Technically the racist and neo-fascist WXUR failed to qualify for a license renewal because it made misrepresentations in its renewal application, but the broadcaster came under FCC scrutiny initially because of a fairness complaint for its extreme views.[14] WXUR expressed offensive views that appalled many Americans, but it also exemplified the diversity of voices, no matter how repellent, that the Fairness Doctrine was supposedly designed to promote. The *Brandywine* decision, one observer commented, "achieved its result at the cost of diminishing controversial programming within the listening area. . . . When Brandywine left the air, there was no substitute station ready to present that amount of controversial programming."[15]

■ Henry Geller, former FCC general counsel, provided expert advice on managing an expanded Fairness Doctrine. In a Rand Corporation report underwritten by the Ford Foundation, Geller confined his recommendations to rules and regulations that the FCC could make on its own without having to go to Congress for further authorization. "The report's suggestions are pragmatic ones, which can be implemented by the FCC within existing law," Geller noted. He advised the FCC to discontinue case-by-case review, which it had adopted in its letter to Oren Harris in 1963. He advised the FCC to return to the original Fairness Doctrine standard of evaluating overall programming only at license renewals. Such a course, Geller wrote, would get the FCC out of evaluating single issues and daily news operations. At the same time, overall review of license renewal ensured sufficient scrutiny to determine whether broadcasters fulfilled their public trustee responsibilities, Geller said. To make this policy work, Geller urged the FCC to require broadcasters to "show in a general fashion" only that they had afforded reasonable opportunities for contrasting views. He also suggested that broadcasters submit a list of ten issues, national and local, that they covered most extensively in the previous year. "Time percentage guidelines" might be more useful than the case-by-case single-issue method. He recommended a complaint procedure less burdensome to complainants.[16] The FCC disregarded his advice.

■ Much as FCC commissioners Jones and Webster had warned in 1949, FCC implementation of the Fairness Doctrine enabled the agency to police the content of broadcast speech. In *Red Lion* the Court reduced broadcasters to public proxies from their earlier status as public trustees. Although still licensees charged with exercising discretion, broadcasters were saddled with contingent access or common-carrier-like obligations, which they had avoided historically, through *Red Lion*. The confluence of access (common carrier) obligations and spectrum scarcity in *Red Lion* hinted at a broad new constitutional interpretation of the First Amendment, specifically that the public's right to receive information, or an "access for ideas" approach to freedom of expression, mattered more than historic First Amendment protections for speakers. Some forty years after Secretary of Commerce Hoover had articulated this concept in terms of structural regulation concerning broadcasters' general public interest obligations, the Court not only applied it to content regulation but also imposed reply obligations. For the Court, broadcast oligopoly and technological innovation concentrated control over the news and public affairs in broadcasters' hands, and *Red Lion* offered a remedial solution.[17]

Spectrum scarcity remained the dominant technological rationale for applying the fairness rule to individual licensees. In *Red Lion* the Court cited the individual broadcasters, not the number of broadcast outlets in a community, as the unit of measurement for fairness violations. The thinking undergirding this measurement was, in turn, that more individuals wished to broadcast than available frequencies, or available technology, permitted.

Candidate Debates, Press Conferences, and Polling

6

Sittin' on the sofa on a Sunday afternoon
Goin' to the candidate's debate
Laugh about, shout about it
When you've got to choose
Everyway you look at it you lose . . .

Where have you gone Joe DiMaggio,
Our nation turns its lonely eyes to you . . .

"Mrs. Robinson," Simon & Garfunkel, 1968 pop hit

Although President Nixon had resigned in August 1974, Watergate loomed over the Republic well into the following year. On May Day, 1975, North Vietnamese troops rolled into Saigon. To thoughtful people the Watergate scandal and the North Vietnamese victory over the US-backed South Vietnamese signaled the disastrous conclusion of an imperial presidency. The Pentagon Papers in 1971 and the Nixon tapes in 1974 exposed its savage remoteness and venality. One could only thank journalists for doing their jobs so well. True to the founders' First Amendment vision, a free press reported and public opinion rid the nation of a cloven-footed chief executive. But something more had to be done to return the presidency to the people, to bring it back to voters, to make it respond to public opinion.

Douglass Cater, director of the Aspen Institute Program on Communications and Society, a think tank on communications issues, pondered the problem. Throughout 1975 Cater advocated televised debates between presidential candidates as one important way to enable voters to assess the next president. Fifteen years earlier as a *Reporter* correspondent, he had been a panelist in the third Kennedy-Nixon debate. In April Aspen and CBS asked the FCC to alter equal time restrictions on candidate debates and presidential news conferences. Unless the FCC changed its equal time rule on candidate debates and news conferences, broadcasters would remain impelled to provide equal time to minority party and fringe candidates, making broadcasts impossible.

■ After the glow of the Kennedy-Nixon debates in 1960, candidate debates languished in the 1964, 1968, and 1972 presidential elections. In 1964 President Johnson killed a televised confrontation with Republican opponent Senator Barry Goldwater (R-Ariz.). A bare Democratic majority in the Senate, weakened by defections by twelve liberals and Southern conservatives, fended off a harsh Republican attack and rejected an equal time waiver for candidate debates by a thin 44–41 vote. A year earlier, before President Kennedy's assassination, each chamber supported a waiver, but it languished until 1964, when Johnson rounded up enough votes to kill it.[1]

Equal time caused problems with broadcast presidential addresses. On Sunday, October 18, 1964, President Johnson addressed the nation on Nikita Khrushchev's downfall and a Communist Chinese atom bomb. Goldwater pressed for equal time. Candidate addresses triggered equal time, he charged. A Democratic FCC sided with Johnson. The president's address was a bona fide news event exempt from equal time because of the 1959 amendments. The FCC cited a 1956 decision by a Republican FCC denying Adlai Stevenson equal time after President Eisenhower made an election season address on the Suez crisis and ignored as best it could criticism that Khruschev's ouster and a Chinese A-bomb were constituted crises on the scale of the Suez crisis. FCC counsel Henry Geller said that the commission believed it reasonable to exempt special presidential addresses to avoid requiring broadcasters to provide equal time to all legally qualified candidates.[2] Johnson appeared on television looking and sounding nonpartisan two weeks before election day.

In 1968 Republican candidate Richard Nixon blocked televised candidate debates. "If the [equal time] problem can be worked out," Nixon said in July, he would willingly debate his Democratic rival. After securing the Republican nomination, he responded positively to a CBS invitation to debate Humphrey "contingent only upon waiver of [equal time] . . . and agreement on time, place and format." Humphrey responded positively to a similar offer. Broadcasters, spearheaded by CBS, launched a major lobbying drive for repeal. The Senate passed a bill waiving equal time for candidate debates in June. It languished in the House until October. By then Nixon believed that debating Humphrey would hurt his chances and said that, as a believer in the two-party system, he would not debate third-party candidate George Wallace.[3]

Reeling from the Chicago convention, Humphrey failed to push aggressively or soon enough to eliminate equal time for candidate debates. Many Democrats, furious over broadcast coverage of their chaotic convention, opposed further liberties for broadcasters. Desperately aware that a televised confrontation with Nixon might salvage his tattered nomination, Humphrey agreed to go along with House backers of American Independent Party candidate George Wallace with new wording of the Senate bill to exempt debates for "nominees" qualifying in thirty-four states, that is, Wallace. Humphrey implored Speaker of the House John McCormick to force a vote on the bill. Republican congressmen eager to insulate Nixon from televised debates, delayed the vote for twenty-seven hours, the longest in House history, save delay action lasting two days and nights in 1854 over repeal of the Missouri Compromise to allow residents of the Kansas and Nebraska territories to vote for free or slave labor. Shortly before dawn on October 10, over protests from minority leader Gerald Ford, the sleepless 76-year-old McCormick ordered the sergeant at arms to seal House doors and locked the congressmen in the chamber until he got a positive vote.[4]

In the Senate Humphrey could not command enough votes for the House bill enabling Wallace to debate. Republican minority leader Everett Dirksen (R-Ill.) instructed Republican senators not to enter the Senate chamber and demanded a quorum, requiring fifty-one senators, which the Democrats could not muster because their ranks were depleted by incumbents campaigning for reelection. Despite a Democratic majority, Nixon prevailed, "We would do well to reject what the House has done, Senator Jack R. Miller (R-Iowa) told his colleagues, "because it is not in the best interests of the two party system."[5] Republican Everett Dirksen (R-Ill.) and Hugh Scott (R-Penn.) ridiculed Humphrey for backing President Johnson's ban on candidate debates four years earlier and declaring them in the public interest in 1968. "If it was fish then, it ought to be fish now. If it was fowl then, it ought to be fowl now," chided the mellifluous Dirksen. Humphrey's behavior was "something like the song, 'La Donna e Mobile,' " Senator Scott teased, "sometimes candidates are mobile, too . . . as circumstances change."[6]

Earlier in that tumultuous year, televised debates figured critically in the presidential nominations. Robert Kennedy (D-N.Y.) dropped his objections to debating Eugene McCarthy (D-Minn.) after McCarthy defeated him in the Oregon primary. Both participated in a televised debate for the California primary. Humphrey, the eventual nominee, was not a primary candidate in California. Kennedy reaffirmed his commitment to Israel, and seventy-two hours later, the night of his California primary victory, Sirhan Sirhan, a foe of Israel, assassinated him. The debate, hosted by ABC, was more of a parallel press conference with journalists questioning both candidates; the only confrontation between Kennedy and McCarthy concerned a McCarthy political ad that misrepresented Kennedy's record. Each agreed on substantial policy issues. Shortly before the Democratic convention, broadcasters dropped a scheduled debate between Vice President Humphrey and Senator McCarthy. George McGovern (D-S.D.), who announced his candidacy as a rallying point for Kennedy forces, and Georgia governor Lester Maddox, who entered the fray for the Democratic presidential nomination that August, rejected network offers of broadcast time outside the debate as inadequate, and both Humphrey and McCarthy backed off. On the Republican side New York governor Nelson Rockefeller sought vainly to lure former vice president Nixon to debate before the Republican national convention. Nixon refused, saying Vice President Humphrey would be the beneficiary and that primary victories had demonstrated his popularity adequately.[7]

In 1972 President Nixon and Congress blocked television candidate debates. President Nixon vetoed an omnibus 1970 campaign reform bill that included equal time waivers for presidential and vice-presidential candidate debates. Congress failed to enact a campaign reform legislation in 1972 that repealed equal time for the president and Congress because House members wanted equal time in their contests.[8] Despite a huge lead in the polls, incumbent Nixon saw no point in risking a televised confrontation with Democratic candidate George McGovern. A debate would have worked to McGovern's advantage by allowing him to appear on the same platform, at presidential level. Nixon rebuffed a McGovern proposal for televised debates pending a congressional waiver of equal time for candidate debates.[9]

■ In September 1975 the FCC granted broadcasters a freer hand in covering candidate debates and press conferences, but only to a point. Responding to Aspen Institute and CBS petitions, the FCC ruled that candidate debates and presidential news conferences were bona fide news events exempt from equal time.[10] In the FCC's *Aspen* decision, broadcasters wrested limited control of candidate debates, and in the collateral *CBS* decision they won control over covering candidate news conferences. Broadcasters could cover candidate debates only if they neither initiated nor controlled them; they could neither host nor determine who would be invited. Such control, the FCC felt, gave broadcasters too much power. The more expedient course lay in a third party hosting debates outside a television studio and broadcasters then exercising their news judgment to cover the debates in their entirety as bona fide news events. This course also protected the FCC to some degree from a potential blast from the US Court of Appeals in Washington for overreaching its authority in redefining bona fide news events. At that time the FCC was reeling from numerous critical Court of Appeals decisions that overruled FCC policy. The League of Women Voters assumed the third party role adroitly; the *Aspen* decision did not assign it host responsibilities. Candidate news conferences proved to be more straightforward.

At the same time the FCC skirted a potential battle with the Court of Appeals, the commission expanded its authority by making an agency rule rather than deferring to Congress. In 1959 Congress pointedly excluded candidate debates and press conferences from the *Lar Daly* exemptions for newscasts, documentaries with incidental appearances of candidates, interviews, and on-the-spot news. Not so, the FCC insisted: Congress originally intended to exempt debates from equal time. Time was the real culprit. Too little time had elapsed between congressional enactment of the *Lar Daly* exemptions in September 1959 and an August 1960 joint resolution, enabling Kennedy and Nixon to debate to have allowed the FCC to rule debates were bona fide news events under the 1959 law. Therefore, the FCC contended, Congress passed a joint resolution to ensure that Kennedy and Nixon could debate without equal time challenges.

In expanding its authority, the FCC acknowledged past interpretative errors. In two 1962 rulings the FCC had ruled that candidate debates triggered equal time. Radio broadcast of a debate between then Michigan governor John B. Swainson and his Republican challenger George Romney required equal time for the Socialist Labor Party candidate. A televised broadcast of a debate between then governor of California Pat Brown and Richard Nixon, his Republican challenger, required equal time for a Prohibitionist candidate. The FCC recognized that radio and television coverage of the debates was "on the spot coverage of bona fide news events" and, as such, seemingly exempt from equal time. But a debate's bona fide status as a news event was not sufficient grounds for live broadcast coverage without equal time.[11] Broadcast coverage placed too much control on the news judgment of radio and television reporters and news directors. Congress intended no such discretion when it came to political debates, the FCC had ruled.

In baring these past sins, the FCC found the necessary precedents for new-found virtue. The real issue, the FCC wrote in *Aspen*, turned on whether a candidate's appearance in a bona fide news event such as a debate was "incidental to" the event. In 1962 the FCC had ruled consistently with the 1959 exemptions that candidate appearances were central to debates, triggering equal time. In 1975, however, the FCC found that Congress had meant all along that a candidate's appearance could be central to a news event, such as a debate, without triggering equal time. It based its reinterpretation on House arguments about exemptions for newscasts, interviews, and news events but not for debates. To get around this, the FCC reasoned that the debates, such as those between Nixon and Brown and Romney and Swainson, were news events. The 1962 rulings, the FCC claimed in self-defense of their 1975 recision, had mistakenly cited a 1959 House report of a version of an equal time bill that had never passed.[12]

On news conferences by campaigning incumbents the FCC majority reversed an earlier decision against CBS (1964), requiring equal time. In 1975 CBS urged the FCC to classify presidential news conferences as exempt bona fide news events and news interviews. The FCC agreed, but not on the grounds CBS pressed. Journalists controlled press conferences by asking questions, CBS contended. No, incumbent candidates controlled press conferences by deciding whether or not to hold them, the FCC ruled. Candidate press conferences were routine news, CBS insisted, that is, "recurrent in the normal and usual course of events" like weekly public affairs programs. No, the FCC responded; Congress meant "regularly scheduled" to mean just that and had not lumped sporadically scheduled candidate press conferences with daily newscasts or weekly public affairs programs. CBS asked the FCC to distinguish between candidate press conferences "called by an incumbent candidate in his official capacity and those called in furtherance of his candidacy." That opened a can of worms on content that the FCC wanted to keep shut. Then the FCC ruled that its 1964 objection in *CBS* no longer held: Candidates' news conferences were bona fide news events exempt from equal time.

Commissioner Benjamin Hooks complained that the *Aspen* majority was overreaching its authority and striking equal time "a severe and, perhaps, mortal blow." Only Congress had the authority to change equal time rules for candidate debates and news conferences, not the FCC, he protested. The ghost of perennial candidate Lar Daly appeared in Hooks's dissenting opinion as he worried about broadcasters' "subjective newsworthiness judgment."[13] Candidates manipulated press conferences; allowing them further latitude was a mistake, he lamented. Candidate debates were not hard news, Hooks insisted, and should be covered in newscasts. Commissioner Robert E. Lee echoed Hooks's position.

Power plays and confusion marked initial implementation of the *Aspen* decision. In planning debates between President Ford and Democratic presidential candidate Jimmy Carter in 1976, the League of Women Voters and the presidential candidates excluded broadcasters from initial meetings. The league acceded to demands from Ford and Carter that the debates be more like parallel press conferences than debates. It drew up a list of journalists, whom candidates could veto, and agreed that television cameras would focus exclusively on Ford and Carter; there would be no reaction shots of the audience. Robbing broadcasters of the last bit of control, the league and the candidates agreed to a pool camera.[14] (A pool camera is a camera or set of cameras that records and feeds video to several broadcasters.)

Broadcasters, jealous that the League of Women Voters was getting all the credit for the debates while reducing them to common carriers, complained vehemently. To Richard Salant of CBS News and Reuven Frank of NBC News the tail was wagging the dog. Sixteen years earlier the networks had hosted the Kennedy-Nixon debates without any intermediary. Now, under *Aspen,* the league was taking control and botching it. How could the league pretend to host so significant an event as competently as the networks with all their experience covering national politics? Could the league really "control" the debate? Its dealings with Ford and Carter indicated otherwise. The league surrendered format and candidate veto of journalists, one of the few prerogatives broadcasters had won in 1960. "Pussycats," Frank whined.

In meetings where broadcasters finally participated, Salant blasted the league for accommodating Ford and Carter. The public was getting cheated, he charged. Surrendering veto power over journalists was the worst sin. In agreeing on veto rights over journalists, the league had unwittingly granted the candidates control over the words that would reach the public. In denying reaction shots, the league had given the candidates control over pictures. How could television do its job under such controlled conditions? League representatives stuck to their guns. Salant walked out of a Friday meeting, raising the specter over the weekend that CBS might boycott the first Ford-Carter debate.[15]

But the networks did not boycott the first presidential debate in sixteen years. On Thursday evening, September 23, President Gerald Ford and former Georgia governor Jimmy Carter debated before a tightly packed audience in Philadelphia's Chestnut Street Theatre and a national television audience of 80 million viewers. Both relied heavily on statistics; neither articulated a convincing vision of where he wanted to lead the country; each firmed up support among constituents.[16] Two polls gave President Ford a slight edge.

Well over an hour into the droning rhetoric, a silence disturbing and unexpected befell both candidates. As Jimmy Carter belabored "a breakdown in trust among our people," debate moderator Edwin Neuman interrupted. "Excuse me, Governor. I regret to have to tell you that we have no sound going out on the air."[17] Both men stopped talking. Each stood at his lectern. Neither said a word to each other nor continued to debate. Sound was out for the theater audience, too. After 27 minutes, sound was restored. The debate concluded.

A twenty-five-cent electrolytic capacitor had broken in one of the twenty-four amplifiers that ABC News was using to transmit sound to seventeen sources fed by pool cameras. The capacitor in itself was not important. Its job was to cut the hum and buzz in a power supply. Once sound was restored, the hum and buzz were not audibly worse despite the broken capacitor. Within the 27-minute interval, ABC News arranged to transmit sound through a CBS News sound line to CBS's New York broadcast center, which then sent it through AT&T phone lines to the seventeen sources so the debate could resume and finally conclude.[18]

Where sound mattered and eventually surfaced was in the *Aspen* decision, which defined candidate debates as bona fide news events. Eugene McCarthy, running as an independent, Lester Maddox, running on the American Independent Party ticket, and Peter Camejo, the Socialist Workers candidate, complained that the debate was not a bona fide news event. If the debate had truly been a bona fide news event, the candidates would not have stopped talking because of an audio technical problem, they complained. Each demanded equal time. Not the Superbowl, the Olympics, or a State of the Union Address had ever stopped because of sound problems, contended McCarthy attorney John Armour. The debate was staged for television, so it could not be bona fide, said Camejo's attorney. The problem showed that the League of Women Voters and broadcasters were colluding, Maddox asserted, commingling the roles of sponsor and carrier.

The debate was a bona fide news event exempt from equal time, the FCC ruled, rejecting all three complaints. McCarthy and Maddox persisted. McCarthy said the Fairness Doctrine enabled him to participate in the second and third debates between Ford and Carter. The FCC and the courts disagreed. Affirming a D.C. appeals court decision, Chief Justice Warren E. Burger ruled that McCarthy and Maddox had "reasonable opportunities to have their views presented in contexts outside debates."

As for candidate press conferences, broadcasters declined live broadcast of an October 22 press conference by President Ford. CBS News pointed out that President Ford had held a news conference only the week before. Broadcasters reported the news conference in newscasts.

The second Ford-Carter debate figured prominently in Carter's success. Carter entered the second debate with a vague theme and a loss of independent and moderate support as he tried to pitch his campaign to traditional Democrats. Questions about Carter's judgment beset the born-again Southerner for agreeing to a *Playboy* interview and then making incautious remarks about his sex drive and harshly criticizing former president Lyndon Johnson. In the debate Carter articulated a winning theme. He launched into Ford for "inadequate presidential leadership." Four years later this would come back to haunt him but it played in 1976. Ford entered the second debate partially buoyed by his better than expected performance in the first debate but embarrassed by racist remarks of his recently fired Secretary of Agriculture Earl Butts. In the debate Ford bumbled by replying to a foreign policy question stupidly, "There is no Soviet domination of Eastern Europe." Carter pounced on that. By failing to correct himself immediately, Ford provided Carter with ammunition for his bumbling president theme that lasted into the next week. In the end Carter stemmed the tide of defections that had been eroding his considerable lead. A third debate and a televised debate between vice-presidential candidates Walter Mondale and Bob Dole were uneventful.[19]

Both Carter and Ford said that the debates helped their candidacies. "[If] it hadn't been for the debates," Carter remarked, "I would have lost. They established me as competent on foreign and domestic affairs and gave the voters reason to think Jimmy Carter had something to offer." The Ford campaign, by contrast, credited the debates with erasing Carter's thirty-point lead in preelection polls.[20]

In 1980 the *Aspen* decision helped major party candidates and accommodated a significant third-party candidate with a following among the middle class. The *Aspen* decision worked the way its advocates and its detractors had predicted. Benjamin Hooks's concern that *Aspen* interpreted equal time "into oblivion" seems quite right if one wishes to sustain an unworkable, egalitarian position on political discourse and ignore the variety of ways, other than nationally televised debates, for candidates to reach voters.

In 1980 Jimmy Carter benefited during the primaries. The FCC and the courts rejected Senator Edward M. Kennedy's bid for equal time to a Carter news conference. Mounting an uphill campaign against Carter for the Democratic presidential nomination, Kennedy charged that Carter staged a White House news conference on February 13, 1980, shortly before the New Hampshire primary, to press his own candidacy safely away from a Kennedy response. Broadcasters turned down Kennedy's request for equal time, saying that news conferences were bona fide news events, so they had no obligation to provide him with reply time. The FCC supported the networks, ruling that Kennedy "failed to offer evidence that the broadcasters were not exercising their bona fide news judgment."[21]

Kennedy pushed for a debate; Carter refused. In early June Kennedy offered to release his delegates if Carter would debate him. At that point, Carter controlled enough votes for renomination but Kennedy had enough votes to make the president's renomination limited and partisan. Both he and Carter cited Carter's refusal to debate as the biggest issue separating them, and at that time each disagreed on such issues as wage and price controls and health care. This was a political struggle, pure and simple, but, if *Aspen* rules had not been in place, Kennedy could have pressed for national television time and Carter may well have had to restrain his transparently partisan use of press conferences.

Broadcasters rejected a Reagan request for equal time following a September 18 Carter press conference. "I don't think there's any legal basis under the equal time provision," said NBC's William Small. Carter opened the news conference with four to five minutes of remarks on administration accomplishments before taking reporters' questions. William Casey, former CIA chief and at that time a high-level Reagan adviser, demanded equal time for former governor Reagan to respond to Carter's "political commercial . . . , an obvious partisan announcement, not responsive to questions from the press, separate from the press conference." The Reagan campaign never complained to the FCC.[22]

In 1980 the League of Women Voters exercised its control over

Newton Minow, FCC chairman for President Kennedy, fairness proponent, and advocate of televised candidate debates. Courtesy of Broadcasting Magazine.

(top left) Justice Byron White wrote the Red Lion decision. Courtesy of the Supreme Court Historical Society.

(top right) Fred Cook, journalist, who declined reply time following the Red Lion decision. Courtesy of Fred Cook.

(bottom left) The Reverend Billy James Hargis, who delivered a blistering attack on journalist Fred Cook, resulting in the Red Lion Decision. Courtesy of the Reverend Billy James Hargis.

(bottom right) Benjamin Hooks, FCC commissioner who opposed exempting candidate debates and press conferences from equal time. Courtesy of Broadcasting Magazine.

Jimmy Carter and President Gerald Ford at a televised candidate debate, 1976. Courtesy of Gerald R. Ford Library.

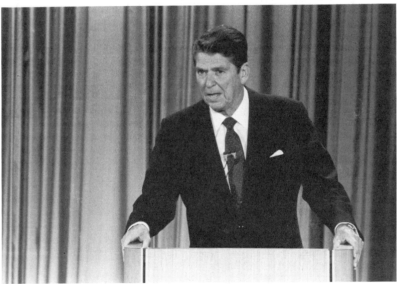

John Anderson *(top)* and Ronald Reagan *(bottom)* at a televised candidate debate, September 1980. Courtesy of the League of Women Voters.

President Jimmy Carter and Ronald Reagan at a televised candidate debate, October 1980. Courtesy of the National Archives, Office of Presidential Libraries.

Walter Mondale and President Ronald Reagan at a televised candidate debate, October 1984. Courtesy of the White House. Photo by Pete Souza.

presidential debates cautiously, for it was caught up in powerful forces. It had to contend with an embattled incumbent, Jimmy Carter, and a highly organized if contentious campaign team surrounding Ronald Reagan. Congressman John Anderson, running on a National Unity ticket, enjoyed measurably more support than former Minnesota senator and independent presidential candidate Eugene McCarthy four years earlier. Both Carter and Reagan wanted to manipulate league invitations to Anderson to benefit their campaigns. The league had to cope with public opinion, too, for if it showed partiality toward any candidate, it would be tarnished. In August the league announced that candidates enjoying a national popularity of 15% would be invited to league-sponsored debates.[23] This figure was low enough to enable Anderson to qualify but too high for other independent candidates, such as Citizen's Party candidate Barry Commoner.

Pollsters jumped on the league for using public opinion polls to set eligibility requirements. The league was bringing polls "into" the political process, Gallup head Andrew Kohut complained. Technical problems like the margin of error in sample findings troubled other pollsters, who worried that polls screened out nonvoters, skewing results to the politically active. "If the League cannot stand the heat of the selection process, it should delegate this responsibility to others who are willing to make tough decisions," simmered Democratic pollster Peter Hart. Ruth Hinnerfeld, the person at the league most responsible for the debates, defended the 15% cutoff: "We were looking for something that had the ability to be applied in a fairly objective way, was simple to understand, and was nonpartisan."[24]

Anderson met the 15% criterion in September for a debate with Ronald Reagan, the league determined, but not in October for one including President Carter. Partisans accused the league of caving in to Carter, who insisted he would not debate Anderson. But the league acted only as it said it would. Indeed the league extended its deadline for the 15% requirement from the end of August to September 10 to help Anderson make the list of invitees.[25]

In the debate Anderson failed to clarify his message to keep any momentum in his campaign. His wry line from a debate eight months earlier in Iowa that Reagan could only balance the budget and spend trillions on defense by using mirrors no longer reflected light. Reagan was the more successful by deflecting concern among moderates and women, in particular, that he was too bellicose.

By mid-October Reagan had reversed his position on a one-on-one debate with Carter. Reagan enjoyed a stable lead, but it was not growing. His advisers wanted to increase his lead. They feared that Carter might engineer a release of hostages, seized by Iranian revolutionaries, shortly before election day and thought a presidential debate would minimize the effect of such a release. They urged Reagan to put to rest as best he could repeated public concern that he would get the United States into a war. Reagan stepped back from sequential one-on-one debates, skirted reporters' questions about his own criticism of the league as recently as September 19 for proposing a one-on-one debate with Carter that excluded Anderson, and agreed to debate Carter.[26]

President Carter lost this critical confrontation. Until the debate, televised on October 28, Reagan enjoyed a solid but not commanding lead in some polls and Carter appeared even or slightly ahead in others. Carter entered as an incumbent underdog and left a corpse. "Hemorrhaging," Carter pollster Patrick Caddell lamented, devastated the president the weekend before election day. When Reagan won all but five states and the District of Columbia, the results were in, painfully.

As in 1976, the League of Women Voters bowed to the wishes of the major party candidates; broadcasters had modest say. The league scrapped plans for three presidential and one vice-presidential debate because candidates would not participate. It acceded to a format dictated by the candidates. It submitted to candidate veto of journalists. Carter and Reagan wanted more confrontation than the six-question format of the Anderson-Reagan debate. Carter's aides, in particular, pushed for rebuttals. Reagan's side agreed, assenting to a number of rebuttals in exchange for moving the debate as close to election day as possible.[27] This arrangement perpetuated the parallel press conference format.

Anderson was the big loser. The Cable News Network telecast his responses to Carter and Reagan, whom he watched on a television monitor. Anderson purchased a half-hour of television time immediately following the Carter-Reagan debate to rebut the major party nominees. His standing in the polls was 8–9%, well below the 15% minimum requirement. Without a dramatic debate confrontation to highlight his differences from Carter and Reagan and with no other significant campaign gesture outside the debate, Anderson's attractiveness and credibility waned.

Nevertheless, one should not hastily conclude that the league treated Anderson shabbily or that voters were disserved by his exclusion. Anderson carried his candidacy quite far and received ample broadcast news coverage. Voters measured an independent against the major party candidates, and, just as important, as a result of the *Aspen* decision, voters measured major party candidates against each other.

■ In 1983 the FCC granted broadcasters the liberty to host candidate debates. Henry Geller, former FCC general counsel and an expert on the FCC's public interest responsibilities, the National Association of Broadcasters (NAB), and the Radio Television News Directors Association (RTNDA) petitioned the FCC to enable broadcasters to host candidates debates without triggering equal time.[28] Geller, then associated with Duke University's Washington Center for Public Policy, had just completed a study showing that in many state elections broadcasters were the best parties to host candidate debates. By 1983 many criticized the *Aspen* decision on debates for promoting an artificial media event, hosted by the League of Women Voters, with no journalistic control. It seemed better to let broadcasters negotiate with candidates and carry debates without an intermediary who had buckled to candidates' wills.

The League of Women Voters, John Anderson, and the United Church of Christ opposed the Geller-NAB-RTNDA petition.[29] The FCC had no authority to grant the petition, they charged; only Congress had authority to exempt candidate debates from equal time, where such action was not likely to take place. Anderson believed he had more of a chance of reaching voters for a prospective 1984 presidential bid under league control. With candidates' debates in its metier, the league had a greater chance of extending its influence and fund raising.

In a legerdemain worthy of successful politics, Geller, the NAB, and the RTNDA argued that the FCC had discretionary authority to modify equal time. Although it is true that Congress intended the FRC and the FCC to exercise discretion, it is just as true that Congress did not include candidate debates in the 1959 equal time exemptions. The league, Anderson, and the United

Church of Christ were correct technically. But metaphorically and politically Geller, the NAB, and the RTNDA carried the day by citing expansive arguments in the *Aspen* decision extending FCC authority and with arguments that congressional risk taking in 1959 enabled FCC risk taking in 1983.

The FCC agreed. Broadcaster-sponsored debates were "on the spot coverage of bona fide news events," the FCC ruled with no evident sense of irony about the artificiality of broadcaster-sponsored media events. Congress had given the FCC authority all along to make decisions like this one, the FCC asserted. Congress took a risk in the 1959 equal time exemptions, that broadcasters might abuse newly gained discretion by promoting political favorites. The FCC could well take a risk now. Court precedents, including rulings rejecting Shirley Chisholm's challenge to the *Aspen* decision, supported broadcaster-sponsored candidate debates and FCC authority to change equal time rules. "In creating a broad exemption to the equal time requirements in order to facilitate broadcast coverage of political news, Congress knowingly faced risks of political favoritism by broadcasters, and opted in favor of broadcaster coverage and increased broadcaster discretion. Rather than enumerate specific exempt and non-exempt 'uses,' Congress opted in favor of legislative generality, preferring to assign the task to the Commission," the appeals court ruled.[30]

By 1983 broadcasters won some of the freedom denied by equal time rules. Ironically broadcasters won a greater measure of their free speech liberties by promoting the regulatory authority of the agency charged with policing them. The D.C. Court of Appeals upheld the FCC's ruling against challenges from the league in 1984.[31]

■ In 1984 candidate veto power over journalists as debate interviewers, dissatisfaction with the parallel press conference format of the debates, and the FCC's 1983 rules approving broadcaster-sponsored debates weakened the league's monopoly on televised presidential debates, setting the stage for other sponsors in 1988. President Reagan and Democratic presidential nominee Walter Mondale exerted control over selection of journalists. Both campaigns ruled out twelve reporters initially proposed by the league and all but three of a supplemental hundred. League president Dorothy S. Ridings complained that both campaigns "totally abused" the selection system and refused to submit any more. CBS, *The New York Times,* and *The Washington Post* subsequently withdrew reporters from consideration. In agreeing to participate as an interviewer in a debate between Vice President George Bush and Democratic vice-presidential candidate Geraldine Ferraro, *Time* correspondent Jack E. White said, "We were given to understand that there was no repeat of the process that went on over the weekend of striking names. Had there been, I would not have accepted the invitation."[32] As in 1980, candidates again dictated format.

During the Democratic primaries, debates increased the legitimacy of Walter Mondale, former Colorado senator Gary Hart, and civil rights activist the Reverend Jesse Jackson. At debates at Dartmouth College and Iowa early in the primaries, Hart articulated his new ideas theme that 1984 was a contest for America's future, not a fight between left and right. Much like President Kennedy, Hart said, "It's time to get this country on the move." In debates Mondale took frontal assaults from John Glenn, another aspirant, for his close ties to organized labor. These broadsides weakened Mondale, did Glenn no good, and created an opening for Hart, whose talk of new ideas appealed to more voters than Mondale's calls for fairness and compassion. Hart came out of Iowa in the second spot and upset Mondale in New England. In New York Jesse Jackson used a debate to attack Mondale and Hart for fighting a "kinship struggle" for Democratic primary votes. They had more in common than not, Jackson charged, and he deserved election as the candidate for a working class majority.

Mondale used a candidate debate to arrest Hart's meteoric success on Super Tuesday, primary voting day for most of the South. "When I hear your new ideas," the stolid Norwegian said coolly, "I am reminded of that ad, 'Where's the beef?' " Although Hart had new ideas on regional security, environmental penalties for hazardous waste producers, industrial policy, and retraining for unemployed workers, voters were more anxious about his identity and character because he had misstated his age and some years earlier had abbreviated his name from Hartpence to Hart and changed his signature to resemble John F. Kennedy's. When the votes were in, Hart carried seven of nine states. Mondale stopped Hart in Georgia and, thanks to support from Birmingham mayor Richard Arrington, pulled out a squeaker victory in Alabama. "Where's the beef?" had punctured Hart's balloon, so much so that the next morning when Hart appeared on NBC's "Today Show," host Bryant Gumbel asked what went wrong in Georgia and Alabama.[33]

In the general election both Mondale and Reagan exploited candidate debates. In the first of two confrontations, Mondale shook up the president by recalling, "There you go again," Reagan's debate attack on Carter four years earlier, and by criticizing Reagan on social security. Borrowing Hart's theme about the future, he laced into Reagan for promoting self-satisfaction and jeopardizing the future. Isn't the real question, he challenged, "will we be better off? Will our children be better off? Are we building the future that this country needs?" Following advice from Pat Caddell, Mondale tried to convince voters that they should retire the amiable Reagan. "It's not what he doesn't know that bothers me, it's what he knows for sure that just ain't so," Mondale quipped, quoting Will Rogers, to try to convince voters that Reagan was no longer competent for executive responsibilities no matter how winning his wave and reassuring his voice.

Mondale narrowed Reagan's seemingly impregnable lead to 9 points. Future confrontations between Vice President Bush and Democrat Geraldine Ferraro and a second debate with Reagan may have made a difference on election day. Ferraro presented facts and figures, placed Bush in the no-win situation by accusing him of patronization, and, polls and pundits agreed, scored a tie.

In the second debate Reagan bounced back, making charges of wimpishness stick to Mondale. Shortly after their first confrontation the "age" issue had surfaced in a *Wall Street Journal* column, documenting Reagan's remoteness. The president's advisers worried. Some blasted OMB chief David Stockman for challenging the president too aggressively and shattering his confidence in rehearsals for the first debate. Nancy Reagan arranged for a supportive coach. Responding to a question in the second debate about fitness for a second four-year term, Reagan responded, "I want you to know also I will not make age an issue in this campaign. I am not going to exploit for political purposes my opponent's youth and inexperience." Then, he pummeled Mondale for being soft on defense, criticizing a Mondale ad that showed Mondale standing on the deck of an aircraft carrier watching jets take off. "If he had his way when the Nimitz was being planned, he would have been deep in the water out there because there wouldn't have been any Nimitz to stand on," again stopping Mondale. An incomplete reverie about the future and a drive along the Pacific Coast Highway cost Reagan little. He stemmed further defection.

In the end, despite Mondale's brief lift in polls following the first debate, televised debates mattered little in 1984. Nominee selection rules worked in Mondale's favor, securing the Democratic presidential nomination even though Hart won nearly as many votes. The economy mattered more in the general election and made the president's reelection a foregone conclusion. Under Reagan, Americans had more disposable income and less inflation. Thankful for this breathing space and anxious lest Mondale's proposed tax increases jeopardize their modest toehold on a mortgaged prosperity, voters rejected Mondale. Admittedly economic growth was slower than under Carter, home mortgage rates higher, unemployment higher, the national debt increasing (from $914.3 to $1,575.6 billion), and more Americans impoverished. But for many voters these were future or distant concerns. On election night Reagan won with a landslide of votes, cutting across lines of gender, age, region, and income (except for the poor). Blacks, Jews, Hispanics, liberals, and urban voters supported Mondale. Few voters thought much about the vice presidency, so Ferraro pulled some votes from women and ethnics but not enough to count. Moreover, the working class did not vote. Wilkie lost with a greater percentage of the potential electorate than Reagan commanded in 1984, so alienated were traditional Democratic voters from their party.[34]

Reagan hit a responsive cord. He presented "a very mythic, very seductive image," rock and roll star Bruce Springsteen observed in *Rolling Stone* the following month. "An image that people want to believe in. . . . I don't know if he's a bad man. But I think there's a large group of people in this country whose dreams don't mean that much to him, that just get indiscriminately swept aside." Springsteen, whose commercial success with creative work attested to how keenly he felt the heartbeat of America in the mid-1980s, continued, "But the difficult thing out there right now is that the social consciousness that was a part of the sixties has become, like, old-fashioned or something. You go out, you get your job, and you try to make as much money as you can and have a good time on the weekend. And that's considered okay."[35]

"Reagan was truly the Teflon candidate," Mondale said months later. "I thought after the first debate I had some momentum. Not that I'd win. Except for a day or two after the convention, I never thought I'd win."[36] And, following his massive rejection, Mondale acknowledged that he had never mastered television. "Modern politics requires television. I've never warmed up to television, and in fairness to television, its never really warmed up to me. I don't believe it's possible anymore to run for president without the capacity to build confidence and communications every night."[37] Less certain success turned on a candidate's use of television or star quality. Speaker of the House Tip O'Neill remarked in postmortems. "I don't believe if we had Paul Newman this year, we could have beaten this fellow to be perfectly honest."[38]

■ By 1988, televised candidate debates became a pervasive fixture of presidential elections. Fully twenty took place between the Iowa caucuses in February and the California primary in June 1988.

The emergence of these debates is due to the FCC's equal time waiver. By placing discretion with journalists to cover debates, irrespective of demands from minor party candidates, the FCC's waiver has increased the flow of political information to the public. From 1976 to 1988 the league provided leadership for the televised confrontations. But the league's experience also showed that candidates had the final say on the number and format of debates. The parties stepped in through the Commission on Presidential Debates. No incumbent sought reelection. Following a Twentieth Century Fund recommendation, advocating that the national parties seize this opportunity to ritualize televised debates under a bipartisan commission, the Republicans and Democrats jumped on the idea. No declared candidate was so strong that he could alienate his party, so most agreed to his party chairman's pitch. As a nonprofit, the commission will have to give significant third-party candidates their own spotlight on the electronic stage or face IRS inquiry about its nonpartisan charter, enabling tax exemption.[39] Commission executives contend that earlier lead time in setting up debates will enable the commission to minimize the problems that beset the league.

Broadcasters also stepped in. CBS and NBC hosted several debates. Many more were carried on PBS and C-SPAN, a public affairs cable channel, during primaries.

■ Uniform poll closing legislation in presidential elections involves technologically driven change in First Amendment law and the media. The plan is simple. All polls from the eastern to the mountain time zone will close at 9 P.M. eastern standard time (8 P.M. central standard time and 7 P.M. mountain standard time). Daylight savings time will be extended for two weeks through the Pacific time zone (California, the Idaho panhandle, Nevada, Oregon, and Washington) during presidential election years. Alaska and Hawaii fall outside the plan. Polls in the Pacific time zone will close at 7 P.M. Pacific daylight time. Because 7 P.M. Pacific daylight time is the same as 9 P.M. eastern standard time, a uniform closing time will be in effect.

The push for uniform poll closings comes from the West. The West feels disenfranchised by the big television networks in the East. On the basis of exit polling, broadcasters can project electoral outcomes and can thus report winning and losing candidates during voting hours. The First Amendment permits broadcasters to televise their projections before polls close.

In fact, in 1980 NBC flashed "Reagan Wins" across the bottom of television screens at 8:15 eastern standard time, or 5:15 P.M. in the West. At 9:45 eastern time, 6:45 in the West, President Carter conceded the election to Governor Reagan. A number of influential Democratic congressmen, who lost reelection in the West, blamed the television networks for discouraging voting.

Like candidate debates uniform poll closing legislation is a constitutionally sensitive area. Broadcasters enjoy free speech protection, and Congress cannot censor them without violating the First Amendment. Voting is the cornerstone of a liberal democracy, and broadcasters are cautious about creating the appearance that they might well diminish the importance of voting merely to be first with election results. Therefore ABC, CBS, and NBC all support the legislation despite intense competition among themselves to be first with the news and uneasiness that other news services not bound by the pledge could well report polling projections and characterizations earlier.

Several issues arise: Will voters in the West, who vote later in the day, be penalized by this shift? Who are the late voters and what impact will the change from an 8 P.M. to a 7 P.M. closing have on political power? Can the networks be trusted to delay their reports of winners until polls close? Will the networks use other techniques to project election results that are not subject to the poll closing agreement?

Evidence shows that no specific group of voters in the West would be discriminated against with earlier closing times. Contrary to the opinion that the working class votes later in the day, a *Los Angeles Times* study shows no difference across racial, class, ethnic, party identification, sex, or religious lines for those who vote earlier or later in the day.

The League of Women Voters is pushing Congress to be more stringent with the networks by demanding that the networks withhold projections and characterizations of elections based on a variety of survey methods, not merely exit polls. The league urges caution about the effects of uniform poll closings and questions findings that few voters would be affected by the change. It recommends further examination of the impact of uniform closings on the recruitment of polling place workers, the cost of election administration, and polling place security. It cautions that longer hours in some areas might skew results in favor of one party.

ABC, CBS, and NBC have promised not to project winners based on exit polling until polls close in a state or, in states with multiple time zones, until the vast majority of polls close. However, in the 1988 New York Democratic primary, NBC's *Nightly News* anchor, Tom Brokaw, seemed to project the outcome, saying that Massachusetts governor Michael Dukakis seemed headed for victory based on information from various candidates' campaign staffs and conversations with voters. John Chancellor, *Nightly News* commentator, then characterized voting results by reporting that Jesse Jackson would carry New York City but lose the state to Dukakis and by providing a demographic breakdown of the vote. Neither ABC nor CBS projected a winner in 6:30 or 7:00 P.M. news feeds and news programs. Congressman Al Swift (D-Wash.), leader of uniform poll closing legislation, reprimanded NBC for "brush[ing] against the line" of an untimely projection and criticized NBC

News for violating the spirit of its agreement with Congress. NBC News president Larry Grossman denied that NBC had projected Governor Dukakis as the winner, acknowledged Congressman Swift's concerns, said NBC News would be more careful in the future, and reasserted his view that implementation of the agreement poses perplexing problems. The Cable News Network and Group W have withheld projections or characterizations in the past and promise to continue this practice.[40]

Uniform poll closing legislation has several holes in it. It ignores local broadcasters. Many of them commission exit polls for their own news coverage of statewide races and their state's voting in presidential elections. It ignores satellite technology. New networks, utilizing this technology, are free to deploy reporters across any number of states and report projections before polling places close and then feed these to local broadcasters who have purchased the service. Finally, the legislation has no mechanism to cope with network failures to honor their commitments. This is important because of buyouts and takeovers, after which new management may ignore its predecessor's commitments. At this writing the legislation awaits Senate action for implementation.

■ Televised candidate debates continued the country's headlong rush into plebiscitary politics within the Democratic and Republican parties in a period of political dealignment. The FCC's 1975 *Aspen* decision weakened the ability of Democratic and Republican incumbents to control absolutely whether debates would take place. Incumbents suffered a relative decline in their control because post-*Aspen* decision making on candidate debates encompassed a much broader group of players and no longer fell exclusively within the perview of an incumbent president's influence in Congress. Following Robert Kennedy's assassination and Hubert Humphrey's failed 1968 presidential nomination, the Democratic Party initiated new rules calling for a grueling primary process.[41] The Republicans could hardly duck the primaries and followed suit. The expansion of primaries, in turn, produced candidate-centered organizations, which became media producers, and relied on such forums as televised debates to advance each politician's candidacy. In primary elections Jimmy Carter, Ronald Reagan, and Gary Hart emerged from their rivals in part because of their debate performances in

1976, 1980, and 1984. Of all, Reagan and Hart were the most successful. In 1980, copping a line from a Spencer Tracy movie, Reagan grabbed the mike from George Bush in a televised candidate debate in the 1980 New Hampshire primary and literally stole the show. In 1984 Hart's imitation of John Kennedy in a debate at Dartmouth College early in the primary season, although offensive to some, was impelling to others and helped to launch Hart's campaign. Thirteen years after *Aspen,* in 1988, the Republican and Democratic national parties are employing a bipartisan commission, charged with hosting candidate debates, as a way to reassert some visible role of their own in this plebiscitary drama.

Major party candidates exerted dictatorial control over the number and format of televised debates and over selection of questioners. Candidate debates did not increase voting in the 1970s and 1980s as they did in 1960. If anything, they became a drone in a seemingly unending campaign.

It would seem that voters lost out in hearing minority views, but inclusion of all legally qualified candidates in candidate debates would not necessarily increase minority candidates' viability or boost participation. In 1976 Jimmy Carter received 40.8 million votes and President Ford 39.1 million. By contrast, Eugene McCarthy won 757,000; he was followed by Roger McBride with 173,000, and Lester Maddox with 171,000. In 1980 John Anderson won 5.7 million votes, Libertarian Ed Clark received 921,000, or 1%. Nearly 44 million people voted for Ronald Reagan, and 35 million for Carter. In 1984 Ronald Reagan commanded 54.4 million votes to Walter Mondale's 37.5 million. Libertarian David Bergland came in third with 228,000, followed by Lyndon LaRouch with 79,000, and Sonia Johnson with 72,000. Although one can assert, in principle, that these candidates have the right to express their views, denying them access to televised confrontations between major party candidates hardly restrains their freedoms. Furthermore, when candidates as different as John Anderson and George Wallace, who won 9.9 million or 13.5% of the vote in 1968, had significant political and organizational strength, major party candidates expressed willingness to include them in debates.

In terms of implementation a contentious national elite—composed of the FCC, network broadcasters, and the League of Women Voters—collaborated to maximize candidate debates between major party politicians. Like many elites the participants had conflicting goals and jockeyed for maximum influence. The FCC expanded its authority at the expense of Congress by altering equal time rules, and the courts backed it up. League claims to sole sponsorship reflect its efforts to sustain the role it created for itself following the *Aspen* decision. Broadcasters' successful moves to eliminate a league monopoly indicate deft manipulation of regulatory policy and law. Similarly, Republican and Democratic National Committee efforts to orchestrate their candidates show that political parties are seizing the opportunity presented in 1988 of no incumbent seeking reelection to advance party influence over candidates.

Although broadcasters gained more discretion, they hardly won dominance. Indeed, broadcasters won a greater measure of liberty in the 1970s and 1980s by supporting the policing powers of the FCC. This differs from their behavior in 1959, when broadcasters and Congress joined ranks against the FCC to modify equal time restrictions. And, when broadcasters did win more discretion, they did so marginally. By requiring a third party, such as the League of Women Voters, to host candidate debates, the FCC exhibited an abiding concern, which has shaped regulatory policy since the 1920s, that mass communications media such as radio and television disproportionately influence election results and shape public opinion. Only in 1983 did the FCC grant broadcasters the privilege of hosting candidate debates that newspapers had enjoyed historically. These freshly gained liberties were part of an institutional move toward deregulation. In the mid-1970s FCC chairman Richard Wiley put the commission on the deregulatory road by calling for deregulation of political programming in large radio markets.

Perhaps as telling, the emergence of televised candidates debates highlights the emergence of video as a rival to print. By producing video, debates provide a supply of assertions, disclaimers, pronouncements, and evasions within the convention of broadcasting for subsequent news and public affairs programs.

Documentaries

7

For better or worse, editing is what editors are for.
CBS v. Democratic National Committee

The documentary is the stepchild of television journalism. In the 1950s entertainment programming generated enormous revenues, pricing news documentaries out of their slots. As television penetrated American homes, an hour of prime time became so valuable that advertisers demanded mass audiences, who preferred entertainment over public affairs. Television existed as a regulated oligopoly. NBC and CBS were the two dominant networks, ABC a diminutive third. The FCC's freeze on ultra-high-frequency (UHF) channels restrained competition from any nascent fourth or fifth network, which could have provided more choice if not necessarily different quality. Although UHF stations, many of which run independently of the networks, emerged in the 1960s and 1970s, they more frequently broadcast movies or reruns of popular entertainment programs no longer syndicated over network television. Cable television exploded in the 1970s amid promises of local programming. Cable television provided more news and public affairs programming with Ted Turner's Cable News Network and C-SPAN's coverage of floor debates first from the House of Representatives and then from the Senate but few documentaries. By the 1980s, competition from independents, cable networks, and video cassette recorders eroded the networks' audiences, prompting intense competition and reducing further time for documentaries on prime time network television.

Broadcast documentaries are uncommon for political and economic reasons. Documentaries explore issues and challenge interest groups and politicians, who then muscle broadcasters through the Fairness Doctrine to contest the documentary. A good documentary can present so vivid a picture of a social or political problem that it disturbs viewers, alienating portions of the all important audience. In these cases broadcast management reins in reporters.

■ Edward R. Murrow stands as a towering figure in American broadcast journalism. An intimate of Churchill, Murrow's dramatic wartime radio broadcasts from London during the Battle of Britain brought the war home and, some say, played a critical role in boosting United States preparedness for World War II. President Roosevelt regarded Murrow's influence so highly that he conferred with him the day Japanese planes bombed Pearl Harbor.

Murrow pioneered broadcast documentaries, and they played a critical role in his demise. CBS network executives feared that Murrow's controversial documentaries would alienate powerful politicians, many of whom insisted on further regulation of television after the quiz show scandals of the late 1950s. Earlier in the 1950s, Senators Joseph R. McCarthy and John Bricker sought to utilize television for their own ideological purposes. Bricker blamed television when his neo-isolationist amendment failed to pass in the Congress. As chairman of the Senate Commerce Committee, he launched a full-scale investigation of broadcast syndication revenues practices, siding with Hollywood movie producers against the New York–based networks, to bully broadcasters into compliant behavior. From CBS president Frank Stanton's point of view at the time of Murrow's documentary on McCarthy, Murrow's journalistic independence jeopardized CBS's survival and aggravated affiliates.[1]

From 1951 to 1958 Murrow produced *See It Now* with Fred Friendly. From all accounts they enjoyed an exceptional collaboration. "They seemed to be completely as one in their understanding of the relationship in television between editorial judgment and the technological basis upon which any television communication must be based," remarked a visiting BBC documentary film producer. "They worked together in such a remarkable way because Ed never relinquished the personal view of any film . . . while Fred was the practical down-to-earth man who could decide in detail how everything could be put together."[2]

Murrow is perhaps as well remembered for "A Report on Senator Joseph McCarthy" as for his wartime radio reports. Murrow feared that Senator McCarthy could energize a neo-Nazi movement in America. McCarthy's assault on due process and demagoguery disturbed him greatly. McCarthy's efforts to chase supposedly pro-Soviet sympathizers and operatives out of the State Department in 1950 were "squalid beyond belief," Murrow opined. Republican leaders Dwight Eisenhower and Ohio senator Robert Taft disappointed Murrow by sanctioning McCarthy's congressional investigations and fervid anti-communist rhetoric. When Eisenhower failed to defend his mentor, General George Marshall, from McCarthy's depredations during a campaign stop in Wisconsin in October 1952, Murrow believed that Eisenhower had turned his back on decency.[3]

Murrow launched a series of television documentaries on the controversial senator and created television news milestones in doing so. In October 1953 *See It Now*'s "The Case of Lieutenant Milo Radulovich, A0589839" marked the first time television tackled a controversial issue. The March 1954 "Report on Senator Joseph McCarthy" was the first broadcast editorial on a controversial national politician and political movement. Other *See It Now* documentaries dealing with McCarthyism made strong editorial assertions for civil liberties.

Murrow wrestled with standards of fairness in making the documentaries. Impartiality was the rule. Paul White, head of CBS News during World War II and a colleague, insisted on neutrality as a broadcaster's best method for conveying information and winning audience confidence. But McCarthyite tactics and the contagion of fear engulfing the nation were so severe that Murrow risked asserting an independent editorial voice, like newspaper columnists Walter Lippmann and Arthur Krock, in the documentaries. "We can't sit here every Tuesday night and give the impression that for every argument on one side there is an equal one on the other," Murrow confided to Friendly.[4] By March 1954 Murrow was so disturbed by White House wavering on McCarthy's attacks that he remarked that President Eisenhower "wasn't going to do a damn thing" about McCarthy, as *See It Now* staffers worked on the report.[5]

Murrow built his campaign by exposing the effects of McCarthyism and then attacking the senator. "The Case of Lieutenant

Milo Radulovich" publicized the plight of an air force lieutenant, asked to resign his commission because of undisclosed allegations that his father read *The Daily Worker* and his sister belonged to a left wing group. For Murrow the documentary pointed out that guilt by association, instilled by McCarthy's vicious and often baseless assaults, had become the norm. During the documentary Lieutenant Radulovich stood by his family, the first time ever a victim of undisclosed accusations during the McCarthy period had a national forum. The air force subsequently reconsidered the accusations, reversed the order the following month, and reinstated Radulovich on *See It Now*. It ignored Murrow's offer of equal time. CBS and Alcoa, Murrow's sponsor, stood by the show despite McCarthy's influence and jeopardy to Alcoa's contracts to supply aluminum to the air force.[6]

In "An Argument in Indianapolis," Murrow focused on civil liberties, highlighting American Legion efforts to prevent the American Civil Liberties Union (ACLU) from using a meeting room in a war memorial building. The legionnaires could not abide use of a building dedicated, in their view, to servicemen who had died fighting communism by a group that upheld the free speech rights of communists. A nearby Catholic church offered the ACLU meeting space; Murrow interviewed the priest, Father Victor L. Goosens, who spoke for minority rights and peaceable assembly.[7]

Coincidentally CBS televised "An Argument in Indianapolis" the same evening that Senator McCarthy made a nationwide telecast to rebut charges from former president Harry S. Truman. A week earlier Truman had coined the term "McCarthyism," labeling the senator's tactics as "the corruption of truth, the abandonment of due process of law." "It is," Truman continued, "the big lie and the unfounded accusation against any citizen in the name of Americanism or security. It is the rise to power of the demagogue who lives on untruth." In the telecast McCarthy overstepped. He challenged President Eisenhower's leadership by saying anti-communism would be a dominant issue in the 1954 congressional elections when Ike had said otherwise. The day before, November 23, President Eisenhower distanced himself from McCarthy in what became known as the "Code of Abilene" speech. "If someone dislikes you or accuses you," President Eisenhower said, "he must come up in front. . . . He cannot assassinate you or your character from behind without suffering the penalties. . . . [T]here must be no weakening of the code by which we have lived. By the right to meet your accuser face to face. . . . By your rights to speak your mind and be protected in it."[8]

Murrow produced "A Report on Senator Joseph McCarthy" amid great tension. CBS chairman William S. Paley told Murrow privately that he wished Murrow would not do it but stood by him publicly. He acknowledged that Murrow's documentary was "exceptional" in the degree of editorial freedom allowed a CBS journalist and defended Murrow's right to editorialize. CBS president Frank Stanton conducted a poll after McCarthy's rebuttal. The poll showed that more people believed McCarthy than Murrow. Stanton presented the findings to Friendly by way of implicit warning not to go too far. Board members worried about a run on CBS stock. Amid gossip of an advertiser boycott, soap manufacturers, heavily committed to advertising slots, stuck with CBS. Alcoa, Murrow's sponsor, expressed support for the show while management took heat from some irate stockholders. "We were getting very good results both from public relations and from the advertising point of view," Alcoa president I. W. Williams remarked, putting the best face on things.[9]

For months before Murrow had been conferring with CBS attorneys in the event that McCarthy might attack him for his outspoken defense of civil liberties. Murrow alerted *See It Now* staffers that anyone with potentially incriminating associations could dismiss himself from working on the report because he was sure they would all be scrutinized after its broadcast. Murrow and Friendly purposely kept details of the documentary from CBS management so that they could deny precise knowledge of the attack. Murrow and Friendly paid for an advertisement in the *New York Times* themselves, an ad without a CBS logo.

"A Report on Senator Joseph McCarthy" made television history on March 9, 1954. At the outset Murrow offered McCarthy equal time. Murrow laid out his case carefully. He showed McCarthy browbeating a witness before his permanent investigations subcommittee. He depicted McCarthy's vulgar humor, impugning Governor Adlai Stevenson by deliberately calling him Alger, a reference to accused spy Alger Hiss. Murrow piled newspaper after newspaper from the American heartland on top of each other, accumulating evidence they were not pro-communist and had no use for McCarthy's high-handed techniques. He looked straight into the camera and told his audience that Americans were not a fearful people and should not tolerate McCarthy's campaign of guilt by association.

Murrow's timing was perfect. The tide was turning against the renegade senator. A week before, in a national television address, former governor Adlai Stevenson, titular head of the Democratic Party after his loss to Eisenhower in 1952, blasted McCarthyism as demagoguery and characterized Republicans as a party, split between Eisenhower and McCarthy. On March 9, the day of Murrow's documentary, Senator Ralph Flanders (R-Ver.) attacked McCarthy for setting up a "one man party—McCarthyism." Murrow cited Flander's comments in the documentary. On March 10, President Eisenhower endorsed Flanders's statement and in a news conference in early April responded to reporters' questions that he thought of Murrow "as a friend." The Republican National Committee nixed McCarthy's demand for equal time to answer Stevenson, choosing Vice President Richard Nixon instead, who took Eisenhower's reservations one step further and accused McCarthy of helping communists through his "reckless" tactics.[10]

In an effort to diminish Murrow's damaging report, McCarthy initially demurred on the equal time offer and proposed William F. Buckley, Jr., as his stand-in. The opportunity was not transferable, Murrow responded, and McCarthy set about putting together a rejoinder. Production help came from Louis B. Mayer, the movie mogul. CBS paid for the production costs and provided a kinescope and transcript of Murrow's documentary. J. Edgar Hoover opened the FBI's file on Murrow to McCarthy, and the State Department's Passport and Security Office provided information on Murrow's travels.[11]

In his rejoinder McCarthy proved all of Murrow's points. Assaulting Murrow as "the leader of the cleverest of the jackal pack which is always found at the throats of anyone who dares to expose individual communists and traitors," McCarthy connected Murrow wildly to the Communist victory in China and accused him inaccurately of membership in the moribund Industrial Workers of the World, "a terrorist organization." He assailed Murrow's association in the 1930s with the Institute of International Education as "a job which would normally be done by the Russian Secret Police." Switching gears, McCarthy accused communists in the government of holding up H-bomb research, a claim President Eisenhower contradicted the following morning by authorizing further H-bomb tests. Holding up a copy of the *Daily Worker,* McCarthy refuted Murrow's accusation that his own tactics gave comfort to America's adversaries and concluded, "If on the other hand Mr. Murrow is giving comfort to our enemies, he ought not to be brought into the homes of millions of Americans by the Columbia Broadcasting System."[12] McCarthy never answered Murrow's charge that his investigations degenerated into persecutions.

McCarthy inevitably came out second because of *See It Now*'s regularity. No single response, no matter how persuasive, could counter such continuity. "It may take a little time before the Senator realizes he was had," *Times* critic Jack Gould remarked.[13] Critics praised Murrow for courage, and professional journalists applauded "the networks . . . for . . . shak[ing] off their habitual timidity."[14] "We leaned over backward to be fair," Murrow told *Newsweek* and doubted if one documentary could change a whole medium.[15] Crowds gathered around the journalist when he appeared on New York City streets, thanking him for the documentary. Murrow later confided to colleague Alexander Kendrick, "It is a sad state of affairs when people think I am courageous to do this."[16] William F. Buckley, Jr., disagreed. "Men who never had the spirit to face up to their mothers-in-law are suddenly aware that they can now earn a badge of courage by denouncing Senator McCarthy, and what is more, their heroism is sure to be immortalized in *The New York Times,*" Buckley disdained.[17]

The week following Murrow's McCarthy report, *See It Now* reported the plight of Annie Lee Moss, a government worker whom McCarthy charged with passing secret defense codes to the Soviets. Annie Lee Moss, a diminutive black woman charged with the offense, knew no encryption, said she had never heard of Karl Marx, and commanded English so poorly that she stumbled over the words in her subpoena. Senator McClellan challenged committee counsel, Roy Cohn, with bringing the woman before the committee on hearsay. *See It Now* cameras showed McCarthy ducking out of the hearing just before things fell apart.

McCarthy was eventually censured by the Senate later in 1954, and Murrow was widely credited with causing McCarthy's downfall. However, Murrow's documentary came when Republican leadership, including President Eisenhower, Vice President Nixon, and GOP chairman Hall were turning on McCarthy. At the time, McCarthy was making preposterous claims that subversives were undermining the army. Eisenhower could no longer abide McCarthy's browbeating of administration appointments. It would seem, therefore, that Murrow's documentary reported ongoing national politics, hastening but hardly causing McCarthy's downfall. This does not detract from Murrow's courage. He and his family were threatened following the documentary.[18]

The McCarthy documentary hastened Murrow's denouement as an independent documentary producer. Six months later, in August 1954, CBS president Frank Stanton established CBS News and Public Affairs to assert corporate management control over all news programming. Three years later, in 1957, the unit developed into the CBS News Division. Roughly a year after the McCarthy documentary, Alcoa bowed out as Murrow's sponsor. *See It Now* had telecast a documentary on corruption in Texas state government. Alcoa planned to locate a plant in Texas and feared alienating local politicians unnecessarily. Alcoa was also moving from ordinance to mass market goods, so entertainment was better suited as an advertising vehicle for its new market. General Motors briefly picked up *See It Now* but dropped it just as quickly amid rumors that Murrow was producing a critical documentary on Vice President Nixon's behavior during President Eisenhower's bout with heart trouble. In June 1955 CBS aired "The $64,000 Question," which boosted advertising revenues and priced *See It Now,* with its comparatively small audience, out of its time slot. That fall, CBS News president Daly offered Murrow six hour-long *See It Now* shows in lieu of its usual weekly broadcast. This shift undercut Morrow's flexibility. Although still autonomous and independent, *See It Now* worked in more confining space. "No longer could we alone decide to do a McCarthy broadcast or a program on South Africa or a report on lung cancer," Friendly remarked.[19]

Murrow saw it coming. In February 1955 Murrow confided his frustrations to his friend David Lilienthal, formerly FDR's chief of the Tennessee Valley Authority and later head of the Nuclear Regulatory Commission, "I get credit for 'courage,' in putting on the

McCarthy show that got me in such a row. . . . [It] should have been a decision of the network, of CBS itself, as a deliberate part of its editorial policy, for which it would be held accountable. Instead, I do this without Paley or Alcoa knowing what I intend to do. The networks say we are only conduits, pipes—they might . . . better say sewers. We carry whatever anyone wants to transmit to the country for a charge, and that is the extent of our responsibility. . . . That's power . . . without assuming responsibility."[20] At the 1956 Democratic convention, Murrow told party activist Vanessa Brown that he no longer had the freedom to produce controversial documentaries and had to "submit ideas in advance to the company."[21] He resigned from the CBS board of directors that fall.

As a vehicle for mass market entertainment, 1950s television antiquated commentators like Murrow. Despite the *Mayflower* ban on licensee editorials, individual radio commentators enjoyed national reputations. Their voices competed with others and filled programming time. By contrast, television adopted radio comedy, a format designed to reach mass audiences, enveloping them in a "trouble free cathode cage,"[22] and commentators lost programming time comparable to the amount they commanded in radio.

Murrow persisted. In January 1956 *See It Now* charged that Eisenhower administration farm policies were driving family farmers out of business. Not so, retorted Secretary of Agriculture Ezra Taft Benson, demanding equal time. CBS granted it over objections from CBS News president Sig Mikelson without consulting Murrow then on assignment in Israel. The decision appalled him. He had used Agriculture Department statistics in the documentary and Benson had expressed administration views at the show's conclusion. In his response Benson blasted "The Farm Problem: A Crisis of Abundance" as "demagoguery of the worst kind" and extolled an administration farm bill. Senators Hubert Humphrey and Clinton P. Anderson demanded time to respond to Benson. Subsequently Eisenhower press secretary James Haggerty said he never thought Benson would get the time.[23]

The final straw came in March 1958. *See It Now* reported on statehood for Alaska and Hawaii. The broadcast angered Congressman John R. Pillion, who demanded time to respond to the broadcast. CBS complied. Murrow fired off an angry note to Paley, defending the show's objectivity and saying he would just as soon sever his relation with CBS. Paley took him up on it. Murrow backtracked and told Paley he only wanted to be consulted on equal time demands. *"See It Now*'s over," Paley said. In his rebuttal, Pillion claimed Hawaiian statehood was "a major objective of the Soviet conspiracy."[24] CBS denied rebuttal time to proponents of statehood, including war hero and later senator Daniel Inouye. *See It Now* concluded a seven-year run that July.[25]

The dominance of news organizations over independent documentary producers took place in the fall of 1958. CBS offered Murrow a documentary show, *Small World,* in addition to his popular interview show *Person to Person.* With this change Murrow lost all autonomy and flexibility. *Small World* was under the CBS News Division and hence under organizational control. Murrow vented his frustration in a well-publicized speech before the Radio and Television News Directors Association in October 1958, further alienating Paley. He asked for a sabbatical in February 1959 and spent the next year interviewing world leaders for *CBS Reports,* a new CBS documentary series headed by Friendly and expressly excluding Murrow from management.[26] In 1961 Murrow joined the Kennedy administration as director of the United States Information Agency, describing himself half-jokingly as the Sachel Page of the New Frontier.

An independent editorial voice, no matter how distinguished and thoughtful, was too dangerous for the organization. The charisma had to be routinized, as sociologists say, and Stanton did so by nurturing CBS News. Stanton imposed high professional standards and hired distinguished professional producers, directors, and reporters. A great tradition of reporting, which Murrow initiated, continued under CBS News management control. Quality, objectivity, fairness, accuracy—all the cardinal virtues of broadcast journalism—remained; only the independent documentary voice was sacrificed.

■ In the late 1960s and early 1970s documentaries came under attacks from Congress for deceptive editing. Although this scrutiny was typical of content regulation in the late 1960s and early 1970s, it is noteworthy first because Congress, the FCC, and interest groups assailed corporate news organizations, not lone documentary producers like Murrow, and, second, because the news organizations successfully won greater First Amendment freedoms and political influence. One controversy, involving NBC, revealed how an interest group seized on the Fairness Doctrine in a failed effort to influence a documentary on pension reform.

■ In a congressional investigation of the documentary "The Selling of the Pentagon," CBS president Frank Stanton fought for his organizational accomplishments equally as much as for First Amendment principles. A colloquy between Stanton and Congressman Harley Staggers, chairman of the House commerce committee charged with broadcasting oversight, highlights the ridicule Stanton endured to protect CBS News.

Dr. Stanton: We try to get the best professionals we can get. We give them the policies under which to operate. We keep a review organization that changes with the time, depending upon the situation. . . .

Congressman Staggers: But Jesus picked 12 disciples and one sold him for 30 pieces of silver, another denied him on the night that he was crucified, and another doubted him when he came back. Now that is the kind of men we have today and that we had then.

Dr. Stanton: I think this is most unfair to refer to our news organization that way.

Congressman Staggers: Being prophets and disciples of Christ?

Dr. Stanton: No; as being traitors.

Congressman Staggers: I don't say they were traitors. I said Jesus had those men and he picked what he thought were the 12 most perfect men he could find.

Dr. Stanton: Then, sir; I misunderstood what you said.[27]

On February 23, 1971, *CBS Reports* broadcast "The Selling of the Pentagon," a documentary produced by Peter Davis and reported by CBS correspondent Roger Mudd. CBS spent $100,000 to produce it, and 165 of 204 affiliates carried it. The Pentagon ran a vast public relations machine, costing taxpayers anywhere from $30 million to $190 million annually, to promote the military, the documentary asserted. "The Selling of the Pentagon" broke no new ground: Senator J. William Fulbright and journalist Fred Cook each had written books highlighting Pentagon publicity operations at the time the documentary aired.[28]

CBS moved quickly to diffuse criticism among Pentagon partisans. CBS featured critical interviews with Vice President Spiro

Agnew, Secretary of Defense Melvin Laird, and House Armed Services Committee chairman F. Edward Hebert and repeated the documentary along with a rejoinder by CBS News president Richard Salant. A "disreputable program," Agnew said, complaining that CBS News was "a runaway bureaucracy that frustrates attempts to control it." For Laird, "a little more professionalism putting the show together" might have gotten CBS off the hook. A "professional hatchet job," Congressman Hebert complained; "the greatest disservice to the military I've ever seen on television and I've seen pretty bad stuff." CBS News president Richard Salant defended the documentary's accuracy.[29]

In making the documentary, producer Peter Davis transposed a Defense Department official's response to one of Roger Mudd's questions. He edited a sequence in which Colonel John MacNeil, an officer who, addressing a civic organization in Peoria, Illinois, for the Pentagon, spoke about the domino theory without indicating that Colonel MacNeil was quoting Laotian prime minister Souvanna Phouma. The transpositions did not misrepresent either man's views. Indeed, MacNeil reiterated the remarks later in the show, prompting Salant to say, "It's difficult to tell where Souvanna Phouma left off and the colonel started."[30]

CBS was tricking the public with deceptive editing, Staggers was convinced. He issued a congressional subpoena, demanding all film, video, reporters' and editors' notes, and outtakes from the documentary. Staggers saw deceptive editing through the lens of quiz show scandals thirteen years earlier. At that time Congress, indeed the commerce committee that Staggers now chaired, protected the public from deceptive practices in quiz shows, or so he believed. The "American public is entitled to know whether what it is seeing on the television screen is real or simulated, edited or unedited, sequentially accurate or editorially rearranged, spontaneous or contrived," Staggers insisted. "[The Selling of the Pentagon] is truly the 'newspeak' of *1984;* the age of Big Brother is already upon us," the subcommittee reported.[31]

Congress had authority to examine CBS editing techniques because of its licensing, Staggers believed. Since the airwaves belonged to the people, not the broadcasters, Congress, as the people's tribune, would be shirking its duties if it allowed CBS to foist a doctored documentary on the public. Television's "potential for electronic manipulation" was so great, Staggers contended, that Congress's investigative powers superseded CBS's First Amendment claims.[32]

Stanton saw the investigation as an inquisition, promoting government surveillance and chilling broadcast news by demanding the electronic equivalent of a reporter's notes. He refused to comply. Stagger's subcommittee cut back and demanded outtakes of material used in the documentary. Stanton refused again. Editing was the journalist's job, he argued.[33] Stanton may well have chosen his ground carefully here because he engaged Staggers rather than Vice President Agnew, who represented a campaign of broadcaster intimidation for President Nixon.[34]

Staggers brought the dispute to the Commerce Committee, which cited Stanton for contempt of Congress. Publicly Stanton stuck to his guns, saying government surveillance would inhibit broadcast journalism. He also sent Staggers a letter, indicating that CBS would not object to providing "other information directly related to outtakes."[35] Unsatisfied, Staggers took the fight to the House.

Staggers suffered unprecedented defeat. For the first time Congress denied a committee chairman's subpoena power. The House rejected the contempt citation with a bipartisan vote of 226 to 181. It averted a constitutional test on whether government could investigate editing practices of broadcast journalists by sending Stanton's controversial contempt citation to the Judiciary Committee, where it died. Congressman John Dingell warned his colleagues unavailingly, "If the committee is denied the opportunity to secure the information it seeks, the Congress will have completely lost control over how and by whom the airwaves will be used. . . . The broadcasters will become trustees and fiduciaries to no one. Deceit and fraud may well run riot."[36]

Lobbying was intense, Staggers's timing faulty. One disgruntled congressman complained, "Fifteen minutes before the vote, you goddamn betcha, [House Minority Leader] Jerry [Ford] told me he was with us. And when the going got tough, Jerry finked. He ran and so did [Speaker of the House] Carl [Albert], and so did [Democratic whip] Hale Boggs. Oh hell, they ran like rats. . . . We would have won if it hadn't been for such tough lobbying."[37] Two weeks earlier, the Supreme Court had upheld *New York Times* and *Washington Post* publication of the Pentagon Papers. Powerful Ways and Means chairman Wilbur Mills, guardian of House traditions, nurtured presidential ambitions, was courting broadcasters, and did not defend Stagger's prerogative as a committee chairman.

Staggers had a weak case. The information that he subpoenaed had been available from the Pentagon all along; the Pentagon also had transcripts of Mudd's interviews. Shortly before the critical vote, CBS issued new guidelines, essentially meeting Staggers's requirements. The guidelines required journalists to inform listeners of transpositions. By the time the House voted, Staggers himself ducked the constitutional question he had championed in committee and said the vote turned on whether the subpoena had been duly issued and refused.

In the "Selling of the Pentagon" dispute the Federal Communications Commission issued a reprimanding letter. It cited rebroadcast as evidence that CBS met Fairness Doctrine obligations to present contrasting views. It found the transpositions troublesome but unworthy of commission action.[38]

■ In May 1968 *CBS Reports'* "Hunger in America," written by Peter Davis and Martin Carr and reported by Charles Kuralt, inspired an FCC inquiry for deceptive editing. The documentary argued that the Department of Agriculture (DoA) failed to use its emergency powers to distribute surplus food to hungry Americans. DoA's surplus commodities program, Kuralt reported, did more to help farmers. Far better, Kuralt suggested, would be for the Department of Health, Education and Welfare (HEW) to oversee food stamps for the needy.

"Hunger in America" explored a major public issue. A year earlier, Senator Robert F. Kennedy (D-N.Y.) brought national attention to the plight of delta blacks in the Mississippi river valley by saying during a visit there that many were "slowly starving." In January 1968 Senator Jacob Javits introduced legislation expanding DoA's food stamp program. In February the *New York Times* ran a five-part series on hunger in the United States. The following year President Nixon put HEW in charge of food stamps, and at a White

House conference on hunger that November, Jean Mayer, Nixon's adviser on food policy, promised substantial food stamp increases.

San Antonio congressman Henry B. Gonzales claimed that CBS misrepresented hunger in San Antonio. The documentary began by panning a maternity ward in a San Antonio hospital, focusing in on a dying infant, while Charles Kuralt narrated, "Hunger is easy to recognize when it looks like this. . . . This baby is dying of starvation. He was an American. Now he is dead."[39] Gonzales asked the FCC to investigate. FCC investigators found conflicting evidence. Hospital records showed that the child died of complications from premature birth after his mother suffered a fall. And hospital officials had told Carr and Davis, investigators learned, that infants died routinely from maternal malnutrition. Further inquiry would be pointless, the FCC reasoned. The FCC took no action against CBS and ruled that no license would be jeopardized short of "extrinsic evidence of possible deliberate distortion or staging."[40]

■ On September 12, 1972, NBC broadcast "Pensions: The Broken Promise." The documentary focused on workers who lost their pensions without warning and were left without benefits they had anticipated. Edwin Newman narrated the documentary, which also included interviews with New Jersey senator Harrison A. Williams, Jr. (then chairman of the Senate Labor Committee), consumer attorney Ralph Nader, labor leader Victor Gotbaum, Bank of America president Kenneth Anderson, and a spokesman for the National Association of Manufacturers. Newman concluded the documentary by calling the situation deplorable.

Two months later, Accuracy in Media (AIM), a conservative media watchdog group, filed a fairness complaint with the FCC, claiming "Pensions" devoted too much attention to "disappointments, . . . failures and . . . embezzlements."[41]

NBC responded to the FCC first by saying that "Pensions" did not present an editorial view on a controversial issue and then by asserting that, even if it did, NBC had presented sufficiently diverse views on pensions in other news programs. Eight months after the telecast in May 1973, the FCC ruled that NBC had violated the Fairness Doctrine.

AIM capitalized on the FCC staff finding. In letters to NBC affiliates, AIM threatened their licenses. "AIM intends to enter . . .

this Fairness Doctrine violation in the file of each station that carried 'Pensions.' Please let us know if you did carry this program and if you have broadcast other programs that provide the requisite balance. If we do not hear from you, we shall assume that you carried the pension program and have not provided any other program to balance it."[42]

NBC appealed to the commission, saying that "Pensions" explored problems in some private plans, not the pension system. Its news judgment was reasonable, NBC said, and as such the FCC should acknowledge that NBC met its fairness obligations. In supporting remarks, journalist David Brinkley commented, "To be found guilty of unfairness for not expressing that most people are not corrupt or that most pensioners are not unhappy is to be judged by standards which simply have nothing to do with journalism."[43] The commission denied the appeal the following month. The commission found that NBC had violated the Fairness Doctrine by criticizing the pension system and advocating stronger regulation. The FCC instructed NBC to make a reasonable good faith effort to present contrasting views in its overall programming.

Conflicting representations of "reasonable" discretion went to the heart of broadcast regulation. The award-winning documentary was balanced and reasonable by NBC's lights, and, as licensees broadcasting in the public interest, NBC retained discretion to produce the documentary according to its news judgment. The FCC, by contrast, asserted it was only "reasonable" that NBC present contrasting information on pension reform. As the federal licensing authority, the FCC retained discretion to discipline broadcasters for fairness violations. NBC immediately asked the court of appeals in Washington to review the FCC's decision.

Two years after "Pensions" was telecast, a court of appeals panel of judges overruled the FCC in September 1972. NBC had acted reasonably, the court said, because as a licensee NBC enjoyed discretion to produce documentaries as it wanted, and, whatever the FCC thought of "Pensions," it could not regulate content without violating NBC's First Amendment rights.

The case became increasingly litigious, wandering far from journalistic content. AIM asked the appeals court to rehear the case *en banc* in October 1974. The whole court reheard the case in December and reversed the panel's decision in April 1975. The FCC approached the court of appeals a month earlier, saying passage of the Employment Retirement Income Security Act made its original fairness violation moot, and asked the court to send the case back so it could drop the fairness violation. The court decided that the original panel should hear the FCC's mootness claim and reinstated the original panel's decision. Then, in July 1975, the panel of judges sent NBC's fairness violation back to the FCC, where it died. AIM did not relent, unsuccessfully pressing for appeals court and Supreme Court review. Three and a half years after the telecast, in March 1976, the FCC dropped the fairness violation.

U.S. appeals court judge Leventhal concluded that the Fairness Doctrine discouraged public affairs. Despite NBC's resources, Judge Leventhal wrote, "It is no answer to say that the license is profitable, because the problem is that the incremental burden will lead a licensee to acquiesce in the government's instruction as to what he should broadcast."[44]

Pension reform was a controversial subject throughout NBC's battle with AIM. Congress was investigating pension systems. Senator Harrison Williams, Jr., figured actively in the effort as did Jacob Javits and George McGovern, both senators with national reputations. In March 1973 President Nixon proposed pension regulation.

In the 1980s documentaries came under sharp attacks for libel as well as unfairness. General William C. Westmoreland waged an unsuccessful $120 million libel suit against CBS. President Reagan demanded a half hour of prime time to respond to Bill Moyers's documentary on Reagan administration budget cuts. Accuracy in Media accused the Public Broadcasting Service of unfairness in a documentary series on the Vietnam War and won a half hour response. The National Endowment for the Humanities disassociated itself from a documentary series on Africa because the commentator, in the NEH's view, treated the West unfairly, and Israel accused NBC of presenting the Palestine question unfairly.

■ On January 23, 1982, *CBS Reports* broadcast "The Uncounted Enemy: A Vietnam Deception," produced by George Crile and reported by Mike Wallace. Like "Hunger in America," the documentary began dramatically. Over pictures of President Lyndon Baines Johnson reviewing troops in Vietnam, Wallace charged that there was "a conspiracy at the highest levels of military intelligence to suppress and alter critical intelligence on the enemy in the year leading up to the Tet offensive."[45]

According to Wallace, General William C. Westmoreland, field commander for American forces, arbitrarily estimated enemy troop strength at 300,000 troops. Reporting accurate figures, Wallace charged, would have been "a political bombshell" undermining President Johnson's ability to sustain American involvement in the war.

General Joseph McChristian (US Army, Retired): Evidently, people didn't like my reporting, because I was constantly showing that the enemy strength was increasing. . . . The North Vietnamese and Vietcong had the capability and the will to continue a protracted war of attrition . . . for an indefinite period.
. . .

General Westmoreland: I did not accept his recommendation. . . . And I did not accept it for political reasons . . .

Mike Wallace: What's the political reason? Why would it have been a political bombshell?

General Westmoreland: Because the people in Washington were not sophisticated enough to understand and evaluate this thing, and neither was the media.[46]

Claiming Crile and Wallace "rattlesnaked" him in their interview, Westmoreland charged in his lawsuit that the documentary libeled him by saying he deliberately deceived the president and the joint chiefs of staff on enemy strength.[47] The general rejected a CBS offer of fifteen minutes of national television time for an unedited national address. This was inadequate, the general said, demanding that CBS produce an approved 45-minute retraction and pay compensatory fees. CBS refused. Westmoreland never contested deceiving journalists or the public.

CBS had its share of problems with the documentary. *TV Guide* published a critical article, indicating that George Crile had disregarded a number of CBS News rules. Burton Benjamin, a senior executive at CBS, looked into the documentary at management's request. Benjamin issued a scathing report, criticizing Crile for coaching interviewees, editing film to distort interviewing sequences, depending too much on Sam Adams, a consultant to CBS who propounded the conspiracy theory, entering the production with a preconceived idea, surreptitiously taping interviewees, including former defense secretary Robert McNamara, and presenting an imbalanced report. Benjamin also blasted CBS News management for poor supervision. Amid rumors that CBS president Wyman wanted Crile fired, CBS News president Van Gordon Sauter suspended him and shelved a documentary on Nicaragua that Crile had in the works. Just before the trial CBS stepped away from the "conspiracy" charge and stood by the documentary's accuracy.

At the trial Westmoreland's attorney, Richard Burt, argued that estimates of enemy strength were both "an honest debate" and "a bitter dispute."[48] In such a construction there was no conspiracy to deceive President Johnson. CBS's attorney David Boies countered that General Westmoreland imposed artificially low figures on enemy strength in 1967. Crile stood by his guns: He believed Westmoreland had reduced North Vietnamese and Vietcong figures for political reasons. Westmoreland did the same: There was no conspiracy, only differences of opinion.

The trial showed lapses on both sides. Crile had excluded interviews with countervailing information from such former presidential advisers as W. W. Rostow. Several army officers testified that they had reduced figures on enemy troop strength, as the documentary had charged. Former CIA analysts said that the general had wrongfully excluded Vietcong self-defense forces from enemy figures and asserted that he had given President Johnson a "grossly misleading" underestimate of enemy strength. Combat veterans backed this up, telling the jury that Vietcong–rigged booby traps killed American soldiers. Major General Joseph A. McChristian reiterated his statement.[49]

Although fairness suffused the controversy, libel mattered at the trial. "The fairness of the broadcast is not at issue," Judge Pierre N. Leval ruled. "Reporters do not comit libel in a public figure case by publishing unfair, one-sided attacks. The issue in the libel suit is whether the publisher recklessly and knowingly published false information. A publisher who honestly believes in the truth of his accusations . . . is under no obligation under the libel law to treat the subject of his accusations fairly or evenhandedly."[50]

Just before the case went to jury, Westmoreland capitulated. In joint and separate statements CBS expressed respect for the general's "long and faithful service to the country," and Westmoreland stated his high regard for CBS's "distinguished journalistic tradition." CBS stood by the fairness and accuracy of "The Uncounted Enemy," paid Westmoreland no damages, and asked compensation for court costs. Amid public assertions of victory, Westmoreland remarked, "I figured [the CBS statement] was the best I could get."[51] Crile reported back to work.

Shortly after the trial ended, the FCC rejected arguments from the conservative American Legal Foundation that CBS had acted unfairly or doctored the news.[52]

In the end, Crile had used his editorial judgment correctly. He had ignored procedural requirements at CBS, but editorially and substantively he was correct. In some ways Crile's transgressions were comparable to Davis's in "The Selling of the Pentagon" eleven years earlier. Davis had edited a quote of Colonel MacNeil, who in turn was quoting Laotian leader Souvanna Phouma, to make it look as though the words were MacNeil's. Crile edited quotes of Gains Hawkins, an army intelligence officer, making Hawkins's dismissal of the accuracy of South Vietnamese army estimates seem as though Hawkins was talking about US army estimates. Neither had fundamentally altered either officers' position. But in other ways Crile had overstepped journalistic bounds, and for this he was suspended.

■ In 1982 the Reagan administration made an unprecedented demand for a half-hour of prime time to respond to Bill Moyers's "People Like Us," a *CBS Reports* exposé exploring the impact of Reagan administration budget cuts on America's poor and ill.

Moyers did not consult the administration while making the documentary, nor had he included an administration spokesman. The administration challenged that half the cases covered in the documentary could not be accurately "laid . . . at Ronald Reagan's doorstep."[53] White House communications director David Gergen denied that the administration would direct the FCC to investigate the documentary as a fairness violation. When pressed by reporters, Gergen did not think it heavy-handed to request a script of "People Like Us" before it was televised. He denied that such an action would be comparable to Senator Joe McCarthy reviewing Edward R. Murrow's "A Report on Senator Joseph McCarthy." Nor was "People Like Us" like "The Selling of the Pentagon." There, at least, Pentagon people were in the documentary. Nor did daily

White House access to the media to present the merits of Reagan's budget cuts constitute sufficient fairness in the minds of some administration officials. Nor did seeking reply time to a documentary set a particularly bad precedent. Gergen dismissed these concerns. He doubted that the White House might next want rebuttal time for critical news stories. No, "People Like Us" differed. "This was a powerful, emotional documentary to which we had no way of responding," according to a White House spokesman. "It hit us like a two-by-four."[54]

CBS responded artfully. CBS News president Van Gordon Sauter rejected President Reagan's request on fairness grounds. "People Like Us," Sauter replied, was just "part of ongoing coverage of issues related to administration economic and budgetary programs." Administration views were covered amply each day, CBS maintained, so no prime time response was necessary.[55]

Congressmen lined up along partisan lines praising or lambasting the documentary. "Having L.B.J.'s press secretary reporting on the Reagan administration is like sending Jack the Ripper to babysit for lonely girls," John H. Rousselot simmered. "This is not journalism; it is CBS letting the Great Society's chief flak . . . have the last hurrah." Acknowledging that he had not seen the documentary, minority leader Robert Michel was hard pressed to recall such sensationalism and emotionalism. "We do not need the seeds of class warfare to be planted in the minds and hearts of people." Democrats Jim Shannon of Massachusetts and Howard Wolpe of Michigan defended the documentary for throwing bright television lights on President Reagan's budget cuts.[56] The FCC took no action.

But in 1986 Moyers left CBS despite overtures from Chairman William S. Paley to remain. By then, network news allowed little room for Moyers to comment on public affairs and prime time became virtually out of bounds for Moyers's documentaries. Moyers returned to the Public Broadcasting System, where he had more time and more freedom.

Accuracy in Media, which had attacked NBC's "Pensions" documentary so successfully in the early 1970s, struck at PBS in 1983 for unfairness, charging that *Vietnam: A Television History* misrepresented American withdrawal from Southeast Asia. According to AIM, Americans withdrew from the Vietnam War because the American media inadequately supported United States involvement.

No Fairness Doctrine violation was ruled. Instead, William Bennett, head of the National Endowment for the Humanities (NEH), which had supported part of *Vietnam: A Television History*, authorized an emergency $30,000 grant to the conservative media watchdog group to begin its rebuttal.

By many accounts, *Vietnam: A Television History* was meticulously balanced. Stanley Karnow, series producer, stated that he had produced the documentaries to help heal the country.[57]

■ In 1986 Ali Mazuri, an expert on Africa, suffered charges of unfairness for a series of documentaries (*The Africans*) negatively depicting the West's dealings with Africa. Lynne V. Cheney, head of the National Endowment for the Humanities, which had provided $600,000 toward the $3.5 million production, demanded that NEH be stricken from the credits so as not to be identified with the documentaries' editorial content. She asserted and some critics agreed that the documentaries "blame[d] all of Africa's moral, economic and technological problems on the West." It depicted Libyan dictator Muammar al-Qaddafi favorably. Mazuri suggested that Africans would get a better deal from the West once they control nuclear weapons, which he saw as the inevitable outcome of majority rule in South Africa. The West regarded Africa at best with pity and more often with contempt, Mazuri charged. In self-defense Mazuri said that the documentaries were fair; they were not produced to be attractive to Americans. Indeed, the series was acclaimed in Britain.[58] At issue was that the NEH guidelines call for "balance" and Mazuri clearly espoused an editorial view. The FCC responded favorably to the NEH's request. *The Africans* was broadcast to negative reviews in America and critical acclaim in Great Britain.[58]

■ In 1987 Israel threatened to withhold interviews with Prime Minister Yitzhak Shamir, Foreign Minister Shimon Peres, and Defense Minister Yitzhak Rabin from NBC in retaliation for alleged unfairness in a documentary on Israel's twenty-year occupation of the West Bank and the Gaza Strip. Entitled "Six Days plus Twenty Years," the documentary angered the Israelis because maverick Parliament member Rabbi Meir Kahane was the only member of the government whom NBC interviewed and because the documentary dwelled unnecessarily on the plight of Palestinians, the Israelis claimed. "What kind of fairness is that?" complained Avi Pazner, spokesman for Prime Minister Shamir. NBC responded that Israel's action "export[ed] censorship to this country." Israel also demanded an hour of rebuttal time from NBC, which the network refused.[59]

■ None of the documentaries under fire dealt with candidates. Only documentaries with incidental appearances of candidates are exempt from equal time. By contrast, a documentary devoted exclusively to a candidate falls under equal time, triggering reply time. To avoid this burden, broadcasters interview candidates on public affairs interview shows, which are exempt from the equal time rule. This format has multiple benefits. A public affairs interview show enables candidates to parry with journalists without risking the in-depth scrutiny of documentaries. By questioning candidates on public affairs interview shows, journalists boost their public recognition, thus contributing to their careers. Public affairs news interview shows, such as "Face the Nation" and "Meet the Press" fit more easily into corporate news management strategies than documentaries because their weekly repetition provides public affairs visibility for network news organizations and their conventional formats enable audiences to grasp public affairs more easily than irregularly scheduled and independently produced documentaries. Beyond equal time problems and institutional dynamics, the Fairness Doctrine inhibited documentaries further as partisans employed fairness to impose their ideological agendas on broadcasters. In particular, politicians such as Staggers and Agnew saw broadcasters as Frankenstein monsters out of control because broadcasters focused critically on a dominant institution, the military. Finally, the media marketplace works against documentaries as broadcasters program lucrative entertainment programming during prime time. Cable producers may step in but are doing so warily.

Advertisements

8

You see the Reagan re-election ads on TV—you know: "It's morning in America." And you say, "well, it's not morning in Pittsburgh. It's not morning above 125th Street in New York. It's midnight, and, like, there's a bad moon risin'."

Bruce Springsteen, *Rolling Stone* interview, *Rolling Stone,* December 6, 1984

Regulatory and legal controversies over product and editorial advertisements reflect the wildly differing perspectives of antagonists as to just what is being sold or proposed. In confrontations beginning in the 1960s and continuing to the present, the large and powerful tobacco, automobile, mining, energy, and utility corporations claimed that they were selling products: cigarettes, cars, coal, oil, and electric power. Any number of environmental and citizens groups disagreed. These corporations, public interest groups charged, were really selling mass consumption as a way of life or, more aptly, as a way of death because of cancer, pollution, environmental destruction, dependency on nuclear reactors of untried reliability, and dangers of "ecocide," that is, irrecuperable despoliation of the world's ecosystems.

A broadcast editorial critical of the 1963 Nuclear Test Ban Treaty prompted the FCC to elaborate broadcasters' Fairness Doctrine responsibilities for editorial advertisements. The Citizens Committee for a Nuclear Test Ban Treaty requested that the Cullman Broadcasting Company's WKUL in Cullman, Alabama, and Walker County Broadcasting Company's WARF in Jasper, Alabama, broadcast a tape promoting the treaty in response to a derisive syndicated commentary, "Life Line," which each broadcaster had carried. Cullman asked the FCC what to do, saying it thought the Fairness Doctrine governed local issues.

In what became known as the Cullman corollary to the Fairness Doctrine, the FCC ruled that Cullman Broadcasting must provide response time free of charge if WKUL management could not locate an articulate spokesman with a contrasting view willing to pay for the time. Although originating in a controversy over an editorial, the Cullman corollary became attached to product and editorial advertising.[1]

Ostensibly expanding the diversity of views reaching the public through broadcast editorials, the Cullman corollary created two unintended consequences. First, it inhibited broadcasters. Broadcasters shied away from airing controversial editorial programs and advertisements for fear of the management time involved in finding or fighting off spokesmen and the cost of providing free editorial rejoinders. They worried erroneously about alienating audiences by peppering their programming with editorial commercials. They fretted about jeopardizing advertising revenues by placing a disturbing editorial message next to an upbeat product advertisement. More important, though, broadcasters were anxious about taking risks with their licenses. In providing rejoinder time, broadcasters gave editorial control to partisans with precise and often strident ideological goals. No matter how many disclaimers that "so and so's views do not reflect the views of station XYZ's management," broadcasters had to deal with the fallout and its impact on meeting public interest standards at license renewal time.

Second, the Cullman corollary subsidized partisans. Interest groups seized the corollary to demand free broadcast time, thus freeing funds for newspaper advertisements, staffing, and campaigning (see chapter 9).

Although the Cullman corollary is the regulatory basis for control of editorial advertisements, the line between product and editorial advertisements is often hazy.[2] Following the surgeon general's finding that cigarette smoking is hazardous to one's health, in 1967 the FCC required broadcasters to air one antismoking message for every three cigarette advertisements and denied tobacco companies any response time. Lest the decision trigger requests for responses to other product advertisements for such pollution-causing products as leaded gasoline, electric power, airplanes, detergents, and disposable containers, the FCC stated that cigarettes were somehow unique and ruled that the public interest rather than the Fairness Doctrine required the ban.[3] A dizzying series of congressional acts, court decisions, and FCC rulings followed. Congress banned cigarette advertising over radio and television effective January 2, 1971. The court of appeals in Washington, D.C., upheld the FCC's decision.

Environmental groups pushed to extend the Cullman corollary to advertisements for other products, and a crazy quilt of regulation and law resulted. Friends of the Earth, an environmental group, pressed WNBC for reply time to advertisements for large automobiles in 1971. To Friends of the Earth the cars were gas guzzlers and pollution contributors, a public issue. NBC said the advertisements promoted a product and were not controversial and in any case the FCC should not extend the cigarette ban to cars. The FCC refused reply time to the Friends of the Earth on the grounds that doing so would create a policy that would undermine commercial broadcasting.[4]

FCC commissioner Nicholas Johnson fired off a heated dissent. Broadcasters were harming the public interest by carrying partial information through automobile and gasoline advertisements, Johnson said. He questioned how the FCC majority could place the prosperity of commercial broadcasting above the fate of the earth and worried that "Americans [were] being grossly oversold an automotive product and lifestyle they neither need nor may really want and which may eventually kill them with its exhaust by-products." Spot advertisements were persuasive, Johnson said, and should be used to promote solutions to social problems, not big cars. Citing counterculture guru Philip Slater, Johnson derided the FCC majority as "old culture" and characterized their decision as granting broadcasters a license to lie.[5]

Friends of the Earth took its complaint to the US Court of Appeals in Washington, D.C. The appeals court reversed the FCC, saying that the Fairness Doctrine could not logically be restricted to cigarette advertisements. Henceforth the Fairness Doctrine would apply to high-powered cars despite the fact that initially the FCC had applied the public interest standard, not the Fairness Doctrine, to cigarette advertisements.[6]

In additional environmental cases the Wilderness Society successfully challenged NBC over several ESSO advertisements promoting exploration of Alaskan North Slope oil fields in 1971. NBC's public affairs program, "Meet the Press" had carried the advertisements. In this case the FCC ordered NBC to present the Wilderness Society's viewpoint on the pipeline because, it reasoned, the advertisements raised controversial issues about the need for Alaskan oil and the ecological effects of oil development.[7] In 1973 the Media Access Project, representing a coalition of tenants and welfare rights and other groups, successfully forced Atlanta stations WJBF and WQXI to provide contrasting views to advertisements by Georgia Power.

The rules of the game for product advertising were clearly growing more complex and less manageable. Broadcasters got the jitters about just what product advertisements they could carry without triggering Cullman complaints. The FCC worried that it was getting too closely involved in regulating product advertising, which had little to do with public issues. Public interest groups were challenging licensee discretion and the commercial advertisements that support American broadcasting.

The FCC reexamined its cigarette advertising decision and issued new Fairness Doctrine guidelines in 1974: Henceforth only advertisements clearly "devoted in an obvious and meaningful way to the discussion of public issues" warranted response time. In most cases these advertisements concerned energy products such as coal, oil, natural gas, and nuclear power. Product advertisements, the FCC ruled, did not "inform the public on any side of a controversial issue of public importance."[8]

Seven years after the cigarette advertising ban, the FCC stepped back from regulating product advertisements. Broadcasters and most product advertisers benefited from the decision; most public interest and environmental groups were losers. So long as products were legal and advertisements contained no fraudulent claims, broadcasters were free to accept or reject them. That, of course, was precisely the rub: What one person saw as a product, others viewed as an issue. In the case of gas guzzlers, where one person saw a handsome car, another saw pollution and environmental devastation.

The test came over snowmobile advertisements in 1974. The FCC denied time to the Public Interest Research Group and the Environmental Law Institute to respond to Ski-Doo, Rupp, Alouette, and Harley-Davidson snowmobile advertisements, aired over WMTW-TV in Portland, Maine. The public interest and environmental law groups argued unpersuasively that the advertisements showed one point of view, extolling snowmobiling as part of "the good life without sufficient attention to safety or consideration of wildlife, vegetation, or noise."[9]

The FCC took a partial step toward enforcing its policy on controversial product advertisements in 1977. The Energy Action Committee challenged Texaco advertisements promoting the deregulation of oil and gas. At the time Congress was wrestling with controversial energy legislation and Texaco wanted to exert its influence over national energy policy. ABC, NBC, and Washington station WRC had all carried the advertisements less than a half-dozen times; each had also presented contrasting views. Not so with Washington station WTOP, which aired thirty- and sixty-second versions of the ad more than fifty times. In keeping with the 1974 guidelines, the FCC ordered WTOP to provide response time and dismissed Energy Action Committee demands for response time from ABC, NBC, and WRC.[10]

In one area, television advertisements for nuclear power, fairness policy was still up in the air. After the terror of Three Mile Island in 1979 and no less so following the Chernobyl disaster in 1986, Americans worried about the environmental risk of nuclear power. Television commercials extolling nuclear power raised provocative regulatory questions because utility companies were promoting a product, electricity, and propagandizing an issue, nuclear power.

In a series of decisions from 1982 to 1987 concerning advertisements for nuclear power, the FCC granted more freedom to broadcasters to decide whether to carry the advertisements and rejected requests for response time from antinuclear and environmental groups. KERO-TV in Bakersfield, California, successfully rebuffed demands for response time to utility ads by arguing that electricity, not nuclear power, was the issue at hand.[11] Similarly, in 1984 the FCC rejected Yes to Stop Callaway Committee demands for response time to pro–nuclear power advertisements, which KTVI in St. Louis, Missouri, had carried.[12]

By far the most critical decision took place in 1987. The FCC discarded its Fairness Doctrine totally (see chapter 9) in a fight pitting a utility trade association against an antinuclear group. The Energy Association of New York purchased advertising time on the Meredith Corporation's WTVH-TV in Syracuse, New York, in 1982 and again in 1984 for spot advertisements touting the Nine Mile II nuclear reactor as a sound investment in the area's future energy needs. The Syracuse Peace Council, an anti–nuclear power group, demanded free time to respond to the advertisements. Initially Meredith denied reply time. Then it granted time. Nonetheless the FCC ruled that Meredith had violated the Fairness Doctrine's Cullman corollary, which required broadcasters to provide time, free if necessary, to citizens to respond to controversial issues, by initially running the electric power advertisements in 1982 without providing time to the Syracuse Peace Council. Meredith challenged the ruling on First Amendment grounds, and the US Court of Appeals sent the case back to the FCC with orders to respond to Meredith's First Amendment arguments.[13]

The FCC took the unusual step of inviting comments. Fairness Doctrine proponents and opponents argued predictably. Among Fairness Doctrine proponents, the Democratic National Committee argued that spot advertisements are convincing. The Fairness Doctrine helped to ensure that the wealthy did not buy all the time reserved for editorial advertisements and thus dominate public discourse, the DNC argued. The American Civil Liberties Union said that the Fairness Doctrine was necessary because of spectrum scarcity: Cable television and video cassette recorders provided more entertainment than public affairs information. Satellites and low-power television were not reaching enough people to contribute meaningfully to public affairs, insisted the ACLU. The Syracuse Peace Council (SPC) warned the FCC that it was overreaching in terminating the Fairness Doctrine as a whole. The SPC argued that Meredith's compliance with the Fairness Doctrine in 1984 exonerated it for its noncompliance in 1982. Accuracy in Media, the conservative media watchdogs, argued that the Fairness Doctrine inhibited broadcast monopolies from "propagandiz[ing] one-sided or foreign viewpoints." The Anti-Defamation League of B'nai B'rith praised the Fairness Doctrine as an "effective tool in responding to . . . personal attacks and anti-Semitic or racist messages." The US Catholic Conference asserted that the Fairness Doctrine inhibited private censorship by broadcasters and promotes the public's First Amendment rights to access to the airwaves. The New York State Consumer Protection Board cautioned that lifting fairness obligations would not necessarily mean citizens would receive more information.[14]

Fairness opponents argued differently. The American Newspaper Publishers Association contended that the Fairness Doctrine inhibited the flow of controversial information to citizens and made broadcasters second-class citizens by denying them First Amendment freedom comparable to newspapers. The Edison Electric Institute (EEI), a utility association, said the Fairness Doctrine promoted censorship because broadcasters invariably refused their advertisements or accepted them only after significant changes. The EEI observed that the public had a more difficult time learning utility companies' positions on energy and nuclear power issues because the Fairness Doctrine made it more difficult for them to get their commercials on television. The Meredith Corporation pointed out that broadcasters who carry controversial editorial commercials incur fairness obligations, whereas those who do not routinely face no challenge.[15]

In a victory for broadcasters and a rout for Fairness Doctrine proponents, the FCC decided to stop enforcing the controversial regulation in its entirety and dropped the 1982 fairness violation against Meredith. The commission responded to relevant legal precedents, particularly the court of appeals decisions that the FCC had to confront the constitutionality of the Fairness Doctrine and had authority to do so.[16] The FCC grounded termination of the Fairness Doctrine in the Supreme Court's observation in *Red Lion* that, if the Fairness Doctrine were found to inhibit rather than promote the flow of news and information to the public, the doctrine's constitutionality would warrant reconsideration. In its *1985 Fairness Report* the FCC had found that the Fairness Doctrine limited public discourse. The FCC responded to an invitation by the Supreme Court in *FCC v. League of Women Voters* to send the court a signal on the doctrine's constitutionality. The commission tended its own turf by stating that policymaking and enforcement are inseparable from constitutional obligations and by holding that it could decide the doctrine's fate well within the Administrative Procedure Act because the fairness rule has always been a memorandum subject to agency revision.[17]

■ Broadcasters have the upper hand in political editorial advertising, that is, spot ads for political causes. In 1973 the Supreme Court ruled in *CBS v. the Democratic National Committee* that broadcasters were free to accept or reject editorial advertisements. The case arose when the Business Executives Move for Vietnam Peace (BEM) filed a fairness complaint against Washington, D.C., radio station WTOP for refusing to sell time for one-minute and thirty-second spot advertisements against the Vietnam War. BEM also charged that WTOP had not met its Fairness Doctrine obligations in presenting contrasting views on the war. Four months after the FCC had turned down the antiwar group, the Democratic National Committee requested unavailingly that the FCC rule that the committee enjoyed the right to impel broadcasters to carry committee editorial advertisements and fund raisers. The Democratic committee maintained that *Red Lion* established a limited constitutional access right to the airwaves for "responsible entities,"[18] and it was willing to pay for the air time.

Both the Business Executives Move for Vietnam Peace and the Democratic National Committee were pushing to establish an absolute access right for political editorial spots beyond broadcasters' control. Each wanted to extend the Fairness Doctrine so that no broadcaster could deny air time for paid editorial advertisements, thus taking the Cullman corollary a step further than the FCC had intended. If the groups succeeded, the FCC would extend the Cullman corollary so that broadcasters would have no choice but to accept political editorial spots.

The FCC rejected the committee's and BEM's claims. WTOP had acted within the Fairness Doctrine. The broadcaster could reject BEM's editorial spots like any other advertising. As for the Democrats, the commission gave the Democratic National Committee the green light under the equal time law for radio and television fund raising but not for political editorial spots.

The court of appeals reversed the FCC on the Democrats' right to purchase editorial spots. As licensees of a scarce spectrum, broadcasters possessed "abridgeable" First Amendment rights. The appeals court ruled it discriminatory to air product but not political editorial commercials. Rather than order broadcasters to carry BEM's or the committee's editorial spots, however, the appeals court sent both cases back to the FCC with orders to develop "reasonable procedures and regulations determining which and how many 'editorial advertisements' will be put on the air."[19] In the meantime the Democratic National Committee took the case to the Supreme Court.

Broadcasters' editorial control was the critical issue facing the Supreme Court. CBS resistance to the Democratic National Committee went to the heart of licensing, pitting broadcasters' editorial control against the FCC's control as licensing authority. By ruling that broadcasters had the right to choose whether or not to carry editorial advertisements, the Court did no more than recognize broadcasters' status as licensees, not common carriers. The Court saw several other problems. The Court saw "no principled means under the First Amendment of favoring access by organized political parties over other groups and individuals."[20] It worried that the FCC would get too closely involved in overseeing broadcasters' daily news operations. The Court cautioned that, if broadcasters were required to sell political editorial spots, control would pass from broadcasters, who are licensed, to unregulated partisans. It pondered that the public interest might deteriorate to contention over passing issues. The Court rejected the notion that every potential speaker is the best judge of what is newsworthy or demands public attention.

Most important, the Supreme Court saw that exposing broadcasters to access demands would inhibit broadcast journalism. Justice Douglas directly addressed the Democratic committee's efforts to approach broadcasters with an FCC ruling that ordered broadcasters to carry editorial spots. "Television and radio stand in the same protected position under the First Amendment as do newspapers and magazines. . . . The Fairness Doctrine has no place in our First Amendment regime. It puts the head of the camel inside the tent and enables administration after administration to toy with television or radio for its sordid or benevolent ends." Justice Stewart was equally gimlet-eyed about FCC scrutiny of broadcast news and commentary: "Those who wrote our First Amendment put their faith in the proposition that a free press is indispensable to a free society. They believed 'fairness' was far too fragile to be left for a government bureaucracy to accomplish. . . . If we must choose whether editorial decisions are to be made in the free judgment of individual broadcasters, or imposed by bureaucratic fiat, the choice must be for freedom."[21]

No matter how strenuously Justices Douglas and Stewart shouted its shortcomings, the Court maintained broadcasters' rights to accept or reject editorial spots, in part, because the Fairness Doctrine required them to present controversial news and views. The Fairness Doctrine was adequate to ensure that the public received a diversity of information, the Court held: No further encroachment on broadcaster editorial control was warranted.

Justice William Brennan dissented, saying interest groups could well use editorial spots to reach the public with novel, unorthodox, and unrepresentative information. He complained that the Fairness Doctrine filtered out too much. Under the Fairness Doctrine, Brennan observed, the public was "compelled to rely 'exclusively' on the 'journalistic discretion' of broadcasters, who serve in theory as surrogate spokesmen for all sides of all issues. This separation of advocate from expression can only serve to diminish the effectiveness of that expression."[22]

■ Candidates enjoy preferential advertising rates for spot advertisements promoting their candidacy and the benefits of "reasonable access" to the airwaves. In 1952 Congress amended the equal time law so that political candidates could purchase advertising at the lowest commercial rate. Twenty years later Congress legislated access rights for federal candidates as part of the Federal Election Campaign Act of 1971 and amended Section 312 of the Communications Act to increase federal candidates' control of their appearances on television.[23]

The 1980 Carter-Mondale campaign tested the reasonable access law. In October 1979 Jerry Rafshoon, media adviser to the Carter-Mondale campaign, wrote to ABC, CBS, and NBC to purchase a half-hour of prime time television in early December for a documentary highlighting President Carter's accomplishments.

None agreed to sell a half-hour; each offered varying amounts of time. The FCC split along party lines, voting four Democrats to three Republicans in favor of the Carter-Mondale campaign. By that time, however, Iranian revolutionaries had seized the American Embassy in Tehran, and the Carter campaign withdrew the half-hour documentary in favor of a shorter pitch.

The FCC ruled that Section 312 required broadcasters to make prime time available to candidates, forbade them from excluding federal candidates from any time periods or spot advertisements, and impelled them to make time available forty-five days before a primary election and sixty days before a general election. Candidates won control over how they were to appear—in other words, in a spot or any other format. In addition, the FCC ruled that public television stations must provide time and that political candidates should act with restraint in their demands on public television.[24]

CBS appealed and lost before the Supreme Court. The Court viewed reasonable access for candidates as a sensible balance, enabling candidates to reach mass audiences without eroding broadcasters' editorial control. Broadcasters could reasonably deny time to a candidate before a campaign, the Court noted. Once campaigning was underway broadcasters could also factor in the amount of time previously sold to candidates, disruption to regular programming, and potential requests from other candidates. But in the end candidates' access, the Court observed, was a limited right, so broadcasters should accommodate candidates' requests. Justice White dissented, saying that the FCC and the Court were granting federal candidates more control over broadcasting than Congress had intended originally.[25]

■ Candidates had no sooner won favorable access when political action committees (PACs) began challenging them, particularly incumbent Democrats. Political action committees got their start as part of reform legislation intended to clean up presidential election fund raising in the wake of the Watergate scandal in the early 1970s. The organizations solicit and channel private contributions to promote causes and advance candidates, particularly congressional candidates; the campaign reform legislation had made it more difficult to contribute to presidential campaigns, and the PACs seeking influence increased spending on congressional elections. In the 1980 election Republicans nominated a winning candidate and won control of the Senate for the first time in twenty-six years, thanks to active involvement by right wing PACs, which successfully attacked several liberal Democratic senators.

Political action committees secured a relative advantage over candidates and political parties through Supreme Court rulings that upheld the right of PACs to spend unlimited funds for candidates and causes so long as a PAC's effort was not coordinated with candidate or referendum campaigns. To hold otherwise, the Court ruled, would compromise freedom of speech.[26] If candidates received public financing, they must campaign within expenditure limits imposed under the Federal Election Campaign Act and Presidential Election Campaign Fund Act. By contrast, the Court freed PACs to spend privately however they wished.

The Court's decisions on PACs assume unfairness. The thrust of the Court's thinking was that First Amendment rights are unabridgeable. Free speech is not a distributive right: One person's free speech cannot subsidize another's. Accordingly the Court ruled that the First Amendment permitted restrictions on contributions to candidates and PACs in order to avoid corruption or the appearance of corruption. And pivotally the Court ruled that the First Amendment authorized unrestricted expenditures as an expression of free speech.

Justice Byron White viewed the majority position as sophistry. The majority's distinction between coordinated and independent expenditures was "blink[ing] at reality," White chided. Successful candidates would inevitably reward supporters whether their efforts were coordinated or not, he insisted. White worried that the Court was gutting the post-Watergate campaign reforms by "transform[ing] a coherent regulatory scheme into a nonsensical, loophole-ridden patchwork."[27]

Political spots figured importantly in the Court's thinking. "The electorates' increasing dependence on television, radio, and other mass media for news and information has made these expensive modes of communication indispensable instruments of effective political speech," the Court observed.[28] Imposing limits on PAC expenditures for mass media hardly differed from "allowing a speaker into a public hall to express his views while denying him the use of an amplifying system."[29]

Justice White objected to the Court's media rationale, too. Unlimited PAC expenditures produced speech, White conceded, but producing spot advertisements differed from political speech. The Court was actually protecting spending to make television commercials, not ensuring free speech, White insisted. Precisely because the majority saw no problem with unabridgeable free speech rights irrespective of the threat of large-scale expenditures to campaigning, White's objections fell on deaf ears. On the other hand, the majority decision assumed that citizens are responsible for evaluating well-financed from poorly financed candidates and for drawing their own conclusions.

Twice blessed and street legal, PACs hit the political scene in the 1980s. The Carter-Mondale campaign and Missouri Democrat senator Thomas Eagleton, two targets of negative PAC spots, challenged them and ran afoul of the Supreme Court rulings upholding the PACs' unabridgeable free speech rights and unlimited expenditures. The FCC rejected both Carter and Mondale's and Eagleton's demands for free time from broadcasters, ruling that the candidates were entitled to purchase time on similar terms, no more. The Court had so ruled. Equal time protected against broadcaster favoritism. Nor was the Fairness Doctrine much use to candidates. It required only that broadcasters provide viewers with controversial news and contrasting views on pressing issues. So long as broadcasters covered candidates, disgruntled candidates could not press for free time to respond to critical PAC spots.[30]

PACs pushed the FCC unsuccessfully in 1982 to impose similar rules for PAC advertisements against candidates during noncampaign periods. The FCC drew the regulatory line there and sided with candidates. It ruled that broadcasters would be liable under the Cullman corollary to provide response time to candidates or to opponents of PAC-backed referendum issues in noncampaign periods. PACs enjoyed a financial advantage during campaign periods, but no more. The Fairness Doctrine protected incumbents from PACs' stinging arrows when they were not campaigning.[31]

By the mid-1980s PACs and broadcasters emerged in relatively stronger positions than candidates concerning spot advertisements. In campaign periods PAC-financed ads triggered equal time if the candidate or a PAC favorable to him wished to respond and, critically, if the candidate had the money to do so—no mean trick if a candidate accepted public funds. With no fairness obligations during campaign periods for carrying PAC advertisements, broadcasters were freer to accept them. Because PAC ads triggered Cullman obligations under the Fairness Doctrine in noncampaign periods and the Fairness Doctrine rested on broadcasters' discretion, broadcasters were free to reject PAC ads so long as they could come up with some plausible rationale for their coverage of the controversial issue in question. The FCC went so far as to say that an incumbent's voting record may not be sufficiently controversial to trigger fairness obligations.

Candidates, by contrast, fared less well. Despite the plebiscitary politics of the 1980s, candidates, who accepted public money, had to live within a budget that balanced private and public donations or rely on friendly PACs. Because most candidates plan on spending their advertising money to counter their opponents, not a PAC, these new rules altered the dynamics of campaigning, particularly through televised spot advertisements. The rules placed candidates with no PAC funds at a relative disadvantage.

Politicians responded by trying to reassert their dominance in electoral politics. Any number of candidates believed it fundamentally unfair to be placed in the position of battling political action committees in addition to opponents. PAC-sponsored negative political commercials were doubly offensive because there appeared to be so little accountability. President Carter and Senator Eagleton had wrestled with the former problem in their failed efforts to have the FCC grant them free time to respond to PAC-sponsored programming. In 1986 Illinois senator Charles Percy suffered from the latter. He lost reelection after a barrage of negative commercials, financed by a Californian unconnected to his opponent, were televised late in the campaign. Similarly, Kentucky senator Walter Huddleston was satirized viciously in a number of spots in his unsuccessful reelection bid in 1984. The spots depicted a baying hound dog sniffing unsuccessfully through the Capitol trying to find the portly Huddleston at work and in the end staring up a tree at the rotund derriere of an actor hired to imitate the incumbent.[32]

One proposal, backed by Democratic majority leader Robert Byrd and Oklahoma senator David Boren, called for a voluntary system to sidestep the First Amendment issues in *Buckley v. Valeo* concerning subsidizing First Amendment rights and has failed repeatedly to win congressional approval. Senate candidates would be free to participate or not. If the proposed legislation became law, only major party candidates with extensive field organizations would be able to raise enough private contributions, specified in the legislation, to trigger public money. Minor party candidates could not realistically make claims on public monies. This insulates Democrats and Republicans alike. Participating candidates would be rewarded by receiving the lowest unit rate for their broadcast advertisements, whereas nonparticipating candidates would be required to pay commercial advertising rates. Should a candidate run a negative ad attacking his opponent, the candidate would be required to make the assertion himself and appear in half the spot. The legislation imposed a requirement on PAC-funded advertisements to carry subtitles, identifying the sponsoring PAC and stating that "the cost of presenting this communication is not subject to any campaign contributions limits."[33]

Senator Boren argued unsuccessfully that PACs push up election costs, make campaigns nastier, stifle challengers by contributing more heavily to incumbents, and increase incumbents' dependency on single-issue money. He missed the mark on several other particulars. Campaign costs have risen, but candidates spend more on organizations and consultants than on television advertisements. Furthermore, many candidates prefer to spend money on ads, which they totally control, than contend with journalists, whom they do not control. Campaigns are faster. It takes only a few hours to produce a spot response to an opponent's commercials. PACs make for more players, but they are hardly nastier than electoral contests earlier in American political history. Incumbents received more money than challengers from interest groups long before PACs. Far from limiting diversity, PACs identify the diversity. With so many players, each required to label itself a PAC in order to contribute, lobbying became more public and more visible.

Aside from these substantive problems, Senate Republicans viewed this anti-PAC reform as a Democratic smoke screen to sustain Democratic domination. Limits on campaign spending would make it more difficult for Republicans to regain control of the Senate, because as the minority party they must spend more money than Democrats to reach and convert voters. Senator Boren's bill also limited party expenditures to $2 million during congressional elections. Since Republicans rely on party support more heavily than Democrats, this was also a disincentive. Finally, the bill concerned itself exclusively with Senate contests; its fate in the House was doubtful.

By the late 1980s independent broadcasters became players briefly in spot debates, not PAC advertisements. In 1987 the Association of Independent Television Stations (INTV) and Washington journalist John McLaughlin petitioned the FCC to waive equal time requirements for brief sixty-second debates on policy issues, appropriately named "60 Seconds." In the spot debate McLaughlin poses a question on a controversial issue such as trade or mandatory AIDS testing, and two Congressmen assert contrasting views on the issue. INTV sought assurance that "60 Seconds" would be exempt from equal time as a "bona fide news interview" despite its brevity. Through the spot debates independent broadcasters increase their influence among Congressmen, politicians raise their visibility among viewers of the many independent high-frequency television stations, independent broadcasters provide public interest programming, and viewers receive contrasting views. However, INTV's spot debates folded before the FCC made a ruling. Larger independent stations refused to guarantee that they would carry the spots, whereas smaller ones embraced the concept. Without commitments from independents in larger markets, advertisers pulled back support, which doomed production.

Editorial advertising is now virtually unregulated. The FCC's 1987 memorandum in *Meredith* (see pp. 140–142 and Chapter 9) frees broadcasters to accept editorial spots for public issues and political editorial spots for political causes without worries about Cullman challenges. As a result, spot announcements for and against controversial Supreme Court nominee Robert Bork, Contra aid, and other public issues typify ideological spot advertising. Whether greater public awareness or continued erosion of political participation will result is unclear. What is clear is that more organizations will be able to get their messages to the American public. This seems wholly reasonable. The founders entrusted citizens with the responsibilities of choosing their representatives and monitoring their actions. Such responsibilities require at a minimum that voters are free to choose for themselves how seriously they pay attention to political advertisements on radio and television.

The Ebbing Tide
of the Fairness Doctrine

9

Somehow the wires uncrossed;
The tables were turned,
Never knew I had such a lesson to learn.
I'm feelin' good from my head to my shoes;
Know where I'm goin' and I know what to do.
I tidied up my point of view,
I've got a new attitude.

Patti LaBelle, "New Attitude," 1985 pop hit

By the mid-1980s a deregulatory tide pulled at the Fairness Doctrine. In 1985 the FCC launched a wholesale inquiry, initiated by Chairman Mark Fowler. In February 1985 Fowler looked out on panels of partisans and experts assembled in the FCC's hearing room. For Fowler the two days of hearings were something of an accomplishment. Through his efforts debate was shifting away from content regulation. Discussion focused less on a governmental role in ensuring fairness in public affairs and more on the marketplace and broadcasters' free speech rights. Things had begun a year earlier.[1]

In 1984 the FCC, riding a deregulatory wave, issued a Notice of Inquiry on the Fairness Doctrine. On a note of caution the FCC stated that it was inquiring into the possibility of altering the Fairness Doctrine and that it would not repeal fairness on the basis of inquiry responses. Taking a provocative tack, the FCC in its notice leaned toward repeal by posing queries that indicated FCC willingness to dispose of the controversial regulation.[2]

The notice reflected the major fairness issues facing the FCC. First, the FCC asked whether the Fairness Doctrine promoted or inhibited public affairs. Second, it queried whether technological innovations, specifically cable and satellites, made the doctrine's spectrum scarcity rationale obsolete. Third, it questioned whether First Amendment law had changed since *Red Lion*.[3] Fourth, and most telling, the FCC questioned whether it had the authority to alter the Fairness Doctrine or whether sole authority to do so resided with Congress. This final query signaled conflict over the Fairness Doctrine's status as a law or regulation because of the ambiguous fairness proviso to the 1959 equal time amendments. If the Fairness Doctrine was a regulation, then the FCC, as the responsible administrative agency, could do with it as it pleased. Agency discretion during this deregulatory period meant certain repeal. If the Fairness Doctrine was instead a law, only Congress could authorize change in the controversial statute, ensuring certain retention. House Democrats were solidly behind it; as recently as 1984, the Republican Senate had refused to change it.

On the first query, whether the Fairness Doctrine promoted or inhibited public affairs, contention turned on the doctrine's "chilling effect," that is, whether it suppressed public affairs by deterring broadcasters from covering controversial issues and expressing editorial views.

Fairness advocates asserted that media economics had more to do with public affairs programming than the Fairness Doctrine. Charles Ferris, Jimmy Carter's FCC chairman, representing the Democratic National Committee, stated that, as an industry dependent on advertising revenues, broadcasting presented material designed to be unoffensive to the largest possible audience and shunned controversy to protect their revenues.[4] Reed Irvine, a conservative critic of the media and head of Accuracy in Media, which had challenged NBC's award-winning "Pensions" documentary, blasted broadcasting as an "oligopoly" pumping the public with "liberal" news. Without the doctrine public affairs programming would degenerate into "political tools," Irvine claimed.

The Fairness Doctrine was remedial and minimally intrusive, proponents claimed. Of the 11,000 broadcasters in the country in 1985, only 25 had received fairness complaints in the early 1980s according to proponents' figures. How could broadcasters possibly call the doctrine "chilling" with so few cases, Ferris asked. An attorney who had represented advocates for beverage bottle deposits in a California referendum asserted that the Fairness Doctrine enabled bottle bill advocates to get media coverage they could not have acquired otherwise because of saturation advertising against the referendum by the beverage industry. Prominent equal rights and abortion rights foe Phyllis Schlafly credited the doctrine with enabling her to negotiate news coverage on both issues. "Of all the coverage on the ERA, over 95% of it on tv was pro-ERA and only 5% of it was against the ERA. If it wasn't for the Fairness Doctrine, we couldn't have gotten even that measly five percent," Schlafly said. A B'nai B'rith attorney claimed that the doctrine diminished racist, anti-Semitic broadcasting, especially important in small towns with few radio and often no television stations. B'nai B'rith used the Fairness Doctrine, he said, to speak with the major networks about news coverage of the 1982 Israel-Lebanon war. Journalists' ethical standards demanded more of them than the Fairness Doctrine, David Rubin, an ACLU attorney, pointed out.

Broadcast journalists and news managers claimed that fairness chilled news coverage, stifled controversial news programming, and inhibited editorials. National news organizations complained that fairness complaints consumed too much management time. Smaller radio broadcasters contended that as small businesses few could afford legal costs responding to fairness complaints, so they shunned public affairs controversy. Former CBS News commentator Eric Sevareid derided fairness as "a weapon in the backpocket of government"; referring to FCC regulators, the silver-haired journalist warned that "people in officious disposition" were a greater danger to the public interest than reporters. "The press doesn't draft you or imprison you or execute you," Sevareid said in a commanding, modulated voice. Someday, Sevareid prophesied, a new generation of reporters would be free of "the little cancerous bit of awareness in the back of their heads" concerning fairness rules. Once burnt, twice shy was the message.[5]

Fairness opponents asserted that the FCC rule intruded directly in news and public affairs. Floyd Abrams, NBC's attorney, blasted the public interest attorney, representing bottle bill advocates, for using the Fairness Doctrine to respond to advertisements. The FCC was wrong, Abrams insisted, to force broadcasters to provide time to bottle bill proponents when broadcasters were already covering the ballot issue in their newscasts. The Johnson and Nixon administrations used the FCC to silence a right wing radio broadcaster in the mid-1960s and to intimidate the *Washington Post* during the Watergate scandal, Abrams charged. In 1984 and 1985 the CIA mounted a fairness challenge, albeit unsuccessfully, to ABC News coverage of an alleged CIA plot to assassinate a former agent. Douglas Ginsburg, President Reagan's failed Supreme Court nominee following the Bork rout and at that time a Harvard Law School professor on leave at the Office of Management and Budget, ripped into the B'nai B'rith attorney for testifying that the Fairness Doctrine enabled B'nai B'rith to make "private deals" with broadcasters on news coverage of the 1982 Israeli invasion of Lebanon.[6]

On the second query, spectrum scarcity, contention turned on what unit of measurement the FCC applied in assessing fairness complaints. Proponents insisted, following *NBC v. US* and *Red Lion,* that the number of people wishing to broadcast compared to the number of broadcast frequencies remain the unit of measurement. Opponents urged the FCC to adopt the number of media outlets in a community as the unit of measurement.

Fairness proponents, ranging from single-issue interest groups to right wing ideologues to major corporations to the American Civil Liberties Union, asserted that cable and satellite channels did not weaken the doctrine's spectrum scarcity rationale. The government granted licenses to individual broadcasters to use scarce spectrum. Because of this limitation, which is sui generis to broadcasting, they claimed that the Fairness Doctrine was necessary. Andrew Schwartzman, representing the Media Access Project, pointed out that broadcasting's success in attracting investment capital indicated that broadcasting would continue to dominate electronic news and public affairs. Henry Geller pointed out that the high prices commanded for television stations indicated scarcity.

Mobil and the National Rifle Association (NRA) punctured the cable cornucopia. Broadcasters reached 98% of American homes, whereas cable reached at best just more than a third in 1985, the NRA claimed. Broadcasting penetration was highest in the areas with the greatest population, because only recently had major cities begun wiring for cable television. And, when cable did program news, specifically C-SPAN and Ted Turner's Cable News Network, the NRA complained that the programming focused on national, not local, issues. Mobil pointed out that most of the newer cable channels programmed entertainment, not news and public affairs. As for the newer technologies, their use and applications are untested, in the future, and at best speculative.[7]

An abundance of broadcast radio and television channels outmoded the Fairness Doctrine's spectrum scarcity rational, fairness opponents rebutted. Quite aside from the newer alphabet soup of communications technologies (LPTV, MDS, SMATV, DBS, VCR, etc.), far more radio and television stations were on the air than in 1949, when the FCC adopted the Fairness Doctrine. In a competitive media marketplace, with these stations vying for listeners, opponents claimed that the public had innumerable opportunities to hear news, information, and a diversity of points of view.

Numbers supported their view. Twelve times as many television stations and four times as many radio stations programmed news and public affairs than in 1950. By the mid-1980s average Americans received at least five channels on their televisions; two-thirds of the country received at least nine.[8]

Tables 9.1 and 9.2 show the increase in the number of broadcast channels by the mid-1980s. In addition to 10,000-odd radio and television stations, 6,400 cable systems served 29 million homes. Subscription television (STV) was in place in seventeen markets. One hundred and five cities had microwave (MDS) service, serving a half-million subscribers. Because of a 1983 FCC ruling permitting MDS operators to operate multichannel systems (multichannel

Table 9.1
Number of radio stations

Stations	1950	1970	1983
Total	2,867	6,889	9,283
Standard (AM)	2,086	4,292	4,723
AM Commercial	–	4,276	4,679
AM Educational	–	25	44
FM	781	2,597	4,559
FM Commercial	733	2,184	3,458
FM Educational	48	413	1,101

Source: Notice of Inquiry, p. 20323.

Table 9.2
Number of television stations

Stations	1950	1970	1983
Total	98	862	1,140
Commercial VHF	98	501	536
Commercial UHF		176	321
Educational VHF		80	112
Educational UHF		105	171

Source: Notice of Inquiry, p. 20324.

MDS), anywhere from eight to twenty-eight more channels were available to MDS users. Direct broadcast satellites (DBS) provided 5 channels and could provide as many as 128. Satellite Master Antenna Systems (SMATV), primarily serving large apartment buildings and hotels, enjoyed nearly 300,000 subscribers in 1984. There were 12 million video cassette recorders in American homes by the mid-1980s.

Adding print to broadcasting, cable, and the new communications technologies, fairness foes showed that 1,700 daily and 6,784 weekly newspapers and 10,809 periodicals circulated in America. That meant that roughly six times as many radio and television stations as daily newspapers provided Americans with information. Many of those newspapers depended on the dominant Associated Press wire service and the financially shaky United Press International, neither of which was under any fairness obligations. (See note 8.)

Invariably, communities had more television and radio stations than newspapers, fairness foes showed. For example, Los Angeles, the second largest broadcast market in the country, supported ninety-five radio and television stations and three daily newspapers. Pittsburgh, the twelfth largest broadcast market, sustained eighty-two radio and television stations and two daily newspapers. Sixty-seven radio and television stations provided Hartford, the twenty-second largest broadcast market, with news, as did one daily paper. Austin, Texas, received its news and information from fifty-one radio and television stations and from one daily newspaper. Austin is the eighty-second largest broadcast market in the United States.[9]

News programming had skyrocketed with the explosion in channels. Regularly scheduled network television news accounted for 60½ hours of network television programming per week. This was two and a half times as much news as the twenty-four hours programmed in 1981 and nearly four times the sixteen hours programmed in the late 1960s. Local television stations boosted their news programming, but not as dramatically as the networks. By 1982 there were, on average, ten hours of locally produced news programming per week, compared with eight in 1971. Independent television stations came on line in the 1970s and early 1980s, providing more local news. By the early 1980s independents devoted eight hours a week to local news, up from three hours in 1974.[10]

This mix of economic and technological issues illustrated administrative problems enforcing fairness. In smaller communities broadcast frequencies were often available, but few applicants had come forward because stations in those communities were unprofitable. In technological terms there was no spectrum scarcity in those communities. In urban areas demand for lucrative licenses created economic scarcity. However, intense competition among broadcasters guaranteed plenty of opportunity for the public to see and hear controversial news.

On the third query, First Amendment law, fairness proponents cited *Red Lion* approvingly and persistently. "It is the right of the viewers and listeners, not the right of the broadcasters, which is paramount," the Supreme Court had ruled, and so the FCC should abide. Spectrum scarcity made it so. "There is nothing in the First Amendment which prevents the government from requiring a licensee to share his frequency with others and to conduct himself as a proxy or fiduciary with obligations to present those views and voices which are representative of his community and which would otherwise, by necessity, be barred from the airwaves," doctrine proponents quoted the Court.[11]

Fairness opponents looked to Supreme Court decisions on libel and access. In the *Sullivan* case (1964), the Court found that print journalists had to willfully and intentionally misrepresent information about a public official—what the Court called actual malice—in order for the individual to bring libel charges. How different, fairness opponents argued, was this standard compared with responsibilities imposed on broadcasters to provide time to reply to their editorial views or to be impelled to do a story over. In the *Miami Herald* case (1974), fairness opponents found unequivocal assertion that the government could not tamper in the editorial decisions of the press. This was the proper standard for broadcasting, they contended. Court rulings from the mid-1970s held that speakers' identity, wealth, persuasiveness, or distastefulness had nothing to do with their right to speak. The right to speak was unabridgeable.[12]

Best of all, in 1984 the Supreme Court invited a retest of fairness in light of the explosion in communications technologies. Justice William Brennan noted that *Red Lion* had left the door open for future reconsideration of the Fairness Doctrine when spectrum scarcity was less pressing. And, noting the changes in the number of channels, Brennan wrote that reconsideration of the Fairness Doctrine may now be appropriate.[13]

A historical view of First Amendment law between the late-1940s and the mid-1980s highlights the differences between contending camps. The Supreme Court initially sustained the FCC's regulatory authority over broadcast content in 1943 in the *NBC* case. In the *AP* case the Court affirmed that a private monopoly could not control the flow of news and information to the public. As commercial enterprises involved in the dissemination of news, information, and entertainment, the print and broadcast media were equally subject to social and economic regulation as any other business, Frankfurter ruled, even if their businesses were those of ideas, opinions, information, and the popular arts. Justice Frankfurter's views followed existing precedent. From the beginning of federal regulation of broadcasting in the 1920s, First Amendment law placed public order above the rights of speakers. In 1927, in *Whitney v. California,* the Court upheld a California statute forbidding communists from recruiting members. In 1925, in *Gitlow v. New York,* the Court ruled that the First Amendment did not protect seditious speech. In 1919, in the *Schenk* decision, the Court articulated the "clear and present danger" standard on freedom of speech, and in *Abrams v. US,* it ruled that the First Amendment did not allow publications during the course of World War I that were critical of the US invasion of the Soviet Union. In 1918 the Court ruled that the First Amendment did not protect newspapers from contempt convictions for publishing articles critical of the legal arguments during pending court cases. In 1907 the Court ruled that, even if allegations of a public official's malfeasance were true, the speaker could still be penalized if the Court deemed the assertions were detrimental to public welfare. And, as far back as 1877, the Court ruled that Congress could exclude publications thought to be immoral from the mails.[14]

Add to this the development early on of radio as an entertainment medium, not as a news media, and Frankfurter's rationale for content regulation is quite plausible. Commenting on the pervasiveness of First Amendment standards, upholding public order over speaker's rights, during the early days of broadcasting, Judge Bazelon noted in his dissenting opinion in *Brandywine Main Line Radio, Inc. v. FCC* that "radio came into the world as a magic box analogized to the telegraph. . . . Broadcasters themselves were viewed as entertainers rather than responsible journalists: certainly they were not 'newsmen.' The Commission felt justified in imposing upon these neophytes a series of obligations to ensure they would act 'responsibly' in the public interest."[15]

These earlier decisions differ markedly from more recent Supreme Court rulings such as *Sullivan, Miami Herald, CBS v. Democratic National Committee,* and *FEC v. NCPAC/FCM* (see chapter 8), increasing broadcasters' discretion and greater freedom of speakers. Coupled with Justice Brennan's invitation to reconsider the Fairness Doctrine, First Amendment law had shifted dramatically to broadcasters' advantage.

On the fourth query, proponents claimed that only Congress could alter the Fairness Doctrine by amending the equal time law. Blasting the FCC as "radical" and "ideological," John Dingell, chairman of the House Commerce Committee, dismissed the inquiry as a fool's errand. "This Commission should have recognized long ago that it is an independent regulatory agency accountable to the Congress, and, as such, it may find that what it thinks is a legal loophole can fast become its own noose."[16] Fairness foes, knowing the FCC's deregulatory agenda under Fowler and anticipating the doctrine's certain end, trumpeted FCC discretion.

The argument devolved into a fight over the ambiguous fairness proviso in the 1959 *Lar Daly* amendments to equal time. Fairness proponents argued the proviso and legislative history proved that Congress had enacted the Fairness Doctrine as law; foes countered that Congress was far more concerned with candidates than public affairs and that the proviso merely left the FCC's fairness policy undisturbed.

■ Later in 1985 the FCC reported on its inquiry. Predictably the FCC found that the Fairness Doctrine was constitutionally suspect, that it chilled public affairs, that an abundance of electronic information outmoded the doctrine's spectrum scarcity rationale, and that First Amendment law no longer supported abridging broadcasters' First Amendment rights. But, on the issue of agency authority, the FCC fudged. The FCC wrote that, although it believed the Fairness Doctrine disserved the public interest, the legislative history of the 1959 amendments was so muddy that it would defer any action on fairness to Congress. Second, the FCC issued a Fairness Doctrine violation against the Meredith Corporation's Syracuse, New York, station, WTVH, for carrying pro-nuclear utility issue advertisements without providing adequate reply time to a group opposed to nuclear power. Third, the Radio and Television News Directors Association brought suit against the FCC for enforcing a rule it had found to be unconstitutional.

The locus of battle moved to the US District Court of Appeals in Washington, D.C. In *Meredith v. FCC,* the court ruled in January 1987 that the commission had to address squarely the constitutionality of the Fairness Doctrine despite heat from Congress. FCC temporizing was too much for the court: "We are aware of no precedent that permits a federal agency to ignore a constitutional challenge to the application of its own policy merely because the resolution would be politically awkward," the court blistered.[17]

In *Radio and Television News Directors Association v. FCC,* decided the same day as *Meredith,* the appeals court ruled that it was willing to review RTNDA's claim that, in light of the FCC's 1985 inquiry, the commission acted capriciously in failing to make a rule killing the Fairness Doctrine but also said that the RTNDA would have to take its petition questioning the constitutionality of the Fairness Doctrine to the US district court.[18]

A year earlier, in *Telecommunications Research and Action Center and Media Access Project v. FCC* (1986), a case testing Fairness Doctrine and equal time applications in teletext, Judge Robert Bork, President Reagan's failed Supreme Court nominee, then an appeals court judge, ruled that the Fairness Doctrine was an FCC rule. In other words, Congress had not enacted it as law in the 1959 amendments; the proviso for equal time had left the Fairness Doctrine undisturbed as an FCC regulation. Judge Bork's ruling prompted Commissioner James H. Quello to remark that the "*TRAC* teletext case stated the Fairness Doctrine is not incorporated in the Communications Act but is only FCC policy which the FCC can eliminate."[19] Bork also challenged *Red Lion*'s spectrum scarcity rationale for the Fairness Doctrine. He wrote, "It is certainly true that broadcast frequencies are scarce but it is unclear why that fact justifies content regulation of broadcasting in a way that would be intolerable if applied to the editorial process of the print media. All economic goods are scarce, not least the newsprint, ink, delivery trucks, computers, and other resources that go into the production and dissemination of print journalism. Not everyone who wishes to publish a newspaper, or even a pamphlet may do so. Since scarcity is a universal fact, it can hardly explain regulation in one context and not another."[20]

■ The Federal Communications Commission once again became the locus of regulatory battles within a week of the Appeals Court's decision in *Meredith*. In January 1987 the commission requested comments on the constitutionality of the Fairness Doctrine, and in August, under new chairman Dennis Patrick, the FCC discarded the Fairness Doctrine in a new *Meredith* decision (pp. 140–142).

Abolition of the Fairness Doctrine was historic. In the August 1987 *Meredith* decision the FCC tackled the historic issue of whether speakers or listeners enjoyed sovereignty of the airwaves. It came out forcefully for speakers, reversing policy dating to the Secretary of Commerce Herbert Hoover and the national radio conferences of the 1920s. It dismissed spectrum scarcity as a valid rationale for fairness obligations. A license to the electromagnetic spectrum did not diminish a broadcaster's constitutionally protected right of free speech. A better standard for a First Amendment issue like fairness was a broadcaster's function in a democracy, not just the physical characteristics of broadcasting. The FCC dismissed economic scarcity as a universal and elided questions of broadcast oligopoly and monopoly. Unlike the equivocal (4–1) vote authorizing fairness in 1949, the FCC voted unanimously (4–0) to discard the Fairness Doctrine.

In repealing the Fairness Doctrine, the FCC relied on the US

(top) Edward R. Murrow, CBS commentator and reporter.

(bottom) Senator Joseph McCarthy (R-Wis.). Courtesy of CBS Television Network.

Vice-President Spiro T. Agnew tells reporters that he has no intention of intimidating the press as he criticizes "The Selling of the Pentagon," a CBS documentary, March 1971. Courtesy of UPI/Bettmann Newsphotos.

Retired general William Westmoreland holds up a statement signed by the principals involved in dropping his $120 million libel suit against CBS for its documentary "The Uncounted Enemy." Courtesy of UPI/Bettmann Newsphotos.

(top left) Justice William Brennan invited reevaluation of the Fairness Doctrine in a 1985 decision. Courtesy of the Supreme Court Historical Society.

(top right) Reed Irvine, a conservative critic of broadcast news and a fairness proponent. Courtesy of Accuracy in Media, Inc.

(bottom left) Herbert Schmertz, Mobil Oil, a fairness proponent and patron of public television. Courtesy of Mobil Oil Corporation.

(bottom right) Congressman John Dingell (D-Mich.), chairman of the House Commerce Committee and a fairness proponent. Courtesy of the United States House of Representatives.

Senator Ernest F. Hollings (D-S.C.), a fairness proponent, pushed to make the Fairness Doctrine a law in 1987. Courtesy of the United States Senate.

CBS commentator and reporter Eric Sevareid, who testified on the chilling effect of the Fairness Doctrine in the mid-1980s. Courtesy of CBS Television Network.

Court of Appeals decision in *Meredith v. FCC* that the FCC had to address the constitutionality of the Fairness Doctrine. It cited *TRAC v. FCC* to claim agency authority to determine the doctrine's fate. Supreme Court statements in *Red Lion* and *FCC v. League of Women Voters* that the Court would reconsider the doctrine's constitutionality if the Fairness Doctrine were found to inhibit rather than promote the flow of news and information to the public provided ample basis for agency review. The *1985 Fairness Report* had found that the Fairness Doctrine limited public discourse.

FCC abolition of the Fairness Doctrine mirrored First Amendment law just as the original *Editorializing by Broadcast Licensees* (1949) reflected rulings from the 1940s. The *Meredith Memorandum Opinion and Order* (1987) relied on *First National Bank of Boston v. Belotti* (that corporate speech is permissible for ballot issues), *Buckley v. Valeo* (that First Amendment rights are unabridgeable and one's First Amendment rights cannot be compromised to advance another's), and Justices Douglas and Stewart's remarks in *CBS v. Democratic National Committee* (that editors rather than government officials should have the final say in news judgment). In *Pacific Gas,* the Supreme Court ruled that a government grant of a monopoly to a utility imposed no fairness obligation. Conversely, *Editorializing by Broadcast Licensees* relied heavily on *Associated Press v. US* (which authorized government intervention in a private communications monopoly to promote public discourse) on *NBC v. US* (which empowered FCC policing of broadcast traffic), and on several FCC cases requiring broadcasters to cover controversial issues.

FCC abolition of the Fairness Doctrine was not too broad. Broadcasters' public interest and equal time obligations were unchanged. Rules on personal attacks and political editorializing remained in force. The Commission stated that it could not separate policymaking and enforcement from its constitutional obligations. The FCC asserted that it could decide the doctrine's fate well within the Administrative Procedure Act because the fairness rule had always been an agency memorandum, subject to agency revision.

Abolition ended a series of anomalous rulings. In *Yes to Stop Calloway* (1984) and *Environmental Defense Fund* (1982), the commission did not find fairness violations for broadcasters carrying pro-utility issue ads. By discarding the doctrine, the commission expanded commercial speech.

Following FCC abolition of the Fairness Doctrine, the *Meredith* case wended its way to the Second Circuit Court of Appeals in New York, where fairness proponents tried vainly to win a hearing on the grounds that Meredith's Syracuse, New York, station was in the court's jurisdictional area. Fairness proponents and opponents also filed motions before the FCC for reconsideration of *Meredith* and for reconsideration of Fairness Doctrine alternatives, which the commission had dismissed earlier as too intrusive.

Of fairness proponents, Henry Geller and Donna Lampert recommended that the FCC adopt a malice test either at license renewal or on a case-by-case basis to determine whether an individual broadcaster acted with malice in failing to meet fairness obligations. They also charged that the FCC was throwing the baby out with the bathwater by discarding the Fairness Doctrine's first prong (providing controversial information) along with its second (providing contingent access opportunities for issue-oriented citizens and organizations whenever broadcasters covered a controversial issue or editorialized) when *Meredith* dealt with the doctrine's second prong.

Fairness opponents claimed that the FCC had not gone far enough in discarding the vestigial regulation. The Freedom of Expression Foundation (FEF) asked the commission to determine whether continued enforcement of the personal attack rule and the political editorial rule (which require reply time) could pass a First Amendment test since each is derived from the Fairness Doctrine. The commission passed over FEF's petition, replying that it was reconsidering the personal attack and political editorial rules in a separate proceeding. It dismissed Geller and Lampert's petition by arguing that the Fairness Doctrine's two prongs were linked inextricably. Acknowledging that a malice test on first-prong Fairness Doctrine violations might be less intrusive than earlier fairness policy, the FCC nonetheless rejected the proposal. The commission asserted that the proposed malice test to enforce issue-responsive programming either at license renewal or on a case-by-case basis was an unconstitutional intrusion on broadcasters' free speech rights. A broadcaster's public interest obligations require issue-responsive programming, the FCC noted, citing its adequacy to ensure that broadcasters provide sufficient news and public affairs to the public.[21]

Fairness proponents and opponents next petitioned the US Court of Appeals in Washington. The Syracuse Peace Council and the Telecommunications Action and Research Center and Henry Geller and Donna Lampert argued variously that the FCC abused its discretion and acted arbitrarily in discarding the Fairness Doctrine in its entirety. They complained that FCC policy on fairness was inconsistent by charging that the FCC based its 1985 report, which found that the doctrine chilled First Amendment speech and was "constitutionally suspect," on faulty information. Eleven years earlier, in a 1974 report, the FCC had found that the doctrine did not chill First Amendment speech. They argued that Congress had codified the Fairness Doctrine in 1959; hence it was statutorily required and beyond the FCC's regulatory perview.

Fairness opponents argued conversely that the FCC acted within its congressionally delegated authority in ending the Fairness Doctrine and concluded correctly that the Fairness Doctrine did more harm than good in realizing First Amendment freedoms.

Beyond these rehearsed and predictable positions, Henry Geller raised the radical question, Did FCC abolition of the Fairness Doctrine relieve broadcasters of their public trustee obligations? If so, then a broadcaster's frequency on the airwaves was essentially private property beyond public reach. If not, then how could the FCC pretend to enforce a broadcaster's public interest obligations without the Fairness Doctrine? This question reaches all the way back to the congressional debates over the Radio Act; it resounds with Justice Frankfurter's ruling in *NBC v. US* that broadcasting uniquely requires public trustee obligations, and it goes directly to the root of the matter by discounting all the facts and figures about spectrum abundance by saying, "Well, so what? How do these broadcasters have to behave?"

Most important, Geller upped the stakes for Fairness Doctrine opponents. They could win a Fairness Doctrine fight but lose the war. If they asserted baldly that spectrum abundance effectively ended broadcasters' public trustee obligations, they risked alienating the US Court of Appeals, the FCC, and the public. A safer course lay in asserting that the general public interest obligations were sufficient to ensure that broadcasters provide the public with adequate news and information. However, the Court of Appeals could then impose "Fairness Doctrine–like" obligations on broadcasters under Section 309 of the Communications Act and order the FCC to come up with new rules and regulations.

Not only would such a ruling make for yet more regulatory skirmishes, but it would also place Fairness Doctrine–like obligations in the law (Section 309), effectively ending FCC discretion to do with fairness as it pleased. Beyond that, a ruling for Fairness Doctrine–like obligations could make license renewal far more difficult by placing charges of alleged fairness violations before an administrative law judge at the FCC rather than among FCC staff, as was the case under Fairness Doctrine regulatory enforcement. As a rule, administrative law judges issue narrow rulings and are reluctant to assert bold positions for broadcasters' First Amendment rights. Furthermore, in awarding new licenses, the current FCC favors minorities, women, and community residents over broadcasters, who are not residents of a community. Accordingly, members of these groups would face far less burdensome procedures in filing for licenses on the basis of alleged unfairness because administrative law judges would be forced to respond narrowly within the FCC's existing preferential policy. Although the Court of Appeals has yet to decide the issue of Fairness Doctrine–like obligations at this writing, broadcasters could find themselves further cowed by interest groups pending the outcome.

■ FCC abolition of the Fairness Doctrine sent Congress into a fury. In the spring of 1987 fairness proponents got busy enacting the Fairness Doctrine into law to head off FCC abolition of the doctrine. Both chambers approved the bills by nearly two-thirds majorities. Furthermore, congressional leaders thought that newly installed FCC chairman Dennis Patrick had double-crossed them; there was a tacit agreement, some believed, that the FCC would take no action on *Meredith* until it had reported back to Congress on fairness alternatives, short of abolition.

Earlier that spring, congressional committees had explored the Fairness Doctrine, the impact of network takeovers on broadcast journalism, and the role of technology in electronic news. Former FCC chairmen Charles Ferris and Newton Minow urged Congress to codify the Fairness Doctrine on grounds that fairness obligations are identical with broadcasters' public interest obligations. Right wing activist Phyllis Schlafly proposed extending fairness obligations to television networks. Consumer advocate Ralph Nader argued that multiple holders of a specific license would produce a flow of diverse news and information to the American public.

On the takeover issue, Congress wanted to learn whether Capital Cities', Loew's chief Laurence Tisch's, and GE's acquisitions of ABC, CBS, and NBC, respectively, had forced reductions in news coverage. If such was the case, the public suffered, so the argument went, because broadcasters were cutting back on their public interest obligations. Beyond that precise question lay broader concerns about anti-trafficking or trading licenses less than three years after their acquisition and cross-ownership among competing media.

Thomas S. Murphy, Capital Cities' chief executive, NBC CEO Robert C. Wright, and now CBS CEO Laurence Tisch assured Congress that their news divisions would remain independent, aggressive, well funded, and competitive. Murphy pointed out that Capital Cities had long been in broadcasting. Wright allayed concerns that GE might interfere with NBC News on sensitive defense and nuclear stories because of GE's rank as the number 2 defense contractor (after General Dynamics). NBC president Lawrence Grossman subsequently pointed out that RCA, NBC's previous owner, did a quarter of its business in defense, approximately the same percentage as GE. Tisch highlighted a competitive media marketplace resulting from the emergence of cable, independents, VCRs, and nascent broadcast networks. He explained that broadcasters could claim 73% of the prime time audience in 1986, compared with 90% in 1980. Such a downward drift produced greater competition for quality programs to attract audiences in order to sustain advertising revenues. In such a competitive environment, CBS News cut back staffing, expanded on-air chores for others, and demanded greater flexibility of its employees in performing assignments.[22]

The National Association of Broadcast Employees and Technicians (NABET), the Writers Guild, University of California (Berkeley) journalism professor Ben Bagdikian, and Columbia University's Fred Friendly all told a different story. NABET's Thomas F. Kennedy blasted lucrative settlements, salaries, and payments for corporate officials ousted in the takeovers. He said the money could be better spent on specialized reporting and on sustaining existing news staff. The Writers Guild's Mona Mangan reported that broadcasters were replacing older, more experienced news professionals with younger and often temporary workers who would "forgo employment benefits and/or work at lower rates." Such a strategy relied on costly anchors to cover the diminished quality. Bagdikian decried media concentration and explained the takeovers as consequences of liquidity resulting from corporate profits and the Reagan tax cut, lax antitrust enforcement, FCC abolition of anti-trafficking, and permissive cross-ownership policies. Friendly described the networks as "mercantile shadows" of their former selves and worried that broadcast journalists are "so tethered by the business of broadcasting . . . their true talents are too often kept from coming forth, to the daily detriment of the citizenry." On technological impacts satellite and independent broadcasters asserted that technology boosted the capacity and flexibility of news organizations to gather and transmit news.

In reporting fairness legislation, Congress asserted that fairness obligations were identical with public interest obligations. Senate and House majority opinions held that (1) the electromagnetic spectrum remained scarce despite the introduction of new technologies, (2) licensees were entitled to use the spectrum by serving the public interest, (3) the Fairness Doctrine enabled broadcasters to speak out on controversial issues and provided a mechanism for others to articulate their views, and (4) the Fairness Doctrine did not chill broadcasters' freedom of speech. Minority reports held that the Fairness Doctrine violated broadcasters' First Amendment rights and diminished coverage of controversial issues and that technological innovation reduced the spectrum scarcity rationale for the Fairness Doctrine to a vestigial argument.

President Reagan vetoed the legislation in June 1987 on the grounds that the fairness in broadcasting bill violated broadcasters' First Amendment freedoms. The president cited increased media outlets. He pointed to Supreme Court decisions in *Miami Herald* and *Red Lion* that the Court opposed government intrusion in the editorial process and had expressed a willingness to reconsider the Fairness Doctrine if increased media outlets could be shown to outweigh justifications for the Fairness Doctrine. He concluded that the First Amendment applied "to the public forum as a whole," rejecting any unique responsibility of broadcasters.

Congress got busy again. Commerce Committee chairman John Dingell pressed unsuccessfully in November 1987 to attach the

Fairness Doctrine bill to "must" legislation, such as a continuing resolution to fund the federal government, which President Reagan would be hard pressed to veto. This effort failed.

Senator Ernest Hollings artfully proposed cutting the deficit and funding public broadcasting by imposing a 2% transfer fee on spectrum users and added codification of the Fairness Doctrine to the legislation. The 2% fee would be applied to cellular phone, microwave, satellite, and cable community antenna relay systems. Broadcasters, however, were subject to higher fees. Those transferring licenses within three years of their last sale would be required to pay a 4% fee. Any licensee who violated the Fairness Doctrine faced an additional 1% fee. It was estimated that the measure would bring in from $125 to $300 million annually. Funds would go into the treasury until 1990 and thereafter to public broadcasting. Hollings's proposal enjoyed something of a boomlet in November but failed. Finally, in the last days of the congressional session just before Christmas 1987, Hollings attached a fairness bill to the budget bill. President Reagan again threatened a veto; weary lawmakers ended 1987 by dropping the fairness law from the bill; fairness partisans vowed to press a fairness law again.

■ The ebbing tide of the Fairness Doctrine has many eddies and cross-currents. Congress perceived a Fairness Doctrine law as a way to slap back at a deregulatory FCC, move into post-Reagan America, and stymie PACs. In its 1987 *Meredith* decision the FCC out-maneuvered Congress and won a temporary political victory. Congress tried to strike back. In 1987 Democrats regained control of Congress for the first time in six years and reasserted Democratic policy across a number of legislative areas. Democrats more than Republicans favor the doctrine not only because key interest groups such as Catholics, Jews, and blacks support it but also because they are not as wealthy as their Republican opponents. They wish to exploit the doctrine to get maximum broadcast coverage. Beyond partisan appeal, incumbents, Democrats and Republicans alike, sought to minimize criticism from potential opponents. If broadcasters chose to promote contenders, such challenges would take place. Newspapers do this all the time; it's part of politics. But politicians do not want radio and television to do so. Politicians view PACs as interlopers and want to use the Fairness Doctrine to suppress them.

A fairness law was easy politically, for it cost no money—no new taxes. Television news is ubiquitous. Virtually anyone, no matter how alienated politically, can venture an opinion on television and radio, but even the most thoughtful of leaders have no idea how to cope with outlying economic problems. Despite a five-year expansion and rising industrial output, the economy was fragile in 1987, with unprecedented foreign investment, white-hot military and consumer spending, modest inflation, the lowest personal savings since 1949, tax cuts, and a declining dollar. In contrast to coping with such difficult problems as the deficit and trade, it was much easier to push a federal law on fairness. The former was ridden with faction; the latter popular and seemingly beneficial.

President Reagan's veto was consistent with Republican policy dating back to Hoover on public affairs programming but odd. As a wealthy minority party, Republicans embrace the principle of equal opportunity based on one's ability to pay. They do not want less-well-heeled organizations getting media time to debate policy issues, which the doctrine supposedly promotes despite its ineffectiveness. President Reagan's veto was odd in that, despite his administration's obsession with official secrecy, its hostility toward freedom of information inquiries, and its haste to use the paper shredder to cover up the Iran-Contra illegalities, Reagan came out a free speech advocate.

Broadcasters won First Amendment freedoms just as they began to lose economic dominance. At the time when broadcasters are most challenged and least monopolistic, Congress is asserting that content regulation on individual licensees is mandatory. Broadcasters are less influential now than in the days of unchallenged broadcast network dominance. By 1988 over half the households in the country received television from cable, and, following unprecedented viewing lows in the summer of 1987, broadcasters failed to recapture viewers, resulting in further erosion of broadcast audiences. Cable is also valued more highly. Total value of the cable industry, net of debt, was roughly $67 billion, and that of broadcasting is about $38 billion.

The FCC changed the unit of measurement for fairness by adopting broadcasters' arguments that the media outlets in a community rather than the number of potential speakers wishing to broadcast constituted scarcity. It discarded Justice Frankfurter's standard of scarcity as broadcasting's "unique characteristic" and measured broadcasting instead with other media. However, should the US Court of Appeals and Supreme Court resurrect the Frankfurter standard that broadcasting requires unique public trustee obligations, specifically Fairness Doctrine–like duties, the individual broadcaster would again remain the unit of measurement for the diversity of points of view in the marketplace.

Given the abundance of news and public affairs, fairness opponents have the better argument. In 1988 nearly 10,000 radio and 1,200 television stations broadcast in the United States. Cable television, satellite channels, and video cassette recorders provide abundant choices. Competition among news organizations challenges the necessity of a fairness rule. Nor is there any compelling evidence that the Fairness Doctrine promoted a diversity of viewpoints in reaching the public. Much of the rhetoric of fairness proponents assumes that the Fairness Doctrine actually worked in achieving the goal of promoting news and public affairs information. However, the instances in which the Fairness Doctrine may have increased the range of viewpoints is slim. In many significant cases interest groups manipulated the Fairness Doctrine to suppress news and public affairs programming, and fairness proved to be so vague a standard, shrouded in definitional ambiguity and evidentiary procedures, that the FCC found it impossible to enforce the Fairness Doctrine effectively.

The Unsettled Question: Who Owns the First Amendment?

10

If the key of E is the people's key
What is the key of the bourgeoisie?
I ask this question most sincerely,
in what key do they play?

. . . let me restate my rhetorical position,
where do they stand on composition?
If the key of E is the people's key
What is the key of the bourgeoisie?

The Central Park Sheiks, "The People's Key," 1976 pop song

The remarkable durability of the Fairness Doctrine and, to a lesser extent, the Equal Time law goes back to the unsettled question of First Amendment rights for broadcasters. Licensing, coupled with these common-carrier-like obligations, enables government to manage the broadcast spectrum with the appearance of minimal intervention. Candidates and interest groups, empowered by fairness regulation, can limit broadcasters' free speech rights. Each claims a superior First Amendment right. "If every dreamer of innovations may propagate his projects," as Johnson wrote in Georgian England, "there can be no settlement."[1] And with broadcast and public affairs, Congress and the courts have yet to decide which stakeholder—broadcasters, politicians, or interest groups—has ultimate claim on the First Amendment. The decision involves ruling on private property and free speech rights in the spectrum.

Legal experts disagree about this First Amendment problem.

Some say scarcity is universal, so it makes no sense to single out the broadcast spectrum as a uniquely scarce commodity. Indeed, Judge Robert Bork's contribution to, or assault on, First Amendment law for broadcasting, depending on your political view, rests squarely in carrying the concept of scarcity as a universal from the textbooks into the law, and applying it to the Fairness Doctrine, with withering results. Other legal scholars are more concerned about media power and influence; they say that media oligopoly and telecommunications innovation centralize control in so few hands that the imposition of Fairness Doctrine obligations on broadcasters is necessary to ensure that a variety of views reach the voting and consuming public. One legal expert discounts spectrum scarcity and calls for content regulation to address media pervasiveness and consumers' privacy, which can be threatened by cable television. Other First Amendment scholars call for flexible First Amendment regulation precisely tailored for differing media—print, broadcasting, cable, and direct broadcast satellites. Still other First Amendment attorneys argue that the granting of licenses either does or does not give the government authority for content regulation: their positions fall out for or against the Fairness Doctrine, respectively.[2]

Media experts disagree about broadcasting's influence over political power and public opinion. Some scholars, following Frankfort School theoretician Theodor Adorno, say that broadcasting is just one more capitalist organization, disposing viewers to accept bourgeois culture by weakening their individuality through repetitive showings of conventional melodramas, ensnaring them as consumers for mass market products, dulling their capacities for life experiences, and diminishing their abilities to confront "the complexity and opaqueness of modern life" through alternately enervating and titillating programs.[3] Others are less harsh; they say that as people become more dependent on broadcasting for news and public affairs, they only become more confused, not necessarily more compliant. Others observe that broadcasting does not tell people what to think, but it does tell people what to think about. Still other experts argue that viewers' class, religious, family, and educational backgrounds dispose them to find reinforcement for their opinions and prejudices in television news and public affairs and to disregard information that challenges their ways of seeing.[4] So many individual and social factors come to bear in formulating public opinion that undue influence cannot properly be attributed to broadcasting.

If there is no settlement in First Amendment law and hearty disagreement among scholars, what explains the Fairness Doctrine's remarkable durability?

Fairness Doctrine supporters believe that every broadcaster has an obligation to air controversial news and information, and to provide contingent access opportunities in return for an exclusive license. This core belief among Fairness Doctrine supporters that each interest group owns a First Amendment right to the airwaves of every broadcaster, irrespective of spectrum abundance and regulatory quagmires, sustains repeated efforts to codify the vestigial rule and to press for it in the courts. Any number of venial and grand motives animate the partisan shrill of these fairness proponents, but all share a common view that the public deserves to hear views, unedited by broadcasters, so that citizens can reach their many conclusions.

Broadcast news is more visible than organizational politics. Presidential primaries, candidate-centered campaigns, political campaign-funding reforms, political action committees, sophisticated polling techniques, and a trend in broadcast advertising to spot advertising have all pushed the role of electronic media at the expense of political parties. From the early Republic to Andrew Jackson's reelection in 1832, the American press carried messages to voters directly because there were no formally organized political parties. Later, from 1832 to 1960, the media complemented healthy political parties, capable of carrying their own messages to voters. Since 1960, because of party de-alignment, the electronic media have assumed the role newspapers played in the era before organized political parties (1789–1832) by carrying political messages and public affairs information to voters directly.[5] Because of this systemic shift in the flow of political information, Fairness proponents want to attach the common-carrier-like obligation to broadcasters.

This broadcast visibility occurs despite audience erosion for ABC, CBS, and NBC in the late 1980s, and jitters by broadcast licensees that cable, satellite, and VCR programming are taking their audiences too. Older terrestrial networks (ABC, CBS, NBC) own and operate stations in the largest cities and broadcast markets. Like all networks, the older terrestrial networks enjoy production and distribution economies, which enable them to produce news and public affairs programming palatable to mass tastes as long as they retain enough of the television audience to attract advertising revenues sufficient to support their operations. Local broadcast licensees, by contrast, turn profits in their news programming, so local news will likely remain an important part of local politics and public affairs. Cable, satellites, and VCRs do provide more channels and greater flexibility in viewing, and PBS provides depth. But for partisans in Fairness and Equal Time fights, local broadcasters and the terrestrial broadcasting networks remain the battlefields.

In an environment of plebiscitary politics, political de-alignment, and a divided government, the Fairness Doctrine provides an illusory mechanism for interest groups to influence public opinion. Voters choose candidates for myriad individual, social, religious, and political reasons, with less regard than in the past for political party or ideological consistency. The de-alignment of political parties is far more pronounced than partisan re-alignment favoring the Republicans. Neither the Democratic nor the Republican party is promoting ideas or enacting laws capable of sustaining a high standard of living in an international marketplace. No candidate comparable to Roosevelt or to either of the slain Kennedys has emerged in the last quarter of the century. Over the long run public welfare, entertainment, civil service, and public higher education have absorbed political parties' functions of assimilating immigrants, providing patronage and entertainment, and promoting upward mobility for party faithfuls.[6] Ronald Reagan's 1980 victory was much more of a conservative revival than a critical realignment, for while the Republicans captured the Senate for the first time in twenty-seven years, they did not win the House, and state government remained under control of the Democrats. In 1984 Reagan accomplished a significant personal victory but failed to bring in significantly more Republicans; two years later several Republicans whom he had carried into the Senate in 1980 lost re-election, and the Democrats regained control of Congress.

This pattern of a Republican president and Democratic Congress continued a trend in a divided government, dating from Eisenhower. Since 1955, when Democrats regained control of Congress following a brief Republican interregnum, divided rather than unified governments have been commonplace in contemporary

America. Nixon, Ford, and Reagan all governed under divided governments; Kennedy had to cope with refractory Democratic segregationist congressmen, whose seniority placed them on key committees and enabled them, under old congressional rules, to block civil rights legislation; Johnson had a year to push Great Society legislation through Congress before Vietnam divided the Democratic majority; Carter ran afoul of energy interests; so even in periods of unified government, problems overwhelmed promises.[7]

Support for the Fairness Doctrine and equal time reflects the abiding fear that broadcast news, politics, and public affairs programming remain the Frankensteins of contemporary American public life. Much as Senator Howell thought of commercial radio in the 1920s, proponents believe that broadcasting requires content regulation to control its monstrous power. No one elected news anchors Tom Brokaw, Peter Jennings or Dan Rather, so some control mechanism, fairness proponents argue, must be placed on individuals who seemingly enter our homes through television to report the news. Their news judgment, so tightly tethered by huge entertainment corporations, is inadequate, Fairness Doctrine advocates contend, to supply citizens with sufficient information to reach rational voting and public affairs decisions.

The longevity of the Fairness Doctrine reflects an inappropriate, groping effort to come to terms with the decline of public intellectuals in contemporary American public life. In the absence of intellectuals like Walter Lippmann, Archibald MacLeish, Robert Hutchins, and other knowledgeable commentators capable of organizing information for citizens, the public turns to broadcast journalists, who are professionally ill-suited and institutionally reluctant to accept the role of public intellectuals. The news, in Walter Lippmann's memorable phrase, "signals an event," no more. By temperament and training, columnists and reporters fare better at signaling, not explaining, events and are reluctant to advocate solutions. If, in a television public affairs show, reporters provide hard-hitting analyses, they run the risk of alienating viewers who may believe the assertive reporter is no longer being objective. Instead, professional reporters go after an interviewee with relentless questions because, if an interviewee divulges information at variance with official policy, that produces news. These interviews provide viewers with information but do not organize it for them. This practice is as far as news can and does go without becoming politically or ideologically partisan. Despite these institutional and professional constraints, many Fairness Doctrine proponents contend that the news is already too partisan ideologically, and they argue for the regulation to promote their own analyses of public issues.

The government prefers to exert power through persuasion and apparently consensual decision making rather than solely through the tax collector or army. The Fairness Doctrine, with its requirement for each broadcaster to balance virtually every story, sustains the appearance of a consensus in an otherwise fractious polity divided by class, race, religion, and region.[8]

Congress is trying to play catch-up to the presidency. About twenty years ago, Senator J. William Fulbright (D-Ark.) complained that television was so powerful and its coverage of the president so persistent that broadcast news reports on the president obliterated the balance of powers. The House allowed television to record official business in 1979, and after a trial period, so did the Senate in 1987. Congressional efforts, as recent as 1987, to impose fairness obligations on broadcasters participates in this broader congressional concern with the media.

In the end, we return to the counsel of Louis Brandeis and Samuel Johnson. None of the Fairness proponents' rationales are adequately compelling to warrant control. Beneficently intended rules of which Brandeis cautioned, such as equal time and fairness, have failed. They inhibited more news and public affairs programming than they allowed. Politicians manipulated equal time for temporary advantage. Interest groups behaved similarly with the Fairness Doctrine. In the fray the public lost. As Johnson had forewarned, prior restraints and censorship cannot work in a liberal democratic polity. Still, unqualified free speech rights leave many squeamish, especially those who view broadcasting as a public utility and who deplore how frequently broadcasters sacrifice news and public affairs programming for more profitable programs.

The fairness fight contests the uses of broadcasting in a democracy. The public has capacities to reach conclusions on its own without government regulation of broadcast content. Technology constantly changes broadcasting, mass communications, and telecommunications. Indeed, the abundance of cable channels, the increased flexibility of satellite news gathering, and the potential for satellite subscription services to provide news and public affairs indicate fewer reasons to hold broadcast journalists uniquely hostage to fairness obligations. Broadcast journalism is neither so dangerous nor so persuasive that a fairness law of dubious constitutionality will accomplish an overriding public good. Although televison and radio news may be pervasive, a law that denies broadcast journalists their First Amendment freedoms diminishes politics and assaults a critical liberty. No law, no matter how beneficently intended, that controls broadcasters' freedom of expression will make citizens any more or less involved in the public life of a great nation than they choose on their own.

Candidate Debates in the 1988 Presidential Election

11

"The most important thing is to have the vision. The next is to grasp it and hold it. You must see and feel what you are thinking. You must see it and grasp it. You must hold and fix it in your memory and senses. And you must do it at once."

President Ronald Reagan, quoting Soviet filmmaker Sergei Eisenstein in Remarks at a Luncheon Hosted by Leaders of the Cultural and Art Community in Moscow, May 31, 1988[1]

The 1988 presidential contest continued the drift of party dealignment, plebiscitary politics, and a divided government. Democratic presidential nominee Michael S. Dukakis, the governor of Massachusetts, failed to mount a campaign sufficiently convincing to wrest the necessary votes from Republican nominee Vice-President George Bush. Continuing economic expansion and a quiet international scene, coupled with lower unemployment than during the early years of the Reagan presidency, proved more assuring to voters than Dukakis's claims that the prosperity of the 1980s was illusory and that the future needed tending. Democrats increased Congressional majorities, gaining two Senate and three House seats, a marked reversal from roughly a dozen House seat losses in presidential election years since 1968.[2]

Candidate-centered organizations, most notably the Bush campaign, dominated campaign discourse with fatal results for Michael Dukakis. Governor Dukakis confronted the same problem that had confounded Illinois governor Adlai Stevenson thirty-six years earlier in his unsuccessful contest with General Dwight D.

Eisenhower. Like Stevenson, Dukakis was less well known than his Republican challenger George Bush, who had faithfully served eight years as vice-president to the inexhaustibly popular Ronald Reagan. Dukakis had to define his agenda—his vision—early on and explain it clearly, simply, and persistently to provide voters with a reason to switch from Republican to Democratic leadership. Dukakis failed to straddle this critical hurdle in his race for the White House. Instead, Bush defined Dukakis and set the agenda with a series of emotional symbolic issues including crime, the Pledge of Allegiance, and Dukakis's membership in the American Civil Liberties Union. Dukakis's twenty-year-old snowblower, of which much was made as a show of the governor's frugality in a promotional film at the Democratic National Convention, proved inadequate to plow through Bush's blizzard of emotionally charged symbols.

Bush's victory was all the more impressive considering how far the vice president had come since early caucus and primary races in Iowa and New Hampshire, where he was routinely criticized for aloofness, vagueness, and for appearing ill at ease with himself.[3] By late May, the vice president held a strategy session with key aides and supporters at his summer home in Kennebunkport, Maine. Bush's negative ratings in the polls were so high that some worried he would lose the presidential election despite having polished off his Republican challengers in Super Tuesday primary contests across the South in March. At the meeting, the Bush campaign charted a strategy to hold Dukakis, the leading Democratic presidential aspirant, to a 25-point lead in political polls going into the Democratic National Convention in July; to concentrate on Republican southern and western redoubts for a substantial share of Bush's electoral college vote; and to contest Ohio and New Jersey vigorously. By early June, the vice-president deftly began attacking Dukakis with charges of being weak on national defense, saying Dukakis opposed a six-hundred-ship Navy and new weapons systems and that these positions were somehow "liberal." At the same time, Bush pollster Robert Teeter held a series of focus groups that showed concern about crime and the environment. The Bush campaign decided early on to hit Dukakis hard on those issues. Finally, a Bush operative, checking the governor's record, discovered that Dukakis had vetoed a bill requiring Massachusetts school children to pledge allegiance to the flag. The Massachusetts Supreme Judicial

Court had ruled any such measure unconstitutional, and Dukakis did no more than uphold his constitutional duties, but here, too, was a powerful symbolic issue, one that would play well in the South and West and serve to define Dukakis negatively among other voters. Bush campaign planners targeted the pledge in June for use against Dukakis later in the summer.[4] That July, Attorney General Edwin Meese resigned after independent prosecutor James McKay questioned his ethics, saving Bush the embarrassment of defending the nation's much-criticized chief law enforcement officer, and in early August, Treasury Secretary James A. Baker III passed his post along to Bush confidant Nicholas F. Brady to become chairman of the Bush campaign, assuring Bush seasoned national campaign leadership.[5]

Baker's arrival proved propitious, for he centralized authority within the campaign and exercised architectural influence in shaping broadcast and print coverage of Bush for the remainder of the campaign. Indeed, Baker orchestrated and controlled the vision, setting the campaign agenda further with a meticulously scripted flow of messages to journalists and equally well-choreographed presentations of candidate Bush for maximum political advantage. Bush kept clear of reporters and stuck to a carefully tailored script, which was designed to convey one theme each day with photo opportunities at planned events for good television, news magazine, and newspaper pictures.[6]

As soon as Dukakis came out of the Democratic National Convention in July with a seventeen-point lead—well within the Bush campaign's damage control parameters—the symbolic attacks began. In August, Idaho Senator Steve Symms blasted Dukakis's wife Kitty for burning the flag at antiwar protests in the 1960s and 1970s. Mrs. Dukakis shot back that the unfounded charge was part of an "orchestrated campaign" conducted with "the full knowledge" of the Bush campaign, which the campaign denied, and complained of repeated coverage of the accusation, "I said it was outrageous when I first heard it; that it was untrue, that no picture could have existed, that I was, in the sixties and seventies, having babies."[7] Following a rumor, which surfaced from volunteers working for Lyndon H. LaRouche, that Governor Dukakis had sought psychiatric counseling following his brother's death and his 1978 gubernatorial primary loss, and a quip from President Reagan that he never criticized invalids, Dukakis took an eight-point nose dive in the polls. "Dukakis Not Crazy—More at Eleven," was how Dukakis campaign manager Susan Estrich described the story. "We had a candidate who just wasn't known. There was nothing backing up the poll numbers. That's why a rumor about his mental health could take you down eight points."[8] That August, Bush also lit into Dukakis for vetoing the pledge bill, putting Dukakis on the defensive and again characterizing the governor's constitutional stand as "liberal," hence somehow weak or unpatriotic. Withering attacks on the Massachusetts prison furlough program and the delayed clean-up of Boston Harbor soon followed.

To Dukakis, these attacks seemed so baseless and manipulative that he mistakenly thought voters would discount them as campaign distortions. To some extent he was a victim of his own earlier success. Dukakis had won the Democratic presidential nomination by running a positive campaign above the fray of other contenders, and he believed a positive campaign in the general election was the surest route to the White House. Hale Champion, Dukakis's chief secretary at the Massachusetts State House, noted that "at first, we used to read this stuff and laugh, and say 'How can this be, why would people take this seriously?' The adjustment by Dukakis to the fact that the demand was not for what he thought the campaign ought to be about was a hard one."[9] Dukakis denied the accusations, but it did him no good because he spoke about Bush's agenda, not his own, and thus vitiated his own vision. Indeed, Robert Dole's acid remark to broadcast journalists to "[tell Vice President Bush to] stop lying about my record" after Bush campaign advertisements had done in Dole's presidential nomination prospects in the New Hampshire primary, could well have been instructive.[10]

Dukakis found himself so badly damaged by late August that he recalled John Sasso to redirect the fall campaign. Sasso had resigned earlier in the primaries over a video that had scuttled Senator Joseph Biden's presidential hopes. Bush had succeeded in defining Dukakis by a liberal caricature, so that Dukakis now trailed Bush in the polls. At this point in early September, James A. Baker III, representing the Bush Campaign, and Paul P. Brountas, Chairman of the Dukakis Campaign, met to decide the number and format of televised candidate debates.

Unlike those of 1984, televised candidate debates mattered in the 1988 contest because so many more voters remained undecided about the major party candidates. The Bush Campaign seized control of these critical forums. So eager were Dukakis forces to put the two men face to face that they conceded virtually all of Baker's points. Baker won concessions on the number, timing, content, and format of debates. He initially won the right to exclude Richard Moe, the Dukakis camp's only experienced negotiator on candidate debates (Moe had advised Walter Mondale four years earlier) on grounds of conflict of interest because of Moe's associations with the Bipartisan Commission on Presidential Debates. Baker then won agreement on two presidential debates within roughly three weeks of each other, ending three weeks before election day, instead of three debates with one as late as October 28th, as Dukakis had wanted. Baker pressed successfully for the first debate to take place during the Summer Olympics and the second during the world series, timing deliberately plotted so that voters would be distracted by other events. Baker and Brountas agreed to open-ended debates and to a panel of journalists, rather than debates on specific issues and a single moderator, as Dukakis wanted. Baker subsequently won concessions on a format that insulated Bush from follow-up questions. Panelists would pose a question to one candidate, who would then have two minutes to answer. His opponent would get one minute to reply, and then the process would be reversed. Both camps agreed on joint veto power over journalists, no candidate-to-candidate questioning, camera locations, ticket allocation, and such procedural matters as candidates' access to dressing rooms. They also agreed on a vice presidential candidate debate in between the presidential debates. On the sensitive matter of who would host debates, both agreed to ask the Bipartisan Commission on Presidential Debates to host the first presidential and sole vice-presidential candidate debate, and the League of Women Voters to host the second presidential debate.[11]

Hosting televised candidate debates remained a sensitive issue, because both campaigns wanted good relations with the league, each wanted to make use of the Bipartisan Commission on Presidential Debates, and neither wanted to hand over host responsibilities to the television networks, where their candidates would have less control. Both candidates' campaigns gambled that the commission and league would agree to candidate-negotiated dictates.

The league bolted. "We have no intention of becoming an accessory to the hoodwinking of the American public," the league's Nancy Neuman told reporters, as she criticized the candidates' concordat. The league wanted a three-way agreement to be hammered out between itself and the campaigns. "The issue is, who's in control of the debate," she protested.[12] The specific issue surfacing in reports focused on the lack of follow-up questions, but the league had favored a single moderator and believed at a minimum that it could have negotiated for follow-up questions if it had to settle for a panel. The league also opposed an agreement by both campaigns that tickets be divided evenly between the two campaigns and the sponsoring organization, in order to assure that the debates would be rowdy. It turned out that the initial Bush-Dukakis debate held the dubious distinction of being the first televised presidential candidate debate since 1976 in which the audience laughed at candidates— twice at Bush for his assertions concerning the Iran-Contra affair and abortion and once at Dukakis for his statements about crime.[13]

For the league, the Baker-Brountas agreement was the final blow in its losing battle to host televised presidential debates. In November 1985, then-league President Dorothy S. Ridings criticized Democratic and Republican National Party efforts to form a bipartisan commission to host televised presidential debates. As momentum for the commission grew, Nancy M. Neuman, Riding's successor, blasted the Twentieth Century Fund in February 1987 for issuing a report backing commission hosting of debates. The league, Neuman claimed, was better suited because it was both experienced and nonpartisan.[14] "I think it will be very difficult for the parties actually to pull off a debate," Neuman told columnist David S. Broder presciently in 1987. "I don't think they realize the difficulty of these negotiations. There has to be an honest broker at the table."[15]

The league then put down $40,000 to secure Shrine Hall in Los Angeles two days after it withdrew as debate sponsor, and offered Shrine Hall to the commission for $90,000, claiming an additional $50,000 for expenses. "What they're telling us is they're willing to spend $40,000 to keep the hall empty. . . . We consider that holding the hall hostage. . . . We're not going to deal with them," the commission's Robert Neuman insisted. He announced shortly thereafter that the Commission would host a second Bush-Dukakis confrontation at Pauley Pavilion on the University of California at Los Angeles campus.[16]

Beyond a skirmish between two elites over institutionalizing the televised presidential candidate debates, the league-commission battle exposed how fully major-party, candidate-centered organizations controlled broadcast debates. Freed of equal time, neither Bush nor Dukakis had to worry about fringe candidates. No third-party candidate of John Anderson's appeal required consideration in 1988. The commission did not live up to its advance billing that it could control candidates. And while the league appeared more virtuous, it criticized the commission for acceding to many conditions that the league itself had accepted in 1976, 1980, and 1988 televised presidential debates.

Dr. Lenora B. Fulani, a thirty-eight-year-old New York City psychologist running for president as a New Alliance Party candidate, unsuccessfully sought a temporary restraining order against the commission for excluding her from the Bush-Dukakis debate. Fulani was a legally qualified candidate in fifty states and the District of Columbia. Evidently mindful of earlier rulings recognizing major party candidate debates as "bona fide" news events, the District Court Judge George H. Revercomb told Dr. Fulani, an associate of Nation of Islam leader Louis Farrakhan and the Reverend Al Sharpton, that an injunction would injure current debate participants and that stopping the debates would not serve the public interest and "orderly political process," since it would prevent citizens from seeing Vice President Bush and Governor Dukakis debate each other.[17] Fulani next asked CBS, NBC, ABC, CNN, and Fox for 45 minutes of free prime time to compensate, contending the debates were not "bona fide news events." CBS, ABC, and CNN defended the debates as news events. Neither NBC nor Fox replied and ABC said it never received her request.[18]

With such candidate-centered organizational control of televised debates, the issue turned next on how broadcasters would behave. Lest NBC stick with its Olympic games coverage while ABC, CBS, and CNN presented the first Bush-Dukakis debate, the Democratic chairmen of two influential congressional committees regulating broadcasting reportedly contacted NBC President Robert Wright to assure full network coverage of the scripted event for the Democrats. The Bush campaign further cowed NBC into withdrawing an advertisement for "Favorite Son," a steamy political mini-series about a callow, neo-fascist senator, which some feared threw an unflattering, if indirect light on GOP vice-presidential nominee J. Danforth Quayle.[19] CBS News President David Burke labeled the debates a "contrivance," lent no CBS broadcast journalists as panelists, and covered all three debates in their entirety.[20] CBS Anchor Dan Rather referred to the debates pointedly as "joint appearances" and "so-called debates."

In the first Bush-Dukakis debate, the governor of Massachusetts seemed to come out ahead. Bush scored on defense, taxes, and crime. He neutralized Dukakis's criticisms for his dealings with Panamanian strongman Noriega by saying, "I will make a deal with you. I will take the blame for the [Iran contra and Noriega scandals] if you give me half the credit for all the good things that have happened in world peace since Ronald Reagan and I took over." Dukakis entered this debate as he did the second with high negative ratings, due in part to the tarring he was taking from negative advertisements produced by the Bush campaign or pro-Bush political action committees. Much like Ronald Reagan in 1980, who suffered from voter anxieties that he would get the country into a war, all Dukakis had to do was appear steady and reasonable to appear the evident winner.[21] ABC's Peter Jennings noted that the technocrat label stuck firmly to the governor and asked him to tell voters why they should entrust the presidency to him. Dukakis provided no convincing answer, was sufficiently steady to win a small fraction of undecideds, and in closing remarks came as close to articulating a vision for his campaign as he did in any address. For this he came out the winner in subsequent polls.[22] All rested on a confrontation between vice presidential nominees Senator Lloyd Bentsen (D-Texas) and J. Danforth Quayle (R-Indiana).

Senator Bentsen showed himself more capable of assuming the presidency than his Republican foe. He delivered a scathing attack on Republican management of the economy and environment ("If you let me write $200 billion in hot checks every year, I could give you the illusion of prosperity, too") and likened Senator Quayle's commitment to the environment to relying on Bonnie and Clyde as crime fighters. He then skewered Quayle with a carefully rehearsed line when Quayle compared himself with former President Kennedy. Although Senator Quayle made no convincing explanation of what he would do should be become president ("First, I'd say a prayer for myself, for the country that I was about to lead, and then I would assemble [the president's] people and talk"), the Republican nominee made no major gaffes. Contrasted to the courtly, poised Bentsen, Quayle did appear wet behind the ears, but he also had no horns, which neutralized, though hardly put to rest, anxieties about him.[23]

The Bush campaign orchestrated a masterful response by way of damage control. The day before, Campaign Chairman James A. Baker III said of Quayle, "We are very, very proud of you. . . . We are very, very proud of the job you're doing for this campaign, and we are very, very proud of the job we know you're going to do tomorrow in Omaha."[24] After the debate, Bush defended Quayle's mediocre performance, saying "this guy [is] under tremendous fire . . . came through with flying colors. . . . Now people can see what I've seen all along."[25] The following day, President Reagan said that Bentsen's withering "Senator, you're no Jack Kennedy" was "a cheap shot . . . unbecoming a senator of the United States."[26] Campaign Chairman Baker acknowledged on CNN, "When you think about what might have happened, we have to be pretty happy."[27] More tellingly, Bush Campaign strategist Lee Atwater shared internal polls with journalists, indicating Bush leads in Michigan and New Jersey, and predicted a six-point victory in Texas, Bentsen's home state, which violated Bush campaign practice not to discuss internal polls publicly. "This race is going to quickly get back to the two candidates for president. . . . There are two gladiators in the arena that are going to count in the end," Atwater said.[28]

Democrats jumped all over Quayle. Senator Bentsen commented that President Reagan's blast was clear evidence that Quayle was the loser. New York Governor Mario Cuomo said on NBC's *Today* that Quayle "looked like Johnny Carson playing Karnac; he started with the answers and looked for the questions." A Dukakis operative in Ohio likened Quayle to Dennis the Menace as a child who "can't tell the whole truth." Betraying his uneasiness with political language, Dukakis said, "I thought he was programmed beyond belief . . . extremely insecure, this fellow. He didn't have a sense of strength or control or anything. . . . Thinking about Quayle being a heartbeat away from the presidency, to watch that, I think, is very, very troubling."[29]

The day after the debate Bush praised his running mate for an "outstanding job" before a morning jog and made no mention of him in his first speech. Instead, speaking in Midland, Texas, Bush returned to attacking Dukakis on prison furloughs, coming up with a twist on the Clint Eastwood line "make my day": Dukakis, he quipped, would tell furloughed inmates "Go ahead, have a nice weekend." By so doing, Bush re-oriented the agenda around social issues.[30]

For his part, Dukakis tried to reassert his vision of "good jobs at good wages" by lacing into Senator Quayle's assertion that international investment created American jobs. Dukakis visited the Moog Automotive Company in Missouri. "Maybe the Republican ticket wants our children to work for foreign owners, pay rent to foreign owners, and owe their futures to foreign owners—but that's not the kind of future that Lloyd Bentsen and I want," he said.[31] But it turned out that the factory was owned by IFI International SA of Luxembourg, which in turn was controlled by Italians. Dukakis seemed to have stumbled unwittingly into confirming the Republican's nostrum and responding to the party's vice presidential rather than its presidential nominee, further diminishing Dukakis's standing.

Dukakis tried further to rally midwestern support in the closely contested heartland. "Ask him [Vice President Bush] what he'd tell a steel worker who lost his job and has to deliver pizzas for a living. Ask him why he opposed the plant closing law . . . in a Dukakis-Bentsen administration, we are going to open the doors of foreign markets to American products and give you a chance to sell. I'm not going to sit while we ship our best jobs overseas, and you can't buy an American-made television."[32]

While providing some badly needed energy in midwestern industrial cities and towns, Dukakis found himself embracing the discredited protectionist policies of his former primary challenger, Missouri Congressman Richard Gephardt. Earlier in the primary season Dukakis had defeated Gephardt, in part, by pointing out that unfair trade practices accounted for 20 percent of trade deficit and that the reasons for the other 80 percent needed tending. In the general election, however, Dukakis never conveyed his vision of what to do about the other 80 percent, and left himself open to counter charges from Bush of embracing protectionism as well as to a slew of negative advertisement.[33]

As the second and final Bush-Dukakis debate neared, the vice president acknowledged explicitly that he had defined the agenda. In a response to a question about his caricature of Dukakis's record, Bush responded, "Three months ago, I remember, some of the great publications in this country had written me off. And what I've had to do is to define not just my position, but to define his. And I hope I've done it fairly."[34] Fairly or not, the Bush campaign had accomplished its goal of setting the agenda. While Dukakis spoke clearly and well, he did not respond well to a question from debate moderator Bernard Shaw about capital punishment and rape, and he exhibited no humor. As Marvin Kalb (Director of the Center for Press, Politics, and Public Policy at Harvard's Kennedy School of Government) later observed, Dukakis was in a sense a victim of unfair expectations, because although he did well he did nothing extraordinary.[35] While some pundits insisted an extraordinary action was necessary to propel Dukakis's candidacy out of the doldrums, it was just as true that Dukakis's high negatives argued for the governor's steady course.

Suffering a tie when he needed a clear-cut victory, Dukakis made no breakthrough in the second debate. Three weeks before election day the Dukakis campaign decided to concentrate on New York, Pennsylvania, Ohio, Michigan, Illinois, California, Massachusetts, Connecticut, Vermont, Rhode Island, Maryland, West Virginia, Iowa, Wisconsin, Oregon, Washington, Hawaii, and the District of Columbia, effectively writing off the South and Rocky Mountain states. Within a week, key operatives were redeployed from New Jersey and Florida to contested states.[36] On election day, despite a valiant rally, Bush carried forty states, winning 426 to Dukakis's 112 electoral votes and defeating the governor of Massachusetts by nearly seven million votes.

Despite much finger pointing about whether television or candidates caused the impoverishment of political rhetoric, it is unclear whether different broadcast coverage of the campaign could have changed its outcome.[37] ABC's Ted Koppel offered time for an open-ended discussion between both candidates, and Dukakis participated in lengthy interviews with network anchors. Candidate-centered organizations controlled the flow of news to the public, and of the two, the Bush people did a better job. Indeed, Dan Rather's tough questioning of Bush during the primaries concerning his knowledge of the Iran-Contra affair seemed to have the perverse effect of elevating the vice president rather than raising questions about him.

The Democrats' problems, too, went far deeper than negative campaign advertisements, catchy sound bites, and a candidate who wished to play above board. Based on a *New York Times/*CBS poll, Bush won the votes of white men and women, whites in each region, professional and white-collar workers, 49 percent of the blue-collar workers, 40 percent of union households, the majority of all families earning more than $25,000 annually, nearly two-thirds of Protestant and over half of Catholic voters, and a majority of high school and college graduates. Like Mondale before him, Dukakis retained blacks, Jews, Hispanics. He improved the Democratic vote among women, among Democrats who had voted for Reagan in 1984, and among whites in each region.[38] Broadcast journalism could not of itself have affected all this.

It seems fitting, in closing, to suggest that candidate-centered organizations, not the broadcasters, are the Frankensteins of modern American politics. In the 1920s, progressives and Southern and Western Democrats had worried that broadcasting would become an uncontrollable monster shaping mass consciousness unless candidates were guaranteed equal time. By the 1980s, media-producing candidate-centered organizations dominated the flow of broadcast news and images. This dynamic between politician and journalist left both open to charges of impoverishing public discourse. When journalists attempted to puncture this balloon, the organizations struck up the band, waved the flags, and whisked away candidates to less threatening turf.

Notes

Chapter 1

1. *Congressional Record* (March 12, 1926), 67:5480. LaGuardia and White were discussing censorship, a critical issue in several radio bills that Congress had considered in 1924, 1925, 1926, and finally 1927. The censorship provision became Section 29 of the Radio Act of 1927 and Section 326 of the Communications Act of 1934. See *US Statutes* (H.R. 9971, February 23, 1927), vol. 44, pt. 2, ch. 169, pp. 1162–1174, and *US Statutes* (S. 3040, June 19, 1934), vol. 48, pt. 1, ch. 651, pp. 1064–1105. Secretary of Commerce Herbert C. Hoover proposed a temporary act until there was adequate time to evaluate radio as a new communications technology in 1924. See *Congressional Record* (January 29, 1927), 68:2572–2573a, cited in Ithiel deSola Pool, *Technologies of Freedom* (Cambridge, Mass.: Harvard University Press, 1984), p. 115.

2. Edward F. Sarno, Jr., "The National Radio Conferences," *Journal of Broadcasting* (Spring 1969), 13(2):189–202.

3. Pool, *Technologies of Freedom*, ch. 6. Radio Act of 1927. See also *Tribute Co. v. Oak Leaves Broadcasting Station* (Circuit Court, Cook County, Illinois, 1926). I am grateful to Thomas W. Hazlett for pointing out this insight on *Oak Leaves*.

4. *New York Times* (April 9, 1922); see also David H. Ostroff, "Equal Time: Origin of Section 18 of the Radio Act of 1927," *Journal of Broadcasting* (Summer 1980), 24(3):367–380.

5. Robert W. McChesney, "Enemies of the Status Quo: The National Committee on Education by Radio and the Debate of the Control and Structure of American Broadcasting in the Early 1930s," paper presented at the Annual Convention of the Association for Education in Journalism and Mass Communications, History Division, San Antonio, Texas, 1987.

6. Writing in *The Century Magazine*, Bruce Bliven contended that "radio broadcasting should be declared a public utility under strict regulation by the federal authorities; and it may be necessary to have the government condemn and buy the whole industry operating it either nationally or locally on the

analogy of the post office and the public school system" ["How Radio is Remaking Our World," *The Century Magazine* (June 1924), 108:149]; E. Pendelton Herring, "Politics and Radio Regulation," *Harvard Business Review* (January 1935), 12:167–178; John Brooks, *Telephone: The First Hundred Years* (New York: Harper & Row, 1975); Joseph McKerns, "Industry Skeptics and the Radio Act of 1927," *Journalism History* (1976–1977), 3:128–131; Pool, *Technologies of Freedom*, ch. 6.

7. See especially Representative Davis's comments in the *Congressional Record* (March 12, 1926), 67:5480–5485.

8. See *Congressional Record*, House (March 12, 1926), 67:5478–5504, for comments by Progressives on common carrier legislation for radio; *Congressional Record*, Senate (July 1, 1926), 67:12497–12505; Brooks, *Telephone*, and Pool, *Technologies of Freedom*, are useful for information on AT&T and common carrier legislation.

9. *Congressional Record*, House (March 12, 1926), 67:5483. General Electric's claim to patriotism provoked scorn from Progressives and Democrats, who viewed it as a veneer for monopolistic practices, and drew praise from some Republicans, who argued that RCA was far less an oligopoly as many charged.
    Representative Arthur M. Free (R-Cal.) reminded his colleagues of Navy Department negotiations with GE. Both Admiral W. H. G. Bullard, director of US Naval Communications, and Commander S. C. Hooper, of the Bureau of Steam Engineering, had approached General Electric, urging GE not to sell the patent for the Alexanderson alternator to the British-controlled Marconi Company in April 1919. Patriotism, Rep. Free asserted, had guided General Electric. Rather than monopolizing radio, Free asserted that RCA and its parent companies competed in different areas of communication. "Each of them," said Free has "to get the use of those patents that pertained to their different lines of the industry." On the basis of these different product lines and specialties, Free asked Democrats and Progressives to quell their concerns about monopoly and the attendant problems of censorship and price discrimination. For example, GE and Westinghouse sold capital equipment and assembly parts to RCA. AT&T reserved the rights to telephone patents.
    See also "Memorandum for the Attorney General Re: *US v. RCA*," Franklin Delano Roosevelt Library, Official File 1314.

10. Radio licensing as a system also raised additional thorny questions. For example, which of the many competing radio broadcasting corporations would receive licenses to broadcast? What criteria would a federal regulatory official or agency use in granting licenses? What quid pro quo would the federal government exact in return for granting lucrative licenses to private corporations for use of a public good like the airwaves?

11. Radio Act of 1927, Section 18; Communications Act of 1934, Section 315.

12. *New York Times* (September 3, 1922).

13. See Thomas W. Hazlett, "The Rationality of U.S. Regulation of Broadcast Spectrum," Working Paper No. 87-4. For a participant's viewpoint, see William J. Donovan, "Origin and Development of Radio Law," *Air Law Review* Vol. II, No. 2, April, 1931, pp. 107–129, No. 3, pp. 349–370, No. 4, pp. 468–477.

14. *Congressional Record,* House (March 12, 1926), 67:5483, cited in Daniel E. Garvey, "Secretary Hoover and the Quest for Broadcast Regulation," *Journalism History* (1976–1977), 3:128–131. See also, Louise Margaret Benjamin, *Radio Regulation in the 1920s: Free Speech Issues in the Development of Radio and the Radio Act of 1927* (Ph.D. dissertation, University of Iowa, 1985).

15. *Proceedings of the Fourth National Radio Conference* (Washington, D.C.: Government Printing Office, 1926), 6–8. See also United States Senate, *Hearings on S.1 and S.1754,* 69th Cong., 1st sess., where the proceedings of the conference are set out in full.

16. *Proceedings of the Fourth National Radio Conference,* pp. 6–8.

17. *Congressional Record* (March 12, 1926), 67:5479.

18. *Congressional Record* (March 12, 1926), 67:5480.

19. *Congressional Record* (March 12, 1926), 67:5479.

20. *Congressional Record* (March 12, 1926), 67:5488.

21. *Congressional Record* (March 12, 1926), 67:5488.

22. *New York Times* (May 7, 1926). The Des Moines radio station WHO blocked Robert LaFollette, Sr., from using its facilities when he ran as a Progressive in 1924. Nor did LaFollette receive time equal to either the Republicans or Democrats. See Ostroff, "Equal Time."

23. *Congressional Record,* Senate (June 30, 1926), 67:12356. Broadcaster discretion over libelous, slanderous, and defamatory political programming also troubled lawmakers. Libelous, slanderous, and defamatory campaign addresses over radio shortly before election day could skew election returns in favor of candidates using radio, some believed. Because of the instantaneous effect of such campaign broadcasts, House Democrats said that the libel, slander, and defamation laws applying to newspapers had become antiquated and that more stringent laws were required for radio. In addition, radio's ubiquity challenged existing law: In a word, radio crossed state lines.

Representative Thomas L. Blanton (D-Tex.) raised the libel issue. He remarked on differing state laws on libel and slander. He noted that Texas distinguished printed from spoken derogatory remarks: Print was subject to civil and criminal charges of libel, whereas spoken remarks were classified as slander and then only when expressed about women. A derogatory expression about a man broke no law in Texas, Blanton said. "The night before election some fellow, who might be favored by the Radio Corporation, could get up in a congressman's district, and with favored access to the radio, ruin any man running for Congress." Blanton expressed greater interest in the political effects of slander than in the more pressing issue of where responsibility appropriately resides for uttering slanderous assertions: with the politician for uttering them or with the broadcaster for transmitting them. In the end the Radio Act held politicians responsible under existing civil and criminal law on the grounds that Congress would be promoting censorship by holding the broadcasters responsible. Broadcasters had argued that they would then have to censor or edit politicians' remarks for fear of being sued by besmirched candidates. The immediate response to Blanton's proposal to make derogatory language transmitted by radio criminal and civil offenses in the states where they were broadcast, however, was to vote it down. Representative White, the Republican floor leader, replied that common law was a sufficient remedy for Blanton's worries, and LaGuardia remarked, "Civil rights are still in existence."

24. *Congressional Record* (March 12, 1926), 67:5483.

25. *Congressional Record* (March 12, 1926), 67:5483.

26. *Congressional Record* (March 12, 1926), 67:5483.

27. *Congressional Record* (March 12, 1926), 67:5483. Harkness testified that "we take the same position that is taken by the editor of any publication. He has the right to accept or reject any material presented to him. You cannot walk into a newspaper office and get them to publish anything you care to present. . . . We do not censor—we edit. We feel if the matter is unfair or contains matter which the public would not care to hear, we may reject it." At the time, AT&T owned eighteen stations and interconnected many more through its telephone lines, reaching nearly 80% of the public.

28. *Congressional Record* (March 12, 1926), 67:5483. The FTC report showed that the major corporations (1) agreed to pool patents among themselves for both wired and wireless telephone and telegraph and for radio until 1945, (2) granted RCA exclusive rights to sell radio apparatus and required RCA to purchase its supplies from other members of the cartel, (3) restricted competition within certain fields so that each company was assured of no competition in its designated specialty, (4) controlled international communication between the United States and abroad, and (5) provided preferential contracts for transoceanic communication among members of the cartel.

29. David H. Ostroff ("Equal Time") discusses Senator Dill's role in fashioning equal time legislation; Donald G. Godfrey's "Senator Dill and the 1927 Radio Act" [*Journal of Broadcasting* (Fall 1979), 23(4):477–489] is also helpful. See Rosalie Jones Dill's *Matthew Dill Genealogy* (Spokane, Wash.: Spokane Public Library, December 1935), preface, for family information, and Ray Tucker and Frederick R. Barkley's *Sons of the Wild Jackass* (Seattle, Wash.: University of Washington Press, 1932) for Dill's activities in Washington state politics. Dill died in January 1978 at the age of 93.

30. *Congressional Record,* Senate (July 1, 1926), 67:12503.

31. *Congressional Record,* Senate (July 1, 1926), 67:12502.

32. *Congressional Record,* Senate (July 1, 1926), 67:12502. Senator Earle Mayfield (D-Tex.) worried that equal time granted too much public affairs programming over radio for dissenters. "If the Senator's amendment is adopted and becomes law and a lecturer desired to deliver a lecture on Bolshevism or Communism, he would be entitled to do so." Equal time applied solely to politicians campaigning for office and specifically excluded discussion of controversial public issues, Dill replied. Acknowledging that he had based his remarks on the Interstate Commerce Committee version for candidates and public affairs—the version adopted following LaFollette's and Johnson's difficulties—Mayfield withdrew his objection. "The original draft had in it language which prevented the operator from denying the use of the radio to

anyone," Mayfield acknowledged. "That is true," Dill responded, "and that is the reason I have offered the new draft" limiting equal time to political candidates.

33. *Congressional Record,* Senate (July 1, 1926), 67:12503–12504.

34. *Congressional Record,* Senate (July 1, 1926), 67:12503–12504.

35. *Congressional Record,* Senate (July 1, 1926), 67:12503–12504.

36. *Congressional Record,* Senate (July 1, 1926), 67:12503–12504.

37. House of Representatives, Report 2106, 72d Cong., 2d sess., 1932.

38. *Third Annual Report of the Federal Radio Commission to the Congress of the United States* (Washington, D.C.: Government Printing Office, 1929). Cited in McChesney, "Enemies of the Status Quo," p. 7.

39. McChesney, "Enemies of the Status Quo," p. 7.

40. In the final negotiations for the bipartisan commission, Dill mollified White, ever loyal to Herbert Hoover and his goal to Commerce Department control over licenses by saying that the commission would be temporary, functioning for only a year and then from year to year until its work was done. At that time the secretary of commerce would assume regulatory authority for radio, Dill promised. But Dill would remark later that he knew that a "temporary" commission was a ruse. "I knew if we ever got a commission, we would never get rid of it," Dill confessed. Subsequently Bethuel M. Webster, second general counsel at the FRC, resigned from the poorly funded commission in disgust, complaining that it was filled with "semi-retired sailors, soldiers or lawyers, men lacking the vision and energy to undertake departures from established notions and routine." Cited in McChesney, "Enemies of the Status Quo," p. 4 n23. Bethuel M. Webster, Jr., "Notes on the Policy of the Administration with Reference to the Control of Communications," *Air Law Review* (April 1934), 5:107–131.

41. Statement of Charles Siepmann before the FCC, National Archives, Record Group 173/8516 Volume 2, p. 85160570.

42. *Congressional Record* Senate (July 1, 1966), 67:12502.

43. By creating licensing with equal time obligations, Republican leadership and Herbert Hoover's efforts as secretary of commerce subscribe to the wry observation of Tories accomplishing Whiggish objectives. As conservative a president as Coolidge articulated the rationale for licensing. At the Third National Radio Conference, Coolidge told participants that "one of the benefits of increased government regulation was that it would permit the Department of Commerce to better insure against the danger of a few organizations gaining control of the airwaves. . . . It would be unfortunate indeed," Coolidge continued in remarks opposing a nationalized broadcasting system, "if such an important function as the distribution of information should ever fall into the hands of the Government." And, taking aim at broadcasters, Coolidge added, "it would be still more unfortunate if its control should come under the arbitrary power of any person or group of persons. It is inconceivable that such a situation could be allowed to exist." Licensing, with the equal time proviso, addressed these problems at the cost of creating many more.

Chapter 2

1. Ted Morgan, *FDR: A Biography* (New York: Simon and Schuster, 1985), p. 376.

2. "Memorandum for the Attorney General, Re: *US v. RCA,*" FDR Library, Official File 1314.

3. Charles Curtis, Jr., *Franklin D. Roosevelt and the Commonwealth of Broadcasting* (Bachelor's thesis, Harvard College, 1978).

4. *Broadcasting* (March 19, 1933), p. 3.

5. Alan Brinkley, *Voices of Protest: Huey Long, Father Coughlin and the Great Depression* (New York: Knopf, 1982); US Senate, Committee on Interstate Commerce, *Hearing to Authorize a Study of the Radio Rules and Regulations of the Federal Communications Commission*, 77th Cong., 1st sess., 1941, p. 361.

6. Lucas A. Powe, Jr., *American Broadcasting and the First Amendment* (Berkeley and Los Angeles, Cal.: University of California Press, 1987), ch. 3; "Memo to the President from James Lawrence Fly, December 23, 1940," FDR Library, Official File 1059-2. "Memo to the President from James Lawrence Fly, October 31, 1941," FDR Library, Official File 1059. See also FCC Commissioner Anning S. Prall's letter to the president, February 19, 1935, documenting the political leanings of newspapers with broadcasting investments. According to Prall's figures, twenty-three Democratic, thirty Republican, and twenty-seven independent newspaper publishers had broadcasting interest. Most of the Democratic papers were in the South FDR Library, Official File 1059-2. Until Fly's term the commission was in the backwater of New Deal initiatives. Roosevelt's initial seven appointments, including a chairman, were undistinguished.

7. Richard W. Steele, *Propaganda in an Open Society: The Roosevelt Administration and the Media, 1933–1941* (Westport, Conn.: Greenwood Press, 1985); see also R. W. McChesney, "Enemies of the Status Quo: The National Committee on Education by Radio and the Debate of the Control and Structure of American Broadcasting in the Early 1930s," paper presented to the Annual Convention of the Association for Education in Journalism and Mass Communications, History Division, San Antonio, Texas, 1987.

8. David Brinkley, "An Age Less Than Golden: Roosevelt vs. the Wartime Press," *Washington Journalism Review* (June 1988), 10:42.

9. *New York World Telegram* (September 16, 1936).

10. John H. Sharon, "The Psychology of the Fireside Chat," B.A. thesis, Princeton University, 1949, Franklin Delano Roosevelt Library, Hyde Park, New York. A. M. Sperber, *Murrow: His Life and Times* (New York: Freundlich Books, 1986), pp. 90–91. Labor Secretary Frances Perkins describes FDR's unparalleled mastery of radio as an ability to see his audience. "When he talked on the radio he saw them gathered in the little parlor, listening with their neighbors. He was conscious of their faces and hands, their clothes and homes. His voice and his facial expression were those of an intimate friend" [Frances Perkins, *The Roosevelt I Knew* (New York: Viking Press, 1947), p. 110]. H. L.

Mencken was less generous. He characterized the chats as "briefs" and found FDR's voice "too tenorish." Sam Rosenman, *Working With Roosevelt* (New York: Harper & Brothers, 1952) provides useful information on the preparation of many fireside chats and speeches.

11. Brinkley, "An Age Less Than Golden: Roosevelt vs. the Wartime Press," p. 42.

12. *Congressional Record*, S. 2910 (May 15, 1934), 78:8843.

13. Interstate Commerce Committee, H.R. 8301, 73d Cong. See McChesney, "Enemies of the Status Quo."

14. Communications Act of 1934, Section 307.

15. *Report of the Federal Communications Commission to Congress on Section 307(c) of the Communications Act of 1934*, pp. 5–6, 9–10. "In order for non-profit organizations to gain the maximum service possible, cooperation in good faith by broadcasters is required," the FCC noted. In making this assertion, the FCC arrogated the policing function.

16. Brinkley, "An Age Less Than Golden: Roosevelt vs. the Wartime Press," p. 44. See also Charles de Gaulle, *The War Memoirs of Charles de Gaulle—Unity 1942–1944* (New York: Simon and Schuster, 1959), pp. 92–97; Robert E. Sherwood, *Roosevelt and Hopkins An Intimate History* (New York: Harper & Brothers, 1948), pp. 680–681, 693–697; François Kersaudy, *Churchill and De Gaulle* (London: Collins, 1981), pp. 254–257. For more on Roosevelt and de Gaulle, see Milton Viorst, *Hostile Allies FDR and Charles de Gaulle* (New York: Macmillan, 1965).

17. Brinkley, "An Age Less Than Golden: Roosevelt vs. the Wartime Press," p. 44.

Chapter 3

1. *Boston Globe* (November 9 and 11, 1939); Massachusetts Acts, 1937, chapter 253. See also Lucas A. Powe, Jr., *American Broadcasting and the First Amendment* (Berkeley, Cal.: University of California Press, 1987), pp. 109–111.

2. *Boston Globe* (November 9, 1939). Cambridge's ex-mayor Richard M. Russell, one of Hurley's opponents in the 1938 gubernatorial campaign, spoke on Bickford's behalf, testifying, "I knew Mr. Bickford as a capable radio commentator." See also Powe, *American Broadcasting*, for information on WAAB.

3. Mayflower Broadcasting Company, 8 FCC 333 (January 16, 1941). Hereafter referenced to as the *Mayflower* decision.

4. *Mayflower* decision.

5. *Mayflower* decision.

6. Great Lakes Company, 3 FRC 32 (1929).

7. In January 1941 the Federal Communications Commission announced its

decision on the Mayflower Broadcasting Corporation's application for WAAB's license. WAAB programmed more news and equally as many editorial commentaries during the period when management policy changed from one promoting editorials in 1937 to one not doing so after 1938. The extent of these editorial commentaries was a portent of the formal impact of the *Mayflower* decision.

For example, on November 9 and 11, 1937, during WAAB's editorializing heyday, WAAB programmed an hour of news each day and a fifteen-minute "Political Talk." WAAB also programmed ninety minutes of public affairs on November 11, including a debate between the Harvard and Yale debating societies on US foreign policy and a report on the Massachusetts economy. At this time, when the Yankee Network was charged with being most flagrant in its editorial commentaries, WAAB featured "Zara's Marimba Melodies"; its rival, WBZ, carried a speech by Mayor-Elect Maurice Tobin. Later on the same day, WAAB programmed "The Vincent Lopez Orchestra" at the time WBZ carried a speech by Ohio governor Martin L. Davey on "The Inside Story of the Ohio Steel Strike" from the Ohio Club of New York.

In 1939, on the day that FCC hearing examiners listened to Massachusetts politicians vilify the Yankee Network for editorial recklessness and to WAAB's avowals never to so trespass again, WAAB broadcast more editorial commentaries than in 1937. In November 1939 WAAB's editorial commentators enjoyed more air time than the fifteen-minute "Political Talk" in 1937. Commentators were nationally recognized, including Elliott Roosevelt, the president's son. Public affairs received more air time. There seemed to be a balance of international and domestic public affairs programming: On November 11, 1939, for example, segments of a parliamentary address by British prime minister Neville Chamberlain and Massachusetts governor Leverett Saltonstall's "State of the State" address were broadcast. In 1939 WAAB's news totaled an hour each day.

In January 1941, when the FCC announced the *Mayflower* decision, WAAB programmed just as many editorials and more news than it had in 1937, when WAAB's editorial programming had elicited so much criticism. News programming was expanded by a quarter-hour, including a BBC feed. President Roosevelt's third inaugural address commanded three hours on January 20. On January 19, perhaps as an expression of the Yankee Network management's own sense of equal time, WAAB devoted a half-hour to a National Republican Women's Club program.

8. Senate Interstate Commerce Committee, *Hearings on S.113,* 77th Cong., 1st sess., 1941.

9. *Hearings on S.113.* Statement of FCC chairman James Lawrence Fly, p. 14. In 1939 Mutual Broadcasting carried the World Series. But, as third network, Mutual lacked affiliates in many communities, and broadcasters with RCA or CBS exclusivity contracts could not purchase the series from Mutual [Charles Siepmann, *Radio Television and Society* (New York: Oxford University Press, 1950), p. 31]. Paley subsequently told a congressional committee that CBS provided the series free to nonaffiliates in areas where it had none.

In claiming regulatory authority for the sweeping report and network exclusivity rules, activist FCC chairman James Lawrence Fly reached back to

Senator Clarence C. Dill's assertions in Senate debate of the Radio Act. "[T]he bill," Fly quoted Dill, "specifically sets out as one of the special powers of the commission the right to make special regulations for governing chain broadcasting. . . . The only way by which monopolies in the radio business can secure control of radio here will be by the commission becoming servile to them. Power must be lodged somewhere, and I myself [Dill] am unwilling to assume in advance that the commission proposed to be created will be servile to the desires and demands of great corporations in this country" (*Hearings on S.113*, p. 15).

10. *Hearings on S.113*, statements of William S. Paley and Sen. Burton K. Wheeler, pp. 217–253.

11. *Hearings on S.113*, Paley's statement. He also remarked that "not only did we publicly strip ourselves of editorial power in the interest of fair service to the American people, we went beyond that and proclaimed that except in political campaigns where the parties want to use . . . time, . . . we would never sell time for the discussion of arguable social ideas. Discarding one of the most tempting opportunities for revenue, we decided instead that . . . lest limited facilities gravitate into the hands of the rich and powerful, we would give such time without charge and would proportion it fairly among all contenders."

12. *Hearings on S.113*.

13. William L. Shirer, *Twentieth Century Journey: The Nightmare Years*, vol. 2 (Boston, Mass.: Little, Brown, 1984).

14. House Interstate Commerce Committee, *Hearings on Proposed Changes in the Communications Act of 1934*, 77th Cong., 1st sess., 1941, p. 231.

15. The Hutchins commission bore the formal title of the Commission on Freedom of the Press and published its recommendations as *A Free and Responsible Press* (Chicago, Ill.: University of Chicago Press, 1947). Jerilyn S. McIntyre explains why commission recommendations were so generally neglected, some of the dynamics of commission meetings, and commission goals in "The Hutchins Commission's Search for a Moral Framework," *Journalism History* (Summer 1979), 6(2):54–57.

16. National Broadcasting Company et al. v. United States, 319 US 190 (May 10, 1943).

17. NBC v. US, p. 228.

18. Associated Press v. United States, 326 US 20 (1945).

19. For supplemental information on earlier precedents, supporting FCC application of the public interest standard to public affairs, see Steven J. Simmons, *The Fairness Doctrine and the Media* (Berkeley, Cal.: University of California Press, 1978).

20. "Public Service Responsibility of Broadcast Licensees," 11 FCC 1458 (March 7, 1946). The FCC published the *Blue Book* in anticipation of more AM and FM radio stations and the commercial emergence of television.

21. United Broadcasting (WHKC), 10 FCC 515 (1945); Sam Morris, 11 FCC 197 (1946); Robert Harold Scott, 11 FCC 372 (1946). The rulings are note-

worthy for the articulation of the Fairness Doctrine because the FCC identified the flow of news and information to the public through controversial public affairs programming with broadcasters' public interest responsibilities as trustees of the airwaves.

In *United Broadcasting* (June 1945), the FCC ruled that overall program scheduling, including controversial public affairs programming, constituted a criterion for renewing a license. Radio station WHKC in Columbus, Ohio, had refused to sell time to Local 927 of the AFL-CIO to discuss labor, racial, and political issues and to solicit memberships. WHKC also censored scripts, a routine practice in radio broadcasting in the 1940s. When Local 927 filed a complaint with the FCC to revoke WHKC's license, United Broadcasting management struck a compromise with the union local. WHKC management agreed to review program requests individually and without discrimination. It agreed to devote some program time to controversial subjects as part of "a well balanced program schedule." WHKC management agreed to allow nonprofit organizations to solicit memberships on radio programs. It agreed to state in writing its grounds for refusing any controversial programming. Finally, United Broadcasting management pledged that controversial programming would be "considered on an overall basis, maintain[ing] a fair balance among the various points of view" and among locally and network-produced shows and between the commercial and sustaining shows provided by the network. The FCC ruled that, because United Broadcasting management had agreed to balance its news and public affairs programming and had ceased censoring scripts, the station was operating in the public interest. The FCC ruled, therefore, that the United Broadcasting Company could retain its license for WHKC.

In *Sam Morris* (March 1946) the FCC reasserted that overall programming, including controversial public affairs programming, was a criterion for license renewal. Sam Morris, a local temperance activist in Dallas, Texas, asked the FCC to revoke Dallas radio station KRLD's license. Morris claimed that radio advertising for alcoholic beverages was offensive, and he objected to KRLD management's refusal to sell time during peak listening hours to individuals and organizations promoting temperance. The FCC ruled against Morris: A single issue, such as temperance, did not constitute sufficient grounds to warrant a special FCC action. Rather, the FCC would review KRLD's license on the basis of its overall programming as it routinely would.

The *Sam Morris* decision expanded the scope of FCC authority over public affairs programming because the FCC ruling required broadcasters to consider the impact of their advertising on their public affairs programming. The FCC rejected as "handy nomenclature" a CBS brief filed in support of its KRLD affiliate. The CBS brief had drawn a distinction between advertising and propaganda. CBS argued that a review of KRLD advertising was beyond the scope of the FCC's regulatory authority concerning public affairs programming because Morris's complaint concerned advertising. The FCC differed. The FCC observed in *Sam Morris* that "advertising . . . is indeed a special kind of propaganda." It went on to say that advertising for alcoholic beverages could "raise substantial issues of public importance." Given the controversy surrounding temperance, the FCC ruled that KRLD had to consider advertising that promoted the consumption of alcohol as controversial and make reasonable efforts in its public affairs programming schedule to address controversial public issues. It also recognized that KRLD provided time for the discussion of temperance issues during local option elections.

In *Robert Harold Scott* (July 1946) the FCC ruled that the broadcasters had an affirmative obligation to present controversial public affairs programming. "The free flow of ideas and information is essential to the effective functioning of democratic forms of government and ways of life," the FCC ruled. "Immunity from criticism" was dangerous to the public interest because "unsound institutions could flourish without criticism." The FCC reasoned therefore that, although broadcasters were not required to grant time to all who requested it, they nonetheless had to grant time for the discussion of ideas "with a high degree of unpopularity." "The public interest criterion precludes removing radio wholly as a medium from the expression of a view protected by constitutional free speech guarantees," the FCC ruled. As in *United Broadcasting* and *Sam Morris,* broadcasters retained discretion in particular cases of access and the FCC increased its authority over public affairs programming, including controversial public affairs programming, within its review criteria for license renewal.

In *Robert Harold Scott* the FCC rejected a petition by Scott to deny license renewals to radio station KPO and KFRC in San Francisco. At the same time, the FCC lectured KPO and KFRC to provide more air time for programs on controversial public issues. Scott had claimed that management at both stations had stifled controversial public affairs programming by denying him time to speak about atheism. In a word, the FCC denied Scott's individual petition for programming advocating atheism and upheld standards that controversial public affairs belonged within a station's news programming.

22. Rufus Cater, "FCC to Review Mayflower Ban, Jan. 12," *Broadcasting* (September 15, 1947), 33:39. So secure was the FCC in its authority to police public affairs that it requested comments on broadcasters' rights to express their views and their "affirmative obligation to be fair and to represent all sides of controversial issues."

23. Statement of Justin Miller before the Federal Communications Commission, National Archives, Record Group 173/8516, vol. 2, p. 85160207.

24. Statement of Justin Miller, p. 85160207.

25. Statement of James Lawrence Fly before the FCC National Archives, Record Group 173/8516, vol. 2, p. 85160325. Broadcasting's influence constituted no grounds to restrain it, Miller retorted. "Does Mr. Fly mean to suggest that because of the powerful influence of radio broadcasting, does it not come, properly within the meaning of the First Amendment?" See "Mayflower Hearing," *Broadcasting* (April 26, 1948), 34:23, 59, 62, 68–70.

26. Caldwell statement before the FCC. Statement of Justin Miller, pp. 85160191, 85160197, 85160204, 85160210. Statement of James L. Fly, pp. 85160544–85160547.

27. Statement of Frank Stanton, National Archives, Record Group 173/8516, vol. 2, p. 85160033. For Woods's testimony, see "Woods' Testimony," *Broadcasting* (March 8, 1948), 34:17, and "Mayflower Hearing," *Broadcasting* (March 8, 1948), 34:23, 59, 62, 68–70. Two-thirds of the respondents to a poll in

Broadcasting, the influential trade publication, said they would be willing to provide reply time to editorials, whereas one-third said they disapproved of an FCC requirement to provide reply time for reinstating their editorial rights. Many radio executives believed that radio enjoyed higher public acceptance than newspapers because broadcasters avoided partisan issues. They wished to preserve radio's impartiality and the resulting revenues. Commentators editorialized routinely.

28. Straus, Novick, and Brown's testimony before the FCC, in "Monday through Thursday Testimony at Mayflower Hearing," *Broadcasting* (March 8, 1948), 34:17, 38, 78–79.

29. Breine and Barnouw's testimony before the FCC, in "Monday through Thursday Testimony." A National Farmers Union spokesman reported that a radio commentator in the Midwest had criticized farmers' cooperatives. See also National Archives, Record Group 173/8516, vol. 2, pp. 85160274–85160307, 85160583–85160602.

Several religious, legal aid, and military groups backed organized labor. The American Jewish Congress warned of anti-Semitic and racist commentaries in the absence of the *Mayflower* ban. The National Lawyers Guild testified that broadcasters who did not comply with the *Mayflower* decision should have their licenses revoked. The American Veterans Committee lauded the *Mayflower* decision as a "logical and necessary extension of the constitutional guarantees of free speech" (National Archives, Record Group 173/8516, vol. 2, pp. 85160567–85160579).

30. Siepmann's testimony before the FCC. Saul Carson, radio columnist of the *New Republic,* expressed concern that radio broadcasters would dominate public opinion if allowed to broadcast news editorials. The *Mayflower* decision should be strengthened, he said, lest the broadcasters gain even more power over the flow of news and public affairs.

31. "In the Matter of Editorializing by Broadcast Licensees," 13 FCC 1246–1270 (1949).

32. "Editorializing by Broadcast Licensees," p. 1256. The FCC cited approvingly Representative White's words that "it is the right of the public to be informed, rather than any right on the part of the government, any broadcast licensee or any individual member of the public to broadcast his own particular views on any matter, which is the foundation of the American system of broadcasting."

33. "Editorializing by Broadcast Licensees," p. 1257.

34. *Broadcasting* (June 13, 1949), 36:48.

35. *New York Times* (March 13, 1947); Walter Isaacson and Evan Thomas, *The Wise Men* (New York: Simon & Schuster, 1986), p. 356.

36. Associated Press v. United States, 52 F. Supp. 362 (S.D.N.Y., 1943).

37. Fly's testimony before the FCC, National Archives, Record Group 173/8516, vol. 2, p. 85160546.

38. Dennis v. US, 341 US 494 (1951).

39. Lawrence Ferlinghetti, *A Coney Island of the Mind* (New York: New Directions, 1955).

Chapter 4

1. "In the Matter of Petitions of the Columbia Broadcasting System, Inc., and National Broadcasting Co. for Reconsideration and Motions for Declaratory Rulings or Orders Relating to the Applicability of Section 315 of the Communications Act of 1934, as Amended, to Newscasts by Broadcast Licensees, Interpretative opinion adopted June 15, 1959," 26 FCC 715–754 (1959). Hereafter referenced to as Intepretative Opinion.

2. "Interpretative Opinion." Lar Daly cited other instances where television newscasts covered his opponents in the Democratic and Republican primaries but had ignored his candidacy: stories on Richard Daley and Timothy Sheehan, his party organization's nomination, interviews with Sheehan and the Democratic Cook County chairman, and Mayor Daley's annual report on the city. Lar Daly included news coverage of Mayor Daley's greeting of President Frondizi and of the mayor's participation in a televised promotion for the March of Dimes. In ruling on Lar Daly's petition, the FCC addressed television news coverage of ceremonial or official and more clearly political activities of campaigning incumbents. See also *Chicago Tribune* (February 20, 22, and 24, 1959).

3. "Interpretative Opinion, cited in House Committee on Interstate and Foreign Commerce, Subcommittee on Communications and Power, *Political Broadcasts—Equal Time: Hearings on H.R. 5389, H.R. 5676, H.R. 6326, H.R. 7122, H.R. 7180, H.R. 7206, H.R. 7602, H.R. 7985,* 86th Cong., 1st sess., 1959, p. 67.

4. "Letter to Allen H. Blondy," 14 RR 1199 (February 6, 1957). "Use of Broadcast Facilities by Candidates for Public Office," Public Notice 63585, 58 FCC 936 (October 1, 1958), question 12, Cited in H. Rept. 802 (August 6, 1959).

5. Senate Committee on Interstate and Foreign Commerce, Communications Subcommittee, *Political Broadcasting: Hearings on Senate Reports 1585, 1604, 1858, 1929,* 86th Cong., 1st sess., 1959.

6. Interpretative Opinion and Senate Hearings.

7. Senate Hearings; *New York Times* (June 18, 1959).

8. "Government: Political Broadcasting Law in Action," *Broadcasting* (July 20, 1959), p. 69; "Government: Political Gag on the Way Out," *Broadcasting* (August 3, 1959), pp. 62–66. Krajewski polled 4,000 votes in his 1952 presidential bid and 1,800 votes in 1956 on the Poor Man's ticket.

9. *Hearings on S. 1585, S. 1604, S. 1858, S. 1929.* Of the bills before Congress, four proposed exempting newscasts and news commentaries from equal time. Five bills proposed exempting newscasts, interviews, documentaries, panel discussions, debates, and "similar type" programming. Of these bills, the Hartke

bill (S. 1585) also specified grounds for determining "substantial" candidates by setting a percentage on votes in previous elections, or 200,000 or 1% of voters' signatures for candidates. The Hartke bill also exempted broadcasters from any liability for libelous or defamatory remarks politicians might make in the course of campaigning—remarks broadcasters could not censor because of anti-censorship provisions (Section 326) of the Communications Act. Amid all this testimony, Senator Pastore of the Senate Interstate and Foreign Commerce Committee, the committee responsible for drafting legislation to cope with *Lar Daly*, complained to Senator Hartke that his bill was too expansive and opened a Pandora's box of election law technicalities by imposing a federal statute on state law, which customarily determined how many votes or petition signatures constituted legally qualified or substantial candidates.

10. *Hearings on S. 1585, S. 1604, S. 1858, S. 1929* (pp. 75, 309n3); *Hearings on H.R. 5389, H.R. 5676* (pp. 13, 122n6).

11. *Congressional Record* 105:14457, 14463 (July 28, 1959). See also S. Rept. 562 (1959).

12. House Rept. 1069 (1959).

13. House Rept. 802 (1959), p. 47. US Code Section 315(a). "A statutes' proviso is generally restrictive and not extending." See Stearns v. Hertz Corp., 326 F 2d 405, 407 (8th Cir., 1964), *cert. denied;* 377 US 934 (1964); Sutherland, *Statutory Construction,* Sections 47.09, 47.12 (4th ed., 1984); RTNDA v. FCC, US Court of Appeals, District of Columbia, Brief of petitioners, 831 F 2d 1148 (D.C. Circ., 1987).

14. Theodore H. White, *The Making of the President 1960* (London: Jonathan Cape, 1962), pp. 281–293; Godfrey Hodgson, *America in Our Time* (Garden City, N.Y.: Doubleday, 1976), ch. 7. CBS's Frank Stanton said CBS would be willing to provide an hour per week for eight weeks before the election for joint use by the major party candidates but would not participate in simultaneous broadcasts with NBC and ABC. ABC suggested that networks rotate an hour each week for the nine weeks preceding the election for debates between the Republican and Democratic presidential candidates; that way each network would produce three hours of time.

15. Senate Interstate and Foreign Commerce Committee, Communications Subcommittee, *Presidential Campaign Broadcasting Act,* 86th Cong., 2d sess., 1960 (S. Rept. 3171). Television network executives disagreed with Governor Stevenson, and all offered time to the major party presidential nominees. NBC criticized Stevenson's proposal as "the wrong way to go about doing the right thing" and stuck to its original offer of eight hour-long shows of "Meet the Press." To support his testimony, Stevenson said that, after one of his commercials in the 1956 campaign had interrupted five minutes of a popular television show, an irate viewer had telegrammed: "I like Ike and I love Lucy. Drop dead."

16. *New York Times* (May 18, 1960).

17. Senator John F. Kennedy (D-Mass.), first presidential candidate debate with President Nixon, Sept. 26, 1960, in *The Great Debates,* Sidney Kraus, ed. (Bloomington, Ind.: Indiana University Press, 1962), pp. 349–350.

18. Nixon's opening statement, in Kraus's *Great Debates*, pp. 350–352. The Eisenhower administration had also built more schools, hospitals, highways, and hydroelectric power plants than any other, Nixon said.

19. Kraus, *The Great Debates*. Kennedy trailed Nixon badly in newspaper endorsements even though he enjoyed the most support of any Democrat since FDR, with 15% of the nation's English-language dailies. Kennedy was also the beneficiary of the unprecedented amount of free television time, made possible by equal time exemptions and the joint resolution waiving equal time for candidate debates.

Political scientist Sam Lubell observed that religion was the most important variable in the 1960 presidential election. Kennedy's sharper vision of America and his concise answers convinced enough voters to put aside momentarily their negative feelings about the suitability of a Roman Catholic to serve as president, Lubell argued.

20. White, *The Making of the President 1960,* p. 293.

21. Austin Ranney, *Channels of Power: The Impact of Television on American Politics* (New York: Basic Books, 1983).

Chapter 5

1. Edward R. Murrow, "Wires and Lights in the Box," Address to the Radio Television News Directors Association, Chicago, Illinois, Oct. 15, 1958, cited in *Documents of American Broadcasting,* third edition, Frank J. Kahn, ed. (Englewood Cliffs, N.J.: Prentice-Hall, 1978), pp. 251–261; A. M. Sperber, *Murrow: His Life and Times* (New York: Freundlich Books, 1986), pp. 538–542; Alexander Kendrick, *Prime Time* (Boston: Little, Brown, 1969), p. 387; for quiz show scandals, see *New York Times,* October 11, 17, 18, 23, 29, and November 3, 5, 7, 8, 11, 14, 15, 1959; for expansion of broadcast news in the late 1950s, see Barbara Matusow, *The Evening Stars* (Boston, Mass.: Houghton Mifflin, 1983), pp. 43–103.

2. "Report and Statement of Policy Re: Commission en banc Programming Inquiry," *Federal Register* (August 3, 1960), 25:7291–7296; 44 FCC 2303, cited in Kahn, *Documents of American Broadcasting,* pp. 262–278.

3. Newton N. Minow, "The Vast Wasteland," Address to the National Association of Broadcasters, Washington, D.C., May 9, 1961, cited in Kahn, *Documents of American Broadcasting,* pp. 281–291.

4. For information on Landis, see Thomas J. McCraw, *Prophets of Regulation* (Cambridge, Mass.: Belknap Press of Harvard University Press, 1984). Fred Friendly, *Good Guys, Bad Guys and the First Amendment* (New York: Random House, 1976), discusses the Democratic National Committee's role in *Red Lion;* Fred J. Cook disputes Friendly's version in his *Maverick: Fifty Years of Investigative Reporting* (New York: Putnam, 1984). The Reverend Billy James Hargis does not dwell on his radio commentary, which started the *Red Lion* case, in Billy James Hargis and Cliff Dudley, *My Great Mistake* (Green Forest, Ark.: New Leaf Press, 1985).

5. "Letter to the Honorable Oren Harris in Reference to the Fairness Doctrine Implementation, FCC 63-851," 40 FCC 582 (1963).

6. Henry Geller, "The Fairness Doctrine in Broadcasting: Problems and Suggested Courses of Action," Rand Corp. Report R-1412-FF (1973).

7. "Letter to Mr. Nicholas Zapple in re Request by Nicholas Zapple, Communications Counsel, Committee on Commerce, for Interpretative Ruling Concerning Section 315 Fairness Doctrine, FCC 70-598," 23 FCC 2d 708 (1970).

8. Office of Communications of the United Church of Christ v. Federal Communications Commission, 395 F 2d 994 (D.C. Cir., 1966), p. 999.

9. United Church of Christ v. FCC.

10. Red Lion Broadcasting Co., Inc., et al. v. Federal Communications Commission et al., 395 US 390 (1969), p. 392.

11. Red Lion v. FCC, p. 391.

12. Red Lion v. FCC, pp. 375–379.

13. Red Lion v. FCC, pp. 383–384. White quotes Pastore: "We insisted that the provision [referring to the fairness proviso] remain in the bill, to be a continuing reminder and admonition to the Federal Communications Commission and to the broadcasters alike, that we were not abandoning the philosophy that gave birth to Section 315, in giving the people the right to have a full and complete disclosure of conflicting views on news of interest to the people of the country." In addition, Senator Hugh Scott (R-Penn.) said that the provision was "intended to encompass all legitimate areas of public importance which are controversial" and elsewhere stated his objection to content regulation.

14. Brandywine Main Line Radio, Inc., 27 FCC 2d 565 (1971), pp. 576–577. aff'd on other grounds, 153 US App. D.C. 305, 473 F 2d 16 (1972), cert. denied, 412 US 922 (1973).

15. Lucas A. Powe, Jr., "Or of the [Broadcast] Press," Texas Law Review (1976), 55:39, 53.

16. Geller, "The Fairness Doctrine in Broadcasting." Geller also told the FCC to revise its personal attacks and political editorial rules and to continue making timely decisions on a case-by-case basis for personal attacks and political editorials, that is, those cases where Cullman, Zapple, or Red Lion were pertinent until it had made newer rules.

17. Benno C. Schmidt, Jr., Freedom of the Press vs. Public Access (New York: Praeger Publishers, 1976), p. 165. Jerome Barron, "Access: The Only Choice for the Media?" Texas Law Review (1970), 48:766.

Chapter 6

1. "No Relief from Equal Time in This Campaign," Broadcasting (August 24, 1964), pp. 70–72. Networks volunteered four hours of time if the waiver passed. Goldwater did not lobby for it aggressively.

2. "Section 315 Hits Political Fan," *Broadcasting* (October 26, 1964), pp. 54–56. In 1956 the networks provided Stevenson time, although not required to do so. The FCC claimed it did not have enough time to rule on Stevenson's request. Then, shortly before election day and well after Stevenson's address, the FCC ruled equal time was unnecessary.

3. "Sec. 315, Pay TV, CPB on Top," *Broadcasting* (September 2, 1968), p. 39.

4. *Congressional Record* (October 9, 1968), 114:30217–30243; *New York Times* (October 10, 1968).

5. *Congressional Record,* Senate (October 10, 1968), 114:30402; *New York Times* (October 11, 1968).

6. *Congressional Record,* Senate (October 10, 1968), 114:30401–30402.

7. *New York Times* (April 26, May 25, 28, 31, June 2, 3, 13, 21, 24, July 1, 3, 10, 11, 14, 21, 22, 23, 25, 26, 27, August 9, 15, 16, 17, 20, 21, 22, 23, 24; all 1968).

8. Newton Minow and Clifford M. Sloan, *For Great Debates* (New York: Twentieth Century Fund, 1987), p. 18.

9. *New York Times* (July 23, 1972). Senator Bob Dole, chairman of the Republican National Committee, sought equal time unsuccessfully for a network telecast after McGovern's announcement that Sargent Shriver would replace Thomas Eagleton as his running mate. Broadcasters responded that McGovern's announcement was a "bona fide news event" not a campaign speech and was thus exempt from equal time (*New York Times,* August 8, 1972).

10. "Petitions of the Aspen Institute Program on Communications and Society and CBS, Inc., for Revision or Clarification of Commission Rulings under Section 315(a)(2) and 315(a)(4), FCC 75-1090," 55 FCC 2d 697 (1975). At Cater's suggestion, the Brookings Institution urged the FCC to reevaluate its equal time regulations on candidates' debates so that debates between the Democratic and Republican presidential nominess could appear on national television without triggering equal time.

11. Chisholm v. FCC, 538 F 2d 349 (D.C. Cir., 1976). The Socialist Labor Party received 1,500 of 3.2 million votes in the 1960 Michigan gubernatorial election.

12. Chisholm v. FCC.

13. Chisholm v. FCC.

14. *New York Times* (Sept. 20, 21, 22, and Oct. 3, 1976).

15. *New York Times* (Sept. 20–22, Oct. 3, 1976).

16. *New York Times* (September 24, 26, 28, 1976).

17. *New York Times* (September 24, 1976).

18. *New York Times* (September 25, 1976).

19. *New York Times* (October 8, 1976). Expert opinion of the 1976 election was that the public was gravely disappointed. Walter Dean Burnham observed that voters were better informed and thus more skeptical. He noted that, in television's saturation presentation of the campaign, television news created

expectations among voters no politician could meet. Marshall McLuhan pointed out that images had taken command: In a "simultaneous information environment," attractive images and promises win more votes than a clearly articulated statement of goals. Candidates' debates mattered only as elements in the new dimension of politics. Margaret Mead complained that television presented so much information that the audience saw it all as advertising. The public was bored, she said, by the "continuous, relentless repetition of what should be fresh experiences for different groups of voters." Roger Mudd called the campaign issueless. He blamed Carter for making trust and integrity into campaign issues and chided Ford for going along with Carter's agenda setting.

20. Minow and Sloan, *For Great Debates,* p. 53.

21. *New York Times* (February 16, 1980).

22. *New York Times* (September 19, 1980). Carter's opening remarks "could not have been a more political commercial if he had paid for the time," Casey complained.

23. *New York Times* (August 10, 1980).

24. *New York Times* (September 14 and 23, 1980); *Washington Post* (August 22, 1980). Among others, the league relied on the Harris-ABC poll, the Roper and Gallup polls, the NBC-AP poll, and the *Los Angeles Times* poll.

25. Dorothy Ridings, remarks at a Conference held at the Institute of Politics, John F. Kennedy School of Government, Harvard University, Cambridge, Massachusetts, January 29–31, 1982.

26. *New York Times* (October 18, 1980). Anderson did suffer from financial problems, which probably had an impact on his performance. The Federal Election Commission (FEC) issued a ruling that Anderson could legally seek bank loans against his election subsidy but that banks could not use the FEC ruling to support the legality of such loans if anybody challenged their legality in court.

27. *New York Times* (October 22, 1980).

28. For a full list of respondents, see 54 RR 2d 1246.

29. 54 RR 2d 1246.

30. See Chisholm v. FCC, 538 F 2d 366 (D.C. Cir., 1976). The FCC also lifted equal time on rebroadcasts of candidates' debates, reversing itself on two earlier rulings.

31. "FCC's Debate Rule Goes to Appeals Court," *Broadcasting* (February 27, 1984), 109(9):55.

32. *New York Times* (October 11, 1984).

33. *New York Times,* (March 1, 1984); *Newsweek Election Extra* (November–December 1984). For more on Jackson and candidate debates, see B. D. Merritt, "Jesse Jackson and Television: Black Image Presentation and Affect in the 1984 Democratic Campaign Debates," *Journal of Black Studies* (June 1986), 16 (4):347–367.

34. *New York Times* (October 9, 1984); Seymour Martin Lipset, "The Elections, the Economy and Public Opinion: 1984, *PS* (Winter 1985), 18(1):28–38; Kathleen A. Frankovic, "The 1984 Election: The Irrelevance of the Campaign," *PS* (Winter 1985), 18(1):39–47 *Newsweek Election Extra* (November–December 1984); William Schneider, "An Uncertain Consensus," *The National Journal* (November 10, 1984, 16(45):2130–2132; Thomas Ferguson and Joel Rogers, *Right Turn* (New York: Hill & Wang, 1986); "Every Region, Every Age Group, Almost Every Voting Bloc," *Time* (November 19, 1984), 124(21):42–45.

35. *Rolling Stone,* December 6, 1984. For a fuller treatment of Reagan's appeal, see Gary Wills's *Reagan's America* (Garden City, N.Y.: Doubleday & Company, 1987).

36. *New York Times* (March 4, 1985).

37. *New York Times* (November 9, 1984).

38. *New York Times* (November 9, 1984).

39. Minow and Sloan, *For Great Debates.*

40. "NBC News Makes Controversial Call," *Broadcasting* (April 25, 1988), p. 39; "TV Networks Again Support Poll Closing Amendments," *Broadcasting* (May 16, 1988), p. 38.

41. For further information on primaries and plebiscitary politics, see Nelson W. Polsby, *Consequences of Party Reform* (New York: Oxford University Press, 1983).

Chapter 7

1. A. M. Sperber, *Murrow: His Life and Times* (New York: Freundlich Books, 1986); Fred Friendly, *Due to Circumstances beyond Our Control* (New York: Random House, 1967); Alexander Kendrick, *Prime Time: A Life of Edward R. Murrow* (Boston: Little, Brown, 1969); David Halberstam, *The Powers That Be* (New York: Knopf, 1979).

2. Sperber, *Murrow,* p. 495. Friendly, an aggressive young producer, and the distinguished broadcaster first teamed up in 1947 when they made a phonograph record, *I Can Hear It Now, 1933–1945.* The record featured a history in sound of the great and not-so-great during the tumultuous mid-century with Murrow's understated narration tying together chaotic events of depression and war. The collaboration was important on both technical and editorial grounds. Friendly experimented with the then new technology of magnetic tape. As things would evolve, *See It Now* was technically innovative, involving complex uses of film, coaxial cable, and microwave communications for live television. For Friendly's thoughts on the McCarthy documentary, see Michael D. Murray, "Television's Desperate Moment: A Conversation with Fred W. Friendly," *Journalism History* (Fall 1974), 1(3):68–71.

3. Sperber, *Murrow,* pp. 383–385, 388–390.

4. Friendly, *Due to Circumstances,* p. 10.

5. Friendly, *Due to Circumstances,* p. 9; Sperber, *Murrow,* p. 431.

6. Friendly, *Due to Circumstances,* p. 9; Sperber, *Murrow,* pp. 415, 416–420, 422, 458; Kendrick, *Prime Time,* pp. 369, 373.

7. Sperber, *Murrow,* pp. 421–423; Kendrick, *Prime Time,* p. 369.

8. Michael Dennis Murray, *See It Now vs. McCarthyism: Dimensions of Documentary Persuasion* (Ph.D. dissertation, University of Missouri, Columbia, 1974).

9. "Television in Controversy: The Debate and Defense," *Newsweek* (March 29, 1954), pp. 50–54; *New York Times* (April 16, 1954). Paley issued the following statement: "In the pattern of mass communications as part of the fabric of freedom . . . a broadcasting station has the same right to editorialize . . . as the free press. . . . The suppression of opinion and independent thought whether . . . in print of over the airwaves limits public understanding." Friendly discusses the McCarthy report in Michael D. Murray's "Television's Desperate Moment."

10. *New York Times* (March 10, 11, 14, 1954).

11. Sperber, *Murrow,* pp. 414–471; in April 1954 Mayer remarked that McCarthy has "done a job to get rid of the termites eating away at our democracy. I don't care how many toes he steps on, including mine, as long as he gets the job done" ["L. B. Mayer Extols Senator McCarthy," *Variety* (April 7, 1954), pp. 3, 63].

12. Sperber, *Murrow,* p. 450.

13. *New York Times* (April 9, 1954).

14. "The Baited Trap," *Time* (March 29, 1954), 63(13):77.

15. "Television in Controversy."

16. Kendrick, *Prime Time,* p. 55.

17. *New York Times* (April 27, 1954).

18. Sperber, *Murrow,* pp. 445–447.

19. Friendly, *Due to Circumstances,* p. 78.

20. David Lilienthal, *The Journals of David Lilienthal: The Venturesome Years* (New York: Harper & Row, 1964), vol. 3.

21. Sperber, *Murrow,* p. 501.

22. *New York Times* (November 13, 1955).

23. Friendly, *Due to Circumstances,* pp. 83–84; *New York Times* (January 27 and February 4, 1956); Sperber, *Murrow,* p. 492.

24. Friendly, *Due to Circumstances,* p. 91.

25. *New York Times* (July 8, 1958).

26. Sperber, *Murrow,* p. 567; Friendly, *Due to Circumstances,* p. 104.

27. Committee on Interstate and Foreign Commerce, Special Subcommitee on Investigations, "Testimony of Dr. Frank Stanton," 92nd Cong., p. 147.

28. *New York Times* (May 16, 1971).

29. Transcript of "The Selling of the Pentagon: A Postscript as Broadcast over the CBS Television Network," March 23, 1971 (published by CBS).

30. Transcript.

31. House of Representatives, *Proceeding against Frank Stanton and CBS, Inc,* Report 92-349.

32. House Rept. 92-349. He added that the First Amendment prohibits prior restraint but imposes no barrier to government investigation of deceptive editing after a documentary is broadcast. In his opening remarks, Staggers dwelled on broadcasters' fiduciary responsibilities to avoid accusations that the committee was intruding on program content. See F. Leslie Smith, " 'Selling of the Pentagon' and the First Amendment," *Journalism History* (Spring 1975), 2(1):2–5, 14.

33. He had complied, he admitted, with earlier subpoenas for film of "Pot Party at a University" and "Project Nassau." "Pot Party," reported on WBBM in 1969, showed students smoking marijuana in a residence near Northwestern University and raised hackles as staged news. "Project Nassau" was more controversial: To make the documentary on a Haitian coup attempt, CBS allegedly provided financial support to adventurers attempting to topple the Duvalier regime. The documentary was never produced. CBS provided a tape of "Pot Party." Because it was televised, there were no outtakes. CBS provided eighteen cartons and two cans of "Project Nassau" film together with a carton of documents because that documentary had never been telecast. In neither case did Stanton believe he had surrendered materials that interfered with editorial discretion. "The Selling of the Pentagon" differed because Congress was reaching boldly into editorial discretion, so critical to reporting.

34. Joseph C. Spear, *Presidents and the Press* (Cambridge, Mass.: MIT Press, 1984), p. 117.

35. "Stanton Contempt Now up to House," *Broadcasting* (July 5, 1971), 81:50–52.

36. *New York Times* (July 14, 1971).

37. *New York Times* (July 14, 1971). Congressman William L. Springer admitted "sixty to eighty Republicans . . . ran to me and asked what the hell was going on. They all had been contacted, most . . . several times by television and radio station people."

38. "In the Matter of Complaints Concerning Columbia Broadcasting System, Inc., Program 'The Selling of the Pentagon,' " 30 FCC 2d 150 (1971).

39. *CBS Reports,* "Hunger in America" transcript (May 1968).

40. "In Re Complaints Covering CBS Program 'Hunger in America,' " 20 FCC 2d 150 (1969). The FBI also investigated the documentary. See *Washington Post* (December 8, 1968) and "CBS 'Hunger' Report Prompts Committee Probe," *Broadcasting* (December 16, 1968), p. 67.

41. Cited in "Comments of the National Broadcasting Company, Inc. in the Matter of Inquiry into Section 73.1910 of the Commission's Rules and Regulations Concerning the General Fairness Doctrine Obligations of Broadcast Licensees," FCC 84-242 (September 6, 1984), pp. 17–18.

42. "Comments of NBC," p. 22.

43. "Comments of NBC," p. 22.

44. "Comments of NBC," p. 27.

45. *CBS Reports,* "The Uncounted Enemy" transcript (January 1982).

46. *CBS Reports,* transcript, p. 6.

47. *New York Times* (November 20, 1984).

48. *New York Times* (October 12, 1984, and February 1, 1985).

49. *New York Times* (January 10, 1985).

50. *New York Times* (December 14, 1984).

51. *New York Times* (February 18 and 19, 1985).

52. "In Re Complaint of American Legal Foundation against CBS Inc.," FCC 85-556 (October 18, 1985).

53. *New York Times* (April 23, 1982).

54. *New York Times* (April 23, 1982).

55. *New York Times* (April 23, 1982).

56. *Congressional Record,* House (April 22, 1982), 128:7527.

57. *New York Times* (October 2, 7, 10, 1983).

58. *New York Times* (September 5, 11, 14, and October 5, 9, 1986).

59. *New York Times* (July 25, 1987).

Chapter 8

1. The FCC did note, however, that if Cullman believed it had presented contrasting views on the Nuclear Test Ban Treaty in its news programming, Cullman had met its fairness obligations. The Cullman corollary contained additional mollifiers. Broadcasters would be required to provide reply time to spokesmen only if they had aired clearly partial programming with no contrasting views in their other news programming. Broadcasters retained control of the format in which the contrasting views were to be aired [Cullman Broadcasting Company and Walker County Broadcasting Company, 40 FCC 576 (1963)].

2. Product advertisements need only promote a legal product and contain no fraudulent or misleading information to avoid regulatory scrutiny or legal action.

3. WCBS-TV [9 FCC 2d 921 (1967)], *aff'd sub. nom.* Banzhaf v. FCC [405 F 2d

1082 (1968) *cert. denied sub. nom.*]. Tobacco Institute v. FCC, 396 US 842 (1969), 90 S. Ct. 50 (1969).

4. "In Re Complaint by Friends of the Earth," 24 FCC 2d 743 (1970).

5. Complaint by Friends of the Earth, p. 744.

6. Friends of the Earth v. FCC, 146 US App. DC 88 (1971), 449 F 2d 1164 (1971).

7. Wilderness Society and Friends of the Earth Concerning Fairness Doctrine Re NBC, 30 FCC 2d 643 (1971), on reconsideration 31 FCC 2d 729 (1971).

8. 48 FCC 2d 23 (1974), 48 FCC 2d 26 (1974). See also, I. M. Ellman, "And Now for a Word against Our Sponsor: Extending the FCC's Fairness Doctrine to Advertising," *California Law Review* (1972) 60:1416.

9. PIRG and ELI v. FCC, 522 F 2d 1060 (1st Cir., 1975).

10. Energy Action Committee v. ABC, NBC, WRC-TV, and WTOP-TV, 64 FCC 2d 787 (1977).

11. Environmental Defense Fund v. KERO-TV, 90 FCC 2d 648 (1982).

12. Yes to Stop Callaway Committee, 98 FCC 2d 1317 (1984).

13. Syracuse Peace Council v. WTVH, Syracuse, New York, 1 FCC 794 (1987). See also Meredith Corp. v. FCC, 809 F 2d 863 (D.C. Cir., 1987).

14. Comments of Democratic National Committee, the American Civil Liberties Union, the Syracuse Peace Council, Accuracy in Media, the Anti-Defamation League of B'nai B'rith, the US Catholic Conference, and the New York State Consumer Protection Board submitted to the FCC in the *Meredith* decision [1 FCC 794 (1987)].

15. Comments of the American Newspaper Publishers Association, the Edison Electric Institute, and the Meredith Corporation to the FCC in the *Meredith* case [1 FCC 794 (1987)].

16. Meredith Corporation v. FCC, 809 F 2d 863 (D.C. Cir., 1987); Telecommunications Research and Action Center v. FCC, 801 F 2d 501 (D.C. Cir.), petition for rehearing en banc denied, 806 F 2d 1115 (D.C. Cir., 1986), *cert. denied* 107 S. Ct. 3196 (1987). Hereafter *TRAC v. FCC.*

17. See *Meredith* decision (FCC 87-266).

18. Business Executives Move for Vietnam Peace, 25 FCC 2d 242 (1970); Democratic National Committee, 25 FCC 2d 216 (1970).

19. Business Executives v. FCC, 450 F 2d 646 (D.C. Cir., 1970).

20. Columbia Broadcasting System, Inc. v. Democratic National Committee, 412 US 94 (1973). The Court noted that "in this sensitive area so sweeping a concept of governmental action [required carriage of editorial spots] would go far in practical effect to undermine nearly a half century of unmistakable congressional purpose to maintain—no matter how difficult the task—essentially private broadcast journalism held only broadly accountable to public interest standards" (p. 127).

21. CBS v. Democratic National Committee, pp. 145–146.

22. CBS v. Democratic National Committee, p. 189.

23. Communications Act (July 16, 1952), Title 47, Sec. 315, *US Code,* p. 510. Congressional modification of Section 312 may be viewed as a response to an FCC ruling in 1972 in which the FCC ruled that members of Congress had no greater access rights to the airwaves than citizens or interest groups. Aside from equal time during campaigns, federal office holders had to rely on broadcasters' discretion under the Fairness Doctrine [The Black Caucus of the US House of Representatives v. ABC, CBS, and NBC, 40 FCC 2d 249 (1972)].

24. 68 FCC 2d 1079 (1978); see also 74 FCC 2d 682 (1979).

25. CBS Inc. v. FCC, 453 US 367 (1981). White's statement is on pp. 397–418.

26. Buckley v. Valeo, 424 US 1 (1976); Federal Election Commission v. National Conservative Political Action Committee (NCPAC), Democratic Party of the United States v. NCPAC, 470 US 480.

27. Federal Election Commission, Democratic Party, and Democratic National Committee v. NCPAC and the Fund for a Conservative Majority, 470 US 480.

28. Buckley v. Valeo, p. 19.

29. Federal Election Commission, Democratic Party and Democratic National Committee v. NCPAC and the Fund for a Conservative Majority. 470 US 480.

30. Carter-Mondale Reelection Committee, Inc., 81 FCC 2d 409 (1980); Thomas F. Eagleton (Senator), 81 FCC 2d 423 (1980).

31. National Conservative Political Action Committee, 89 FCC 2d 626 (1982).

32. More important, Senator Percy suffered from tepid support among right wing Republicans, many of whom stayed away from the polls because they believed Percy was not sufficiently supportive of President Reagan despite a near-perfect voting record on Reagan measures. He also lost the Jewish vote because of perceptions that he was not sufficiently supportive of Israel. His challenger, Illinois Democrat Paul Simon was able to pull enough rural, traditionally Democrat, and liberal votes to win.

33. Senate Rept. 100-58, 2.

Chapter 9

1. Fairness proponents charged that Fowler had invited more fairness adversaries to the panels. Phyllis Schlafly, a longtime Reagan supporter and fairness proponent, blasted Fowler for "stack[ing] [the] deck . . . for predetermined results" (Statement of Phyllis Schlafly, "In the Matter of Inquiry into Section 73.1910 of the Commission's Rules and Regulations Concerning the General Fairness Doctrine Obligations of Broadcast Licensees," Docket no. 84-282, before the Federal Communications Commission, Washington, D.C., Feb. 7, 1985). All subsequent quotes referring to the inquiry will be referenced as "Inquiry Comments."

2. "General Docket 84-282, FCC 84-140," *Federal Register* (May 14, 1984), 49(94):20317–20344. Hereafter referred to as "Notice of Inquiry."

3. Among other cases the FCC cited Supreme Court decisions that held that the First Amendment granted robust freedom of speech, irrespective of the identity of the speaker or the persuasiveness or social undesirability of his speech [First National Bank v. Belotti, 435 US 765 (1978); Linmark Associates, Inc. v. Township of Willingboro, 431 US 85 (1977)]. The FCC also noted that a recent Court ruling held that the First Amendment was fundamental, absolute, and unabridgeable and, important for the Fairness Doctrine, forbade limiting any individuals' freedom of expression in order to enhance another's [Buckley v. Valeo, 424 US 1 (1976)]. In a word, the Court ruled that the First Amendment is absolute, not distributive. It also noted apparent First Amendment incompatibility of two Supreme Court decisions, one [Miami Herald Publishing Co., Division of Knight Newspapers, Inc., v. Tornillo, 418 US 241 (1974)] denying political candidates access rights to newspapers on the First Amendment grounds of freedom of the press and another [Red Lion Broadcasting Co. et al. v. FCC et al., 395 US 367 (1969)], citing freedom of speech, that imposed citizens' access rights on broadcasters (Notice of Inquiry).

4. Perhaps overplaying his hand, FCC commissioner James H. Quello challenged Ferris on whether broadcast economics are the cause of noncontroversial news and public affairs programming. Quello remarked that years before becoming an FCC commissioner he had worked as a radio news manager. He had granted an antifluoridation advocate an opportunity to rebut his station's editorials advocating fluoridation. Criticism from medical and dental experts and confusion among the public over the station's editorial policy resulted. The station dropped editorializing entirely; the Fairness Doctrine, not broadcasting economics, limited editorials.

5. Inquiry Comments of Eric Sevareid.

6. Inquiry Comments of Floyd Abrams and Douglas Ginsburg.

7. Inquiry Comments of the National Rifle Association, Inquiry Comments of Henry Geller and Donna Lampert, Inquiry Comments of the Media Access Project.

8. Inquiry Comments of Columbia Broadcasting System, Inc., and reply comments of Columbia Broadcasting System, Inc.

9. Inquiry Comments of the National Association of Broadcasters; CBS Inquiry Comments, pp. 48–50; Notice of Inquiry, p. 20324.

10. CBS, the dominant network at that time, telecast nearly 2,000 hours of regularly scheduled news in 1983, up from approximately 550 hours in 1980 and 400 hours in 1969. See CBS Reply Comments, p. 27.

11. Cited in Statement of Erwin Griswold, press conference, February 2, 1985. See also Red Lion Broadcasting Company, Inc. v. Federal Communications Commission, 395 US 367 (1969).

12. First National Bank v. Belotti, 435 US 735 (1978); Linmark Associates, Inc. v. Township of Willingboro, 431 US 85 (1977); Buckley v. Valeo, 424 US 1 (1976); CBS Inquiry Comments; Inquiry Comments of NAB.

13. Federal Communications Commission v. League of Women Voters of California, 468 US 364.

14. Whitney v. California, 274 US 357 (1927); Gitlow v. New York, 268 US 652 (1925); Schenk v. United States, 249 US 47 (1919); Abrams v. United States, 250 US 616 (1919); Toledo Newspaper Company v. United States, 247 US 402 (1918); Paterson v. Colorado, 205 US 454 (1907); Ex Parte Jackson, 96 US 727 (1877).

15. Brandywine Main Line Radio, Inc. v. Federal Communications Commission, 473 F 2d 17 (D.C. Cir., 1972), pp. 71–72.

16. Statement of the Honorable John D. Dingell, press conference, February 6, 1985.

17. Meredith Corporation v. FCC, 809 F 2d 863 (1987).

18. Radio and Television News Directors Association v. FCC, 831 F 2d 1148 (1987).

19. "Communications and Policymaking in the 100th Congress," a speech by James H. Quello, February 4, 1987, cited in Richard Zaragoza and Jonathan Emord, "Electronic Media May Get Same Protection as Print Journalists," *Legal Times* (March 7, 1987), pp. 15–17.

20. Telecommunications Research and Action Center and Media Access Project v. FCC, 801 F 2d 501 (D.C. Cir., 1986), petition for rehearing 801 *en banc* denied, 806 F 2d 1115 (D.C. Cir., 1986), cert. denied 107 S. Ct. 3196.

21. Federal Communications Commission, *Memorandum Opinion and Order in Re Complaint of the Syracuse Peace Council against Television Station WTVH, Syracuse, New York*, FCC 88-131/37344 (March 24, 1988); *Memorandum Opinion and Order, in the Matter of Inquiry into 73.1910 of the Commission's Rules and Regulations Concerning Alternatives to the General Fairness Doctrine Obligations of Broadcast Licensees*, Mass Media Docket 87-26, FCC 88-130/37343 (March 24, 1988).

22. For inside looks at these policies, see Ed Joyce, *Prime Times Bad Times* (New York: Doubleday, 1988), and Peter J. Boyer, *Who Killed CBS?* (New York: Random House, 1988). For a longer-term view, see Lewis J. Paper, *Empire: William S. Paley and the Making of CBS* (New York: St. Martin's Press, 1987).

Chapter 10

1. See preface.

2. Ronald H. Coase, "The Federal Communications Commission," *Journal of Law and Economics* (1959), 2:1–40; Telecommunications Research and Action Center and Media Access Project v. FCC, 811 F 2d 501 (D.C. Cir., 1986); Jerome Barron, "Access: The Only Choice for the Media?" *Texas Law Review* (1970), 48:766, 769–771. See Lucas A. Powe, Jr., *American Broadcasting and the First Amendment* (Berkeley, Cal.: University of California Press, 1987), ch. 12, for a discussion of contending arguments; see also comments of various parties

for the 1985 fairness inquiry, cited in chapter 9, for information on the last group.

3. T. W. Adorno, "How to look at Television," *Quarterly of Film, Radio and Television* (1954), 8(3):213–235.

4. Herbert I. Schiller, "Critical Research in the Information Age," Jay G. Blumer, "Communications and Democracy: The Crisis Beyond the Ferment Within" (pp. 166–173), Vincent Mosco, "Critical Research and the Role of Labor" (pp. 227–248), and Ithiel deSola Pool and Herbert I. Schiller, "Perspectives on Communications Research: An Exchange" (pp. 15–23); from the *Journal of Communications* (Summer 1981), vol. 31, no. 3. Todd Gitlin, *The Whole World Is Watching* (Berkeley, Cal.: University of California Press, 1980); David L. Paletz and Robert M. Entman, *Media Power Politics* (New York: Free Press, 1981); Michael Robinson, "Public Affairs Television and the Growth of Political Malaise," *American Political Science Review* (1976), 70:409–432; Maxwell McCombs and Donald L. Shaw, "The Agenda Setting Function of the Mass Media," *Public Opinion Quarterly* (1972), 36:176–187; Edwin Diamond, *Good News, Bad News* (Cambridge, Mass.: MIT Press, 1978). Mike Chappelle and David Barsamian, "Corruptions of Empire: An Interview with Media Watchdog Alexander Cockburn" (pp. 16–17, 30), *The Bloomsbury Review* (May/June, 1988), vol. 8, no. 3.

5. I am grateful to Joseph P. McKerns for this insight.

6. Arthur M. Schlesinger, Jr., *The Cycles of American History* (Boston, Mass.: Houghton Mifflin, 1986).

7. *New York Times* (October 7 and December 24, 1984, February 2, 4, 1985); Thomas Ferguson and Joel Rogers, eds., *The Hidden Election* (New York: Pantheon Books, 1981); Walter Dean Burnham, Philip E. Converse, Jerrold G. Rusk, and Jessee F. Marquette, "Political Change in America," *American Political Science Review* (1974), vol. 68; Walter Dean Burnham, *Critical Elections and the Mainsprings of American Politics* (New York: Norton, 1970); *Newsweek Election Extra* (November–December, 1984); T. H. White, "The Shaping of the Presidency," *Time* (November 19, 1984), pp. 70–83, and E. Thomas, "Every Region, Every Age Group, Almost Every Voting Bloc," *Time* (November 19, 1984), pp. 42–45; Laurily K. Epstein, "The Changing Structure of Party Identification" (pp. 48–52) and David W. Brady and Patricia A. Hurley, "The Prospects for Contemporary Partisan Realignment" (pp. 63–68), both in *PS* (Winter 1985), vol. 18, no. 1; Jerry Brown, Walter Dean Burnham, Kevin Phillips, and Arthur M. Schlesinger, Jr., "The Election and After," *The New York Review of Books,* (August 16, 1984), 31(13):33–38; Lloyd N. Cutler, "Party Government under the Constitution," in *Reforming American Government,* Donald L. Robinson, ed. (Boulder, Col., and London: Westview Press, 1985). See also, Ferguson and Rogers, *Right Turn* (New York: Hill & Wang, 1983), and Nelson Polsby, *Consequences of Party Reform* (New York: Oxford University Press, 1983); Robert Kuttner offers a Democratic remedy in *The Life of the Party* (New York: Viking, 1987).

8. William Graebner, *The Engineering of Consent* (Madison, Wis.: University of Wisconsin Press, 1987).

Chapter 11

1. "Remarks at a Luncheon Hosted by Leaders of the Cultural and Art Community in Moscow, May 31, 1988," *Weekly Compilation of Presidential Documents*, Monday, June 6, 1988, 24(22):702.

2. *New York Times* (November 10, 1988).

3. *New York Times* (February 16, 1988).

4. *New York Times* (November 12, 1988).

5. *New York Times* (July 19, August 6, 1988).

6. Mark Hertsgaard, "Electoral Journalism: Not Yellow, but Yellow Bellied" *New York Times* op-ed, 10/21/88. Baker built on his experience in the Reagan White House in which he coordinated political and public information activities. See Mark Hertsgaard, *On Bended Knee* (New York: Farrar Straus Giroux, 1988).

7. *New York Times* (August 24, 1988).

8. *New York Times* (November 12, 1988).

9. *Ibid.*

10. *New York Times* (February 17, 1988).

11. "Closing in on a debate schedule," *Broadcasting,* Sept. 12, 1988.

12. *New York Times* (October 4, 1988).

13. "Debate Judges Give the Edge to Dukakis—Barely," AP Wire (September 26, 1988).

14. 11/26/85 League of Women Voters Education Fund News Release; Letter from Nancy M. Neuman to Murry Rossant, February 4, 1987, "JFK School Plays Role in '88 Debates Debate," *Cambridge Chronicle*, February 19, 1987; "RNC and DNC Establish Commission on Presidential Debates," Republican National Committee News 87–104, February 18, 1987. Former Vice President Walter Mondale agreed with Neuman, saying, "What forces a candidate to debate is the threat that his recalcitrance will be made public [by the sponsoring organization]. If the parties are handling the arrangements, a candidate would be able to wiggle out by having his party representative make impossible demands while appearing publicly to be cooperative." David S. Broder, "Party Run Debates" *Washington Post* 1/25/87. See also *New York Times* (November 27, 1985) and *The Christian Science Monitor* (November 27, 1985). The Commission also recommended a one-time national holiday for voting day in 1988, and that the President and Congress designate National Voter Registration Day on a weekday in September or October, 1988.

15. *Washington Post* (January 25, 1987).

16. "League Demands $90,000 to Turn over Debate Hall," AP Wire (October 6, 1988). Robert Neuman announces 2nd debate in Pauley Pavilion at UCLA for Commission, Political Round-Up, AP Wire (October 7, 1988).

17. Dr. Lenora B. Fulani et al. v. Commission on Presidential Debates et al. Civil Action No. 88-2649, filed September 23, 1988. "I . . . see myself running against the two-party system that is tremendously unresponsive to most American people, and definitely to blacks," Fulani said.

18. *New York Times* (October 26, 1988).

19. NBC's Debate Decision: No Applause Please," Reuven Frank, *New York Times* (September 23, 1988). *New York Times* (October 21, 1988).

20. *Broadcasting* (October 24, 1988).

21. *New York Times* (September 25, 1986).

22. PBS's Jim Lehrer served as moderator. Panelists included ABC's Peter Jennings, Anne Groer of the *Orlando Sentinel* and John Mashek of the *Atlanta Constitution*.

23. Judy Woodruff of the MacNeil-Lehrer Newshour served as moderator. Tom Brokaw of NBC News, Jon Margolis of the *Chicago Tribune*, and Britt Hume of ABC News were panelists.

24. AP Wire, Donald M. Rothberg, "Bentsen, Quayle Head for Debate; Bush, Dukakis spur long distance," October 3, 1988.

25. William M. Welch, Debate Roundup, AP Wire (October 5, 1988).

26. Terence Hunt, PM-Debate Roundup, AP Wire (October 6, 1988).

27. *New York Times* (October 7, 1988). The *Wall Street Journal* noted speculation that Baker opposed Quayle's selection as the Republican Vice Presidential nominee. According to a *Journal* story, there was speculation that Baker lieutenants leaked Quayle's name to journalists as a likely vice presidential candidate to derail Bush's consideration of the junior senator as his running mate, but so few took the possibility seriously, the ploy failed. *Wall Street Journal* (October 22, 1988).

Although Bush selected Quayle to appease right-wing elements in the Republican Party who doubted Bush's conservatism, attention focused more on Quayle's military and academic records and his boyish good looks. Jim Ciccone, an issue strategist for Quayle, acknowledged that Senator Quayle "fights the pretty face thing almost like a woman does. There's a predisposition to think he doesn't have a brain. He's really very intelligent, and that's going to come out in the course of the campaign." "Quayle's Looks: Do Women Care?" Jill Lawrence, AP Wire (September 27, 1988).

28. *Ibid.*

29. *New York Times* (October 6, 1988) and Political Roundup, AP Wire (October 7, 1988).

30. David Espo, AM-Political Roundup, AP Wire (October 6, 1988).

31. *New York Times*, October 7, 1988.

32. Joe McDonald, AM-Dukakis-Ohio, AP-Wire (October 17, 1988).

33. John B. Judis, "Gephardt Grasped the No. 1 Issue" *New York Times* (February 11, 1988).

34. *New York Times* (October 15, 1988). CNN's Bernard Shaw was moderator, ABC's Ann Compton, NBC's Andrea Mitchell and *Newsweek*'s Margaret Warner were panelists.

35. *New York Times*, October 15, 1988.

36. AM-Political Roundup, AP Wire (October 16, 1988); *New York Times* (October 24, 1988).

37. For further analysis, see Kathleen Hall Jamieson, *Eloquence in the Electronic Age* (New York: Oxford University Press, 1988) and Kathleen Hall Jamieson and David S. Birdsell, *Presidential Debates* (New York: Oxford University Press, 1988).

38. *New York Times* (November 10, 1988).

Index

Nader, Ralph, 125, 171
National Association of Broadcast-
ers, 29, 41, 43, 48, 73, 100, 101
National Association of Broadcast-
ing Employees and Technicians
(NABET), 173
National Association of Manufac-
tures, 125
National Broadcasting Company
(NBC), 16, 19, 21, 28, 36, 39, 40,
41, 56, 66, 67, 72, 88, 91, 106,
107, 108, 111, 121, 125, 126, 127,
132, 133, 137, 138, 139, 144, 152,
153, 172, 179
NBC News, 88, 108
NBC Nightly News, 107
National Broadcasting Company v.
United States, 39, 49, 50, 73, 76,
154, 158, 168, 170
National Endowment for the
Humanities, 127, 132
Nationalization, 2, 4, 6, 17, 19, 20,
21, 36, 49
National Rifle Association (NRA),
154, 155
National States Rights Party, 70
National Unity, 98
Niebuhr, Reinhold, 39
New Deal, 20, 49, 73
New Frontier, 73
New, Harry S., 2
Newman, Edwin, 89, 125
Newman, Paul, 105
New Republic, 2
News, 33, 36, 37, 38, 41, 42, 43, 45,
47, 50, 51, 54, 55, 56, 57, 66, 67,
69, 72, 73, 74, 75, 76, 79, 85, 86,
87, 90, 101, 106, 108, 110, 111,
118, 130, 131, 133, 141, 147, 153,
157, 158, 159, 168, 169, 170, 171,
172, 175, 176, 179, 180, 182, 183
News conferences (press confer-
ences), 82, 85, 86, 87, 90, 91
Newsweek, 117
New York State Consumer Protec-
tion Board, 141
The New York Times, 102, 115, 117,
124
Nine Mile II nuclear reactor, 140

Nixon, Richard, 56, 65, 67, 68, 69,
70, 81, 82, 83, 84, 85, 86, 116,
118, 123, 124, 127, 154, 181
North Vietnamese, 81
Notice of Inquiry on the Fairness Doc-
trine, 151
Novick, Morris, 44
Nuclear Nonproliferation Treaty, 73
Nuclear Test Ban Treaty, 135

Oligopoly, 3, 12, 31, 48, 79, 111,
152, 161, 178
O'Neill, Thomas P., 105

Pacific Gas, 168
Paley, William S., 20, 26, 36, 37, 38,
115, 119, 120, 131
Panel discussions, 56
Pastore, John O., 57, 64
Patrick, Dennis, 161, 171
Payne, George Henry, 28
Pazner, Avi, 133
Pearl Harbor, 112
"The Pentagon Papers," 81, 124
Percy, Charles, 148
Peres, Shimon, 132
Perkins, Frances, 20
Personal attack rule, 76, 77, 78, 168,
169
"Person to Person," 120
Petty, Herbert L., 20
Phouma, Souvanna, 122
Pillion, John R., 119, 120
Playboy, 90
Political Action Committees
(PACs), 145–150, 174
Political editorializing, 168, 169
Political programming, 45, 50, 51,
55, 66, 73
Polls, 88, 90, 98, 99, 103, 104, 179
Poor Man's Party, 56
Presidential Election Campaign
Fund Act, 146
Price discrimination, 5, 9, 10, 11,
41, 49
Print media, 16f, 178
Priority-in-use property right, 2
Prior restraint, xi, 43, 46, 47, 49, 182
Privacy, 178